# Subtle Webs

# Subtle Webs

*How Local Organizations Shape US Education*

JOSE EOS TRINIDAD

OXFORD
UNIVERSITY PRESS

Oxford University Press is a department of the University of Oxford.
It furthers the University's objective of excellence in research, scholarship,
and education by publishing worldwide. Oxford is a registered trade mark of
Oxford University Press in the UK and in certain other countries.

Published in the United States of America by Oxford University Press
198 Madison Avenue, New York, NY 10016, United States of America.



Library of Congress Cataloging-in-Publication Data

Names: Trinidad, Jose Eos, author.
Title: Subtle webs : how local organizations shape US education / Jose Eos Trinidad.
Description: New York, NY : Oxford University Press, [2024] | Includes bibliographical references.
Identifiers: LCCN 2024055386 (print) | LCCN 2024055387 (ebook) | ISBN 9780197786086 (hardback) | ISBN 9780197786093 (paperback) | ISBN 9780197786116 (epub) | ISBN 9780197786123
Subjects: LCSH: Dropouts—United States—Prevention. | Community and school—United States.
Classification: LCC LC143 .T75 2024 (print) | LCC LC143 (ebook) |
DDC 371.2/9130973—dc23/eng/20241223
LC record available at https://lccn.loc.gov/2024055386
LC ebook record available at https://lccn.loc.gov/2024055387

DOI: 10.1093/9780197786123.001.0001

Paperback printed by Integrated Books International, United States of America
Hardback printed by Bridgeport National Bindery, Inc., United States of America

The manufacturer's authorised representative in the EU for product safety is Oxford University Press España S.A. of El Parque Empresarial San Fernando de Henares, Avenida de Castilla, 2 – 28830 Madrid (www.oup.es/en or product.safety@oup.com). OUP España S.A. also acts as importer into Spain of products made by the manufacturer.

*For Philip and Ellen,*

*and the subtle ways you showered us with love.*

# Contents

# Preface

That's interesting! In late 2021, I was reading about EWIs or *early warning indicators*, which were data systems designed to help predict and prevent dropping out of high schools. As I was learning more about these EWIs, I noticed that many papers referred to the work done in Chicago and Philadelphia. Although I was initially interested in how these EWIs worked *in* schools, I noticed that what was more interesting was what happened *outside* schools. Friends and mentors in graduate school would often ask what I was working on. (It was a common occurrence that often filled many, including me, with much anxiety.) As people asked me about my research project, I slowly started to shift from talking about the data systems to discussing the people and organizations behind them. This started my fascination with organizations outside schools, and how they might influence what happened in schools.

This book is a product of that fascination and tries to take readers on a different starting point in organizational, policy, and education research. While traditional studies in organizations often focus on what happens inside them, this book starts with what happens outside the focal organization. While policy research often highlights the effects and the implementation of policies, this book focuses on how they came about in the first place. While the common informants for studies in education are students, teachers, and school leaders, this book draws on and foregrounds the experiences of researchers, nonprofit leaders, philanthropic managers, school coaches, data strategists, and community organizers. By looking at a different starting point, I aim to let new ideas emerge, particularly ideas that can expand our ways of thinking about organizational, sociological, policy, and educational research.

This book is about the *web* of individuals and organizations that create an almost invisible infrastructure to support and influence educational institutions. One of my informants called it an "exoskeleton," conjuring an image of a turtle's shell with interlocking plates that try to protect the sensitive organs underneath. Such a constellation of outside actors also transacts and negotiates with various actors inside the system. But this web does not just refer to the connections among individuals and organizations, such as when research organizations depend on philanthropic support, or when school coaches work with data strategists, or when researchers need data from the school district. The web also refers to ideas and routines that are being spun and knitted to support the changes inside the system.

If I were to characterize these webs, I would suggest the word *subtle*—drawing on at least three senses of the word.

The webs are subtle in that they are almost *imperceptible*. Many school leaders, teachers, students, and parents take school practices for granted—not knowing their provenance and not knowing that webs of outside organizations have helped research, test, advocate, and contest these practices. In the case of these early warning systems, principals and schoolteachers often do not mention the work of these outside organizations. Many just note that they have been using them or that other schools have used them. Thus, organizations are often in the background, with few taking the spotlight for their work. Yet even with this indiscernibility, the consequences of their actions are often felt in everyday routines and interactions.

The subtlety of the webs also means that they have a *complex structure*. Organizations have unique divisions of labor within and across them. Different individuals and organizations play different roles, adding to the complexity of the web. But, like a spider's web, these webs do not just emerge at random. There is a certain structure to them, a certain logic, if you will. Further on in the book, in Chapter 4 to be exact, I show the different ways these webs are structured, often depending on the local contexts and the types of change being instituted.

The webs are also subtle in that they are quite *discreet*. The webs of outside organizations are intentionally careful with their interaction with schools and districts. They often do not have the powerful tools of top-down accountability or even the radical strategies of bottom-up social movements. They rely instead on personal and long-standing connections with principals, district leaders, and other nonprofit actors. While some are arguably powerful and influential players in local school politics, many have simply continued their own work: researching schools, supporting classroom practices, coaching principals, and shifting school routines.

As I talk about the actions of these organizations to change data systems and transform the dynamics of dropping out, I am aware of the potential problems with such an enlarged role of private organizations in public education. In parts of the book, I highlight these concerns and even show how researchers, nonprofit leaders, and philanthropic managers are themselves cognizant of these concerns. But I also show how individuals and organizations try to work *with* and not against the system to support meaningful changes, and how gradual shifts happen through social learning and collective responsibility. In the case of EWIs, while the organizations are not perfect and while changes in dropping out are affected by other factors than simply their work, these efforts to catalyze changes provide some hope that civic initiatives can bear fruit. In what follows, I aim to accurately portray the work of researchers, leaders, coaches, and philanthropists. It will be clear that I have a lot of respect for their work, but I also do not romanticize these organizations as the book also documents their challenges and potential risks.

This book explores these subtle webs of outside organizations in the context of these EWIs. But it also makes a larger, and hopefully more interesting, argument about how local organizations are key to shaping not just schools and districts, but also the larger institution of US education. The case of EWIs provides a way of understanding larger processes of organizational change in a decentralized system. It illustrates how and when local actions can have national consequences, which is particularly important as the US has become more politically fragmented and polarized. Most importantly, the book offers hope for how meaningful change can emerge from various actors working and learning together.

Writing a book is never easy, but I wrote this book because I believe the story and the argument are much too important to be left unwritten. On one side, the story of research, nonprofit, and philanthropic organizations in Chicago, Philadelphia, and New York City provides important lessons for working with schools, connecting with local school districts, engaging outside actors, crafting new data tools, and framing the problems and solutions to dropping out. On the other side, the argument about the role of local organizations in shaping US education provides critical new lenses to view changes in education and other public policies in decentralized systems. The story and argument are intertwined, aiming to spark dialogue and ideas about the role local organizations play in improving larger institutions.

As with any written work, this book aims to reach a number of different audiences. For education researchers, the empirical case of EWIs and the theoretical case about the role of local organizations can contribute to our understanding of school data use, dropout prevention, and district politics. For sociologists of organizations, I try to further our understanding of institutional theory by illustrating how technologies, templates, routines, and spatial dynamics expand our explanations for institutional change. For public policy scholars, the book's discussion regarding the role of local organizations can highlight the power of nimble actors to support larger policy changes. For leaders of nonprofits, schools, districts, and other organizations, this book aims to provide an accurate depiction of their important work while suggesting lessons for how meaningful collective changes can be achieved. For curious readers, I hope you find the book's questions exciting and the answers, interesting.

# Acknowledgements

The present organizational research would not have been possible without the people in the organizations I studied. I am especially grateful for their permission and continuing engagement with this project. Over the years, our initial interviews opened doors for continued conversation as I shared drafts of this project and emailed them to update where it was going. I write here some of the leaders in these organizations who have generously offered their time and support: Elaine Allensworth, John Q. Easton, Alex Seeskin, Sarah Duncan, Arne Duncan, Krystal Payne, Bob Balfanz, Nikki Giunta, Bob Hughes, Alyn Turner, Becky Cornejo, Penny Sebring, Chuck Lewis, Sara Stoelinga, Jim Kemple, Judy Lorimer, Paige Ponder, and Tony Bryk. To them and to the many others who have generously offered their time, thanks for all your work in improving schools and school systems in Chicago, Philadelphia, New York City, and the United States as a whole. I hope this research provides a careful and accurate analysis of the work you have done.

The project started out as an idea nourished by graduate school mentors in Chicago. Steve Raudenbush and Guanglei Hong were my advisors as I did a joint program in two departments, Sociology and Comparative Human Development. Steve sent long e-mails, some ten paragraphs sometimes, telling me what worked, what didn't work, and what I actually wanted to say. The clarity of his thinking has shaped the primary insights of the book. Guanglei was meticulous in the details of the project, leaving drafts with many comments, challenging me to collect more data, and believing that the work was worth sharing to others. Elisabeth Clemens's influence has also been important as the organizational and comparative aspects of the project owe a lot to our conversations. Finally, Micere Keels challenged me to think about how all these mattered for teachers and students on the ground, and how these initiatives in the three cities illustrate various aspects of social movements.

The mentorship I gained from graduate school at the University of Chicago was not limited to these individuals. I have been so blessed to find various "homes" that provided me intellectual nutrition. The courses and interactions I have had with these professors subtly shaped this project's direction. At the Department of Sociology, I wish to thank Andreas Glaser, Neil Brenner, Julian Go, Marco Garrido, Linda Zhao, Andrew Abbott, Robert Vargas, Kimberly Kay Hoang, Jenny Trinitapoli, and Kristen Schilt. At the Department of Comparative Human Development, I wish to thank Jennifer Cole, Michele Friedner, Eugene Raikhel, Eman Abdelhadi, Susan Levine, Susan Goldin-Meadow, Chiara Galli, Sevda Numanbayraktaroglu, and Margaret Beale Spencer. At the Committee on Education, I thank Lisa Rosen, Marshall Jean, and Anjali Adukia. Of course, all the administrative personnel across the university have been so helpful, particularly Janice Pavel, Linnea Martin, Crystal Todoroff, Lauren Russell, Kathrin Kranz, and Shannon Smith. Thanks also to my research assistants, who worked on the project to transcribe and code the interviews, including Emilio Borromeo, Isid Victor Alngog, April Jewel Domingo, Bianca Mikaila Aguilar, Sofia Isabella Rome Nagrampa, and Mariane Desiree Avendano.

During the COVID-19 pandemic, I reached out to various professors to share about this work and get their thoughts—sometimes in person but often over Zoom. I thank them for encouraging me to undertake the project and sharing their ideas with me. At the university, I'm thankful for comments from Jennifer Mosley, Nicole Marwell, Derek Neal, Ron Burt, Eve Ewing, Elizabeth Branch Dyson, and John Padgett. Beyond the university, I'm grateful for Jim Spillane, Don Peurach, Chandra Muller, Ken Frank, John W. Meyer, Anna Mueller, Tim Hallett, Sarah Reckhow, Patricia Burch, Tricia Bromley, Joanne Golann, Charles Payne, Sarah Cashdollar, Meg Bates, Susanna Loeb, Jeff Guhin, and Adam Gamoran. I am also thankful for funding bodies that have supported this research: the American Sociological Association/National Science Foundation, National Academy of Education/Spencer Foundation, Mansueto Institute for Urban Innovation, and the Charles R. Henderson Fund. Special thanks to Maria Gahan and Carolyn Vasques Scalera for facilitating these.

When I moved to my faculty position at the University of California Berkeley, the same intellectual energy was sustained because of conversations with friends and colleagues. As I was finishing the first draft, I led a book workshop with a diverse group of sociologists and education scholars who helped refine different parts of the book. Thanks to Tony Bryk, Heather Haveman, Amanda Datnow, Bruce Fuller, and Jenny Nagaoka! I am grateful for the support of our school's leadership, with a special mention to Michelle

Young, Glynda Hull, Rebecca Cheung, and Jabari Mahiri, who believed so much in the project to help fund the expenses of this workshop. Of course, I am grateful for the friendship and conversations I've had with colleagues, students, and staff who have cheered on this book project. I also want to take this opportunity to thank James Cook, editor at the Oxford University Press and his wonderful team, including Emily Benitez and Megan Smith, who have shepherded the draft. Thanks also to the anonymous reviewers who have helped refine the ideas and implications of this work.

More personally, I am grateful for friendships that sustained this long project. Thanks to friends in graduate school: Kevin Zheng, Xiaogao Zhou, Angel Boulware, Anna Prior, Zihao Lin, Erika Prado, David Boze, Zikui Wei, Siyanda Mohutsiwa, Jacy Anthis, Anna Fox, Priyanjali Mitra, Joshua Silver, Hyunku Kwon, Niquo Santistevan, Alex Koenig, Mengyuan Liang, Johan Rocha, Ashley Uphoff, Shruti Vaidya, Ana Vasan, Stephanie Ternullo, Lauren Beard, Maurice Bokanga, Liang Cai, Likun Cao, Ryan Dai, Tim Elder, Hong Jin Jo, Karlyn Gorski, Xiangyu Ma, Allison Reed, Diana Sandoval Siman, Simon Shachter, Andrew Swift, Nicolas Torres-Echeverry, Kailey White, and Jimin Joon. I'm grateful for friends from the Catholic Student Association, from the Filipino students' association called *Kababayan*, from the Social Sciences Computing Services, and from family friends I've cultivated in Chicago. Thanks to Fr. Andrew Wawrzyn, Matt Moran, Ben Yates, Michael Le Chevallier, Danny Wasserman-Soler, Milo Magno, Joe Bonni, Zhizhan Tian, Petrus Wang, Sophia Carino, Reese Villasor, Jeremy Dumalig, Ethan Yu, Nichos Molnar, Josh Hackney, Michelle Cully, Megan Barnett, Blake Sanders, Geoff Parriott, Khanh Nghiem, Hongkai Mao, Kurt Soucek, Jisheng Zhang, G.S. Yang, Tony Warfield, John McCraney, Noreen Gojar, Frennie Gonzalgo, and the Meneses, Dihiansan, and Rodriguez families. Thanks also to other friends like Chengzhang Li, Weijie Xu, Randy Gao, Jake Rivera, Andre Tsai, Mela Yaranon, Patty Andom, Kia Opinion, Andy Zhao, Jon Jacob, William Chen, William Zhu, Hongding Zhu, Hongkai Mao, Yang Shan, Elliot Lin, Nigel Gomes, Josh Romo, Noella D'Souza, Nathan Tang, Jonathan Young, Zara Anwar, Sophie Regan, Dalia Neri, Brian Lam, and Abby Roberts. And thanks, too, to Marcus whose constant companionship has supported me and this project.

Now to family, I am grateful for the support and love from my immediate family and extended relatives. To my dad and mom, Philip and Ellen Trinidad, thanks for all your hard work, sacrifices, and love for us. To my siblings, Ino, Yya, and Ely, know that *kuya* is proud of you and grateful for your support. To relatives in the United States, the Abdons, Trinidads, Rodriguezes, Yagos, Balanags, and Lees, thanks for opening your home to me and being my family here in this country. To relatives back home, thanks for your support that crosses seas.

AMDG.

# List of Abbreviations

| | |
|---|---|
| CBOs | Community-Based Organizations |
| CPS | Chicago Public Schools |
| CSOS | Center for the Social Organization of Schools |
| CUNY | City University of New York |
| EWIs | Early Warning Indicators |
| IES | Institute of Education Sciences |
| JHU | Johns Hopkins University |
| NCLB | No Child Left Behind Act |
| NCS | Network for College Success |
| NYC DOE | New York City Department of Education |
| PERC | Philadelphia Education Research Consortium |
| RELs | Regional Educational Laboratories |
| RFA | Research for Action |
| TDS | Talent Development Secondary |
| VAM | Valued-Added Modeling/Model |

# Introduction
## Dropouts, Data, and the Subtle Webs that Transform Them

In 2002, almost 1,000 high schools in the United States failed to graduate half of their freshman class and many of these served racially minoritized students. Nearly half of African American students and 40 percent of Latino students attended what some scholars have called "dropout factories"—schools where less than half of the high school freshman students graduate on time.[1] However, in less than twenty years, graduation rates in the United States have steadily increased, with many large urban school districts seeing significant double-digit increases.[2] For example, in Chicago, graduation rates have increased from 54 percent in 2002 to 85.6 percent in 2024.[3] During the same time span, Philadelphia's graduation rates rose from less than 50 percent to 81 percent.[4] In New York City, high school graduation rates increased from 54 percent to 82.8 percent between 2004 and 2024.[5] What makes these statistics more impressive is that many of these changes and improvements happened in urban districts plagued with massive bureaucracies, critiqued for political dysfunctions, and catering to largely disadvantaged and minoritized student populations.[6] This begs the question, how and why did this happen?

Scholars have suggested various potential reasons for this change. A skeptical reader may suggest that some form of strategic behavior may have been at play. After all, if one were to artificially increase graduation rates, one could easily change the numerator or the denominator of the fraction. To influence the numerator, schools may make it easier to graduate high schools through the likes online "credit recovery" programs that inflate graduation rates.[7] To influence the denominator, schools may remove students from the accountability metric similar to strategies used to prevent students from taking standardized tests to inflate their school's statistics.[8] However, in a 2023 article—"Is the Rise in High School Graduation Rates Real?"—scholars suggest that even if some of these factors may be at play, these artificial ways of increasing graduation rates do not explain the magnitude and significance

*Subtle Webs*. Jose Eos Trinidad, Oxford University Press. © Oxford University Press (2025).
DOI: 10.1093/9780197786123.003.0001

of the increase. Economist Douglas Harris and his colleagues found that "the recent and fast rise in graduation rates reflects some strategic behavior, but the preponderance of evidence suggests a large increase in the nation's stock of human capital."[9]

Even sociologist Charles Payne agrees with this assessment, stating that "in the last ten years, what body of research has had the most positive impact on the lives of poor children? . . . I would nominate the work that has led to the prolonged rise to the national graduation rate, which passed 80% for the first time in 2012 . . . . The research supporting this work is mostly predictive, not causal, [but it] is hard to think of a body of research . . . with so much meaningful change."[10] Payne was referring to the research on dropout prediction and prevention systems, which used new technologies to both identify students at risk of dropping out and motivate changes in the social organization of schools.

Part of the story is about technology. In the early 2000s, researchers in Chicago and Philadelphia found that performance early in middle school and high school were predictive of a student's eventual graduation.[11] This insight initiated the development of dropout prediction systems called ninth-grade *early warning indicators* (EWIs) that used data on students' attendance, behavior, and course performance to predict who was at risk of dropping out of high school (see Figure I.1).[12] Over time, schools used these new technologies to promote school accountability, identify students in need of help through color-coded indicators, create teacher teams to discuss student progress, and introduce a variety of tiered interventions.[13] This is the part of the story about data and dropping out.

But the other part of this story is about people and organizations. Often, studies in education focus on either a top-down understanding of the policy's effects or a bottom-up account of the changes inside schools and classrooms.[14] In the case of EWIs, we see similar studies in top-down investigations of the effects of these technologies on chronic absenteeism, course performance, and graduation outcomes,[15] as well as studies on how EWIs were implemented by teachers and schools, which emphasize the practices and challenges that came along with it.[16] Although many of these studies highlight what happened inside the school system, this book interrogates a different set of actors. The book foregrounds the often invisible and subtle infrastructure of "outside" research, philanthropic and nonprofit organizations, which have arguably become powerful players in education policy and

| Name | Ds and Fs | Current GPA | Daily Attendance | Discipline | Suspension |
|---|---|---|---|---|---|
| Student A | 0 | 2.88 | 91.67% | 2 | 0 |
| Student B | 0 | 3.36 | 98.48% | 2 | 0 |
| Student C | 0 | 3.76 | 88.20% | 0 | 0 |
| Student D | 4 | 2.13 | 64.37% | 0 | 0 |
| Student E | 2 | 2.75 | 75.23% | 8 | 0 |
| Student F | 0 | 3.01 | 100.00% | 3 | 1 |
| Student G | 1 | 2.99 | 90.87% | 4 | 0 |
| Student H | 0 | 3.42 | 99.24% | 2 | 1 |
| Student J | 0 | 3.33 | 86.22% | 1 | 0 |

**Figure I.1** Example of an Early Warning Indicator Dashboard
Rendering by the author.

politics since the beginning of the 21st century.[17] In particular, I interrogate their role in the initiation and spread of these EWIs to understand how local organizations participate in the transformation of education. This is the part about how organizations, particularly local nonprofits, shape US education.

This book offers a case to understand theoretical questions on educational change, organizational strategy, and technological adoption. It uses the example of EWIs to highlight how education policies change and how new school innovations spread in the relative absence of a centralized educational bureaucracy and grassroots social movement. It highlights a theory for *how* and *why* local organizations have become crucial actors in this space, and how this happens with various initiatives across the political spectrum, from computer science education and alternative teacher preparation programs to charter schools and anti-critical race theory organizing. Many of these initiatives have been driven by organizations external to the school system, and this book provides a framework for interrogating why. In this way, the book deepens our theories for understanding institutional changes and education transformations—a core concern for education researchers, public policy scholars, sociologists, political scientists, critical scholars, and other social scientists.

More than providing a theoretical perspective for understanding change, the book also answers practical questions by showing the invisible processes and hidden strategies organizations used to bring about consequential changes. It is a book that systematically investigates how particular practical actions had crucial contributions to improving schools and changing systems. It offers an account of how change happened neither from top-down nor from bottom-up, but from outside-in. By understanding and documenting organizational strategies that spread and sustain EWIs, the book offers key lessons regarding organizational and institutional change for school leaders, policymakers, philanthropists, organizational leaders, and nonprofit practitioners.

Although the book uses the case of EWIs, it is neither an evaluation of their effectiveness nor is it a study of their implementation. Although it documents the work of particular organizations, it is not a story with clear protagonists and antagonists, or victors and villains. Rather, this is a book about making sense of the processes, systems, and changes in education. It is a book about challenges, conflicts, and cooperative ventures that led to discernible transformations in education systems. And while the consequences for EWIs have been predominantly constructive, we caution that there may be spaces where outside intervention on US education is neither optimal nor helpful.

## Core Question and Central Argument

Education researchers, policymakers, and organizational leaders have often asked some version of the same question regarding how one can bring about intentional changes in education. Some scholars highlight the importance of top-down system-wide changes that address clear problems, mobilize significant public constituencies, and build the necessary educational infrastructure to effect change.[18] Other scholars argue for the role of bottom-up initiatives of grassroots actors like teachers, school leaders, and individual districts.[19] Although both are obviously important, relying on either one in a decentralized education system like the United States has unique limitations. Top-down policies often fail to change practices on the ground while bottom-up practices often fail to scale beyond a singular school or a district.[20] It thus begs the question, *how do education changes happen in the absence of a centralizing authority and grassroots social movement?*

One example of a top-down change in US education is the case of test-based school accountability, where the federal government has set up ways to monitor and incentivize schools for their performance in standardized tests.[21] Social scientists have long debated how accountability has arisen as a policy and has influenced changes on the ground. Sociologist Jal Mehta has highlighted how the shift toward test-based accountability was driven by a shared paradigm regarding the central role of education in national and individual economic success.[22] Economist Eric A. Hanushek has leveraged compelling quantitative evidence to show the efficacy of holding schools accountable and using standardized tests in the process—all important factors to support national testing regimes.[23] However, historian Diane Ravitch has critiqued the practice because of its ill consequences for the profession of teaching and the morale in schools.[24] Others have also studied various unintended consequences of test-based accountability systems—from gaming tests to outright cheating—that make this top-down policy less constructive than initially thought.[25] Thus, even with the centralized role of the federal government in testing, education scholars like David K. Cohen and Susan Moffitt argue that the US government has failed to develop instruments for a central state agency to guide and direct what happened inside classrooms.[26] In this way, while centralized top-down policies are important, they are not enough to bring about instructional and pedagogical changes.

On the other end, grassroots initiatives are often started and spread by individual teachers and school leaders. But while changes are possible with the collective action of teachers, many of these actions fail to scale beyond the school or district. For example, network scholars like Kenneth A. Frank and Yong Zhao emphasize the role of teachers' social networks in the spread of new innovations, but this is often limited to spreading practices within the school.[27] Education scholars Cynthia Coburn and Jennifer Lin Russell uncover how the spread of instructional innovations can be affected by policy supports that change teachers' social networks, but many of these interactions happen at the district-level and not beyond it.[28] In his 1975 classic book *Schoolteacher*, sociologist Dan C. Lortie noted how teachers have often focused on their own students to the exclusion of others.[29] Although more recent practices and more recent studies have challenged this view about teachers focusing exclusively on their students, it does hint at their rather limited horizon because teachers center mostly on the students in front of them—often just in their classroom or their school.

If top-down and bottom-up processes are limited in their ability to contribute to educational changes in a decentralized and disjointed public education system, what explains the spread of several educational initiatives? EWIs have spread to many schools and districts, and even 43 US states have adopted these systems.[30] Charter schools have steadily spread, both in terms of the number of schools and the average share of students enrolled in them, with 78,000 charter schools enrolling more than 3.7 million students.[31] Computer science education has steadily expanded, with 18 states that have statewide plans, 37 states that have defined their computer science standards, and 40 states that have had teacher certification processes for K–12 computer science.[32] Alternative teacher preparation and certification programs, like Teach for America and The New Teacher Project, have also expanded through the years, particularly with teacher shortages and the difficulty of attracting or retaining teachers in public schools.[33] More recently, the spate of what some have referred to as anti-critical race theory organizing has also spread to different communities and schools, with one estimate finding 165 groups initiating them.[34] Many of these examples cannot be easily explained by top-down or bottom-up theories for educational change.

Here, I propose a different way of theorizing educational change that emphasizes an "outside-in" perspective. I argue that in the absence of a centralizing authority and grassroots social movement, *ideas are spread, innovations pushed, practices standardized, and changes shaped by networks of school improvement organizations, many of which are concentrated in local areas but have consequences beyond them.* While case studies of nonprofit and philanthropic networks in New York City, Los Angeles, Chicago, Atlanta, New Orleans, and other American school districts have highlighted the enlarged influence of these organizations in education, my argument is more extensive as I illustrate how the very interconnections of these organizations across various places have contributed to an invisible infrastructure—a *subtle web*—for ideas to spread and for practices to be standardized.[35] It shows not only the power of organizations to affect their local school districts but also their ability to change the larger institution of public education in the United States.

To make this argument, I analyze the data collected through more than 90 interviews and close to 3,000 pages of documents in a period spanning

20 years to provide a picture of the transformation of EWIs from the initial research in Chicago, Philadelphia, and New York City to the national growth of the initiative fueled by a variety of nonprofits (see Methodological Appendix). Rather than a linear history, I present an analysis of the *source*, *scale*, and *space* of change. I start by challenging traditional studies in education that too often focus on what happens inside schools and classrooms by highlighting how the source of these changes was often from outside the system. I then talk about the strategies of these organizations from the macro-level of framing to the meso-level of organizational networks to the micro-level of organizational routines. Finally, I show how these processes and strategies have a spatial component because organizations are connected across places in this decentralized system (see Figure I.2).

In presenting this perspective and using the case of EWIs, I contribute to and take inspiration from studies investigating school improvement organizations, institutional theory, and dropout prevention systems. First, I attempt to expand our understanding of external actors in education by highlighting these organizations' strategies, successes, challenges, and limitations. Second, I integrate various elements of institutional theory to provide an analytic structure for explaining how outside organizations are able to institute changes in education. Third, I analyze and theorize early warning indicators, both in terms of their effects and implementation and in terms of their emergence. The next sections illustrate how this research speaks

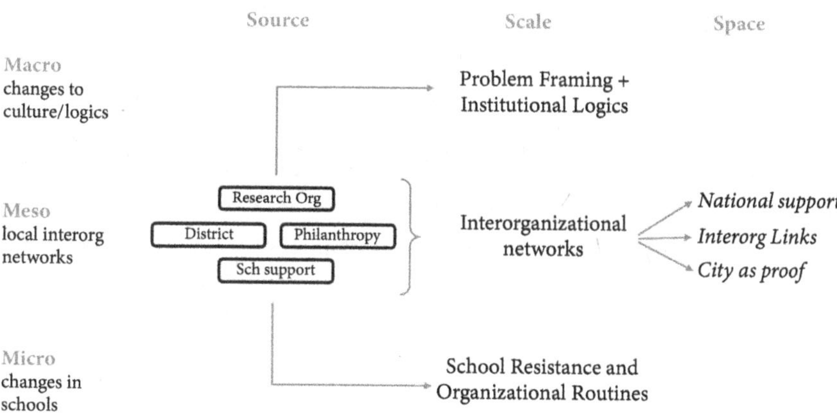


**Figure I.2** Conceptual Framework

to, connects with, and situates itself alongside other studies in education, sociology, and organizational science.

## Private Organizations and Public Education

Organizations outside schools have long been part of American education. As early as the 1800s, parent–teacher associations have dotted the United States such that there subsequently developed the National Congress of Mothers and Parent–Teachers Association, which was described as "the pioneer organization in studying and promoting every phase of child welfare."[36] In the early 1900s, African American women interested in education and social reform helped start two organizations: the National Association of Colored Women and the National Congress of Colored Parents and Teachers.[37] Between 1914 and 1931, nearly 5,000 schools were constructed for rural Black children as an initiative by Chicago philanthropist Julius Rosenwald.[38] Alongside the national establishment of public schools, private Catholic schools have also been a core presence in the United States since the 18th century.[39] Such examples illustrate the various roles nongovernmental organizations have taken in early American education.

While always a basic part of the education system, these organizations have recently grown not just in number but also in influence.[40] Local schools and districts receive sizeable additional support from parent–teacher associations, alumni associations, school foundations, and local endowments—making this a potential space for inequalities to arise between places that receive more or less funding.[41] Large philanthropies, like the Gates, Broad, Ford, and Kellog Foundations, have also supported educational initiatives of different scales.[42] Universities and research groups have initiated research-practice collaboratives since the early 1990s and are now organized with the National Network of Education Research–Practice Partnerships.[43] School reform and school support organizations have provided coaches, strategists, and other forms of professional development in schools.[44] Organizations have also started new models for alternative teacher certification that sought to augment the teaching workforce.[45] Since the turn of the 21st century, these organizations have taken on larger roles in public education with many referring to them as school improvement organizations, intermediary organizations, or external actors in education.[46]

On the face of it, these organizations seem beneficial to public education. But scholars have also noted the risks and problems with such private action on public goods.[47] Foundational research like the work of Brian Rowan, who coined the term "school improvement industry," highlights how these organizations have regularly introduced new programs and policies but have done little to change the instructional core of schools because of the industry's incentives toward inertia.[48] Meredith Honig conceptualized them as "intermediary organizations," describing how they mediate between two parties like policymakers and implementers, and she highlighted the resources these organizations provided and the constraints they faced to bring about changes.[49] Patricia Burch spoke more broadly about the "hidden market" of firms that provide tests, remedial instruction, management consulting, and staff development—and how they might conflict with the public purposes of schooling.[50] More recently, work by Christopher Lubienski and colleagues has highlighted the blurring line between "internal actors" and "external actors," particularly as outside organizations can control some parts of education governance and as some actors, like parents and teachers, can function as both internal and external agents.[51] Taken together, these organizations are arguably important players that complicate our understanding of the present educational ecosystem in the United States.

The enlarged role of private organizations—both for-profit and nonprofit—in public education has brought both benefits and threats, which may at times be two sides of the same coin (see Table I.1). Three common aspects scholars often interrogate include organizations' ability to open democratic opportunities, provide expertise, and contribute to institutional stability. Yet the same aspects can also be problematic because these organizations can be critiqued as undemocratic institutions that contribute to inequitable distribution of resources through the destabilization of public institutions.

**Table I.1** School Improvement Organizations

| **Benefits** | **Threats** |
|---|---|
| Democratic participation | Undemocratic and unaccountable |
| Expertise and financial resources | Inequitable distribution |
| Stability and innovation | Destabilization with institutional challengers |

A common reason for encouraging private and civic organizations is their supposed role in a healthy democracy. One of the earliest observers of this was French political theorist Alexis de Tocqueville, who, in 1838, wrote about the importance of civic associations for American life.[52] More recently, Robert Putnam, in the book *Bowling Alone*, sounded alarm bells regarding the decline of community activities and how such a decline has led to a host of negative individual and community outcomes.[53] Applied to education, civil society groups made of community members, philanthropists, local leaders, and concerned individuals can be an antidote to revitalize engaged democratic participation.[54] But some scholars have critiqued this perspective by showing the threats of civic organizations and philanthropies on democratic participation. For example, philanthropic interests may funnel money on specific initiatives and consequently shape public opinion and political races.[55] Large philanthropic gifts have been critiqued for sidelining community voices, an antithesis to the supposed democratic potential of civic organizations.[56] Others also criticized the power of organizations to influence education policies and practices, given that such organizations are accountable neither to public voters nor to government bureaucrats.[57] While civic organizations may ideally contribute to democratic participation, this can be limited in reality.

Another reason used to justify school improvement organizations is their role in directing expertise and financial resources. On one end, organizations are able to draw on their expertise to do research, create trainings, lead coaching, and support struggling students.[58] They are able to focus on particular programs and initiatives as well as sustain initiatives through their dedicated work. On the other end, these organizations have also been crucial in contributing financial resources to schools and districts, funding programs like after-school extra-curricular activities and supplementary educational services.[59] Although the provision of expertise and financial resources contribute to school improvement efforts, they may exacerbate already existing inequalities between schools that can or cannot leverage these additional resources. In a national study of school-supporting nonprofits, public policy professors Ashlyn Aiko Nelson and Beth Gazley found that school districts that already had more resources had higher chances of having supportive nonprofits and having higher per-pupil additional contributions.[60] In studying schools in New York City, organizational theorist Ebony Bridwell-Mitchell found that well-endowed schools are more likely to partner with civic organizations, potentially exacerbating the structural inequalities in the city.[61] In a study of North Carolina schools led by Brittany Murray, researchers found that high-revenue parent–teacher associations more often form in predominantly white and affluent schools.[62] Taken together, these studies provide a caveat to how increased "outside" supports for schools and districts may lead to disproportionate and inequitable outcomes.

School improvement organizations have likewise functioned as a source of innovative practices. In his book *Just Giving*, political scientist Robert Reich suggests that one of the goals of philanthropic organizations is to bring about democratic experimentalism as philanthropists fund innovations that can be risky and can have a longer time horizon than those set by government programs.[63] Moreover, these organizations can become a stabilizing force as politicians and political appointees in government can easily come in and out of office, which threatens the sustainability of innovations and programs.[64] However, some organizations were set up to do exactly the opposite: to destabilize districts and schools by creating what Sarah Reckhow and Jeffrey W. Snyder called "jurisdictional challengers."[65] Organizations like charter schools are called such because of their role in competing with and offering alternatives to public sector institutions like traditional public schools.[66] Such competitive stances against public institutions may then lead to larger educational problems rather than solutions.

In all these examples, what remains apparent is the large influence of these external actors, nonprofits, and school improvement organizations. Scholars have often studied how these organizations impact specific schools and school districts. In *How A City Learned to Improve Its Schools*, Anthony Bryk and colleagues recounted the work of the "exoskeleton" of organizations in helping improve Chicago schools.[67] In *When Schools Work*, sociologist Bruce Fuller highlighted the contribution of community leaders, ethnic nonprofits, and progressive organizations in transforming public education in Los Angeles.[68] In *Charter School City*, economist Douglas Harris documented the complex results of transforming New Orleans schools into charter schools, and how nongovernmental organizations were crucial in this transformation.[69] Many of these studies concentrate on local case studies of how organizations transformed local schools and local school districts. But this book opens with a different argument. It argues that these local changes can have national consequences.

Private organizations do not just impact local public education; they impact the shape of the very institution of education in the United States.

The next section describes some of the ways this could happen using concepts from institutional theory.

## Institutional Theory from the Macro-Level to the Micro-Level

The story of early warning indicators—and the larger story of the rise of private organizations in public education—is a story about the adaptation of schools to their environment and the transformation of outside organizations alongside changes in schools. To analyze this history, I draw on new institutional theory that investigates how practices, technologies, and organizational forms become distributed and adopted across different organizations.[70] In the 1977 classic article, "Institutionalized Organizations: Formal Structure as Myth and Ceremony," sociologists John W. Meyer and Brian Rowan highlighted how organizations incorporate practices and procedures not because of their efficiency or effectiveness but because they conform to rules set by the larger environment; that is, the institution.[71] Furthering this argument, sociologists Paul DiMaggio and Walter W. Powell suggested how a set of organizations emerge as a field through coercive, mimetic, and normative processes. In other words, organizations change and become similar through bureaucratic pressures, organizational imitation, or professional adoption.[72] Both of these foundational texts try to explain social transformation and change as organizations become more similar with each other.

These works have also inspired various other ways of thinking about institutions. *Institutional fields* focus on the set of organizations that constitute a recognized cluster of institutional life—inclusive of suppliers, consumers, producers, and regulatory agencies.[73] *Institutional logics* highlight an inter-institutional account of organizations as they draw on cultural elements, frames of reference, and justifications for action, which attach with particular institutions like the market, religion, or state.[74] *Institutional entrepreneurship* focuses on the work of individuals and organizations as they leverage their social position and social skills to transform the institutions they belong to.[75] *Inhabited institutionalism* emphasizes the importance of social interactions and struggles over meaning, and problematizes the idea of an individual's actions being simply controlled by the organization and the institution to which one belongs.[76]

While one can easily write an essay on each of these perspectives—and many scholars actually have—I take a different route by attempting to integrate them into an analytic framework to study the transformation of an institution like public education. Rather than go into depth on each perspective, I privilege breadth and interconnections in illustrating how these varieties of new institutionalism speak to each other.

One of the ways to think about their interconnections is to understand the scale at which change happens. First, theories of institutional fields and logics emphasize the *macro-level* transformation of how we talk about and what we expect of social institutions. In education, for example, studies highlight how American educational policy shifted to emphasize outcomes-based accountability because a change in "paradigm," when education came to be seen as an economic good for both the individual and the larger society.[77] Second, the study of institutional entrepreneurs highlights how changes are driven by *meso-level* strategies of individuals and organizations that collaborate, compete, and conflict with each other. For example, philanthropic foundations as institutional entrepreneurs have significantly contributed to the spread and legitimation of charter school organizations.[78] Finally, the study of inhabited institutions highlights *micro-level* interactions, routines, challenges, and processes of organizations. For example, Tim Hallett's ethnography of an urban elementary school has shown how school routines and processes became more linked to previously symbolic institutional gestures as a consequence of new accountability regimes.[79] While each of these perspectives have elements beyond what I ascribe here, the present framework provides a coherent aid to understanding their connections (see Figure I.2 for visual depiction). Moreover, while I focus on specific "levels" in particular chapters, the lines between macro-, meso-, and micro-levels are usually porous, and the concepts often interconnected.

At the macro-level, I highlight the role of institutional logics being transformed to subsequently bring about changes in educational practices, processes, policies, and expectations. Early theorists of institutional logics, Roger Friedland and Robert Alford described them as the "set of material practices and symbolic constructions . . . which constitute [an institution's] organizing principles."[80] In this perspective, society is composed of varied institutions like the economy, religion, state, education, arts, and kinship, and each one has a set of defining characteristics, practices, and rule structures that motivate individual behavior and cognition.[81] For example, a "market logic" may emphasize competition and quantification while a "community logic" may emphasize cooperation and mutual support.[82] Logics may also be more specific. For example, medical education can be understood as emphasizing "care" or "science" logics, and nonprofit centers can emphasize "professional" or "business" logics.[83] Organizations often choose, combine, or change these institutional logics, depending on a host of factors.[84] These organizations may also have two logics competing with each other, such as when one subgroup emphasizes a managerial logic while another uses a community logic.[85] For the study of EWIs, I investigate how changes in institutional logics emerged through the variety of technologies that characterized the early warning data system.

At the meso-level, I investigate the role of institutional entrepreneurs in initiating and sustaining these changes. DiMaggio introduced the concept of institutional entrepreneurs, describing them as actors interested in particular institutional arrangements and able to mobilize their resources to transform or create new institutions.[86] These actors—often, individuals or organizations—leverage their social position and social skills in the construction of new institutional forms, rules, and processes.[87] Examples include the work and strategies of an organization that transformed photography from a highly specialized activity to an everyday hobby, of French chefs who moved from classical cuisine to nouvelle cuisine, of activists in Canada who used their subject positions to transform HIV/AIDS treatment advocacy, and of mid-level bureaucrats who were the unreported agents of institutional change in Mexico's small business finance ventures.[88] They create changes by building innovative technologies, collaborating with other organizations, framing policy problems, and legitimating their proposed solutions.[89] In the case of EWIs, I study how organizations collaborated to spread and sustain practices in an institution so known for its inertia and resistance to change.[90]

At the micro-level, I emphasize the role of organizational routines and interactions in transforming not only the behaviors of individuals but also the meaning-making that supported institutional change. Organization scholars like Martha S. Feldman and Brian T. Pentland have reconceptualized routines as crucial for change rather than as sources of inertia.[91] Most research on these repetitive patterns of action emphasize how they promote efficiency, stability, consistency, and sustainability.[92] Studies have also highlighted the importance of process in initiating and maintaining these routine dynamics.[93] In the context of education, key routines can structure teachers' work practices and subsequently provide stability, even in the face of regular reforms being introduced in schools.[94] For EWIs, organizational routines have often been introduced by nonprofits that experienced the initial resistance of teachers and school leaders. I investigate what factors have led to changes in the reception of these tools and how specific routines figured prominently in this transformation.

While I draw on and take inspiration from the rich literature on institutional theory, the book's chapters will illustrate the subtle ways the EWI case diverges from the expectations of institutional theory. I show how institutional logics change not only because of shifts in individuals' understanding but also because of the shift in information technologies. I explain how institutional entrepreneurs employ different templates of networked collaborations for specific changes, particularly as they focus on technical or cultural fixes. Finally, I highlight how routines can often be a precursor to, rather than a consequence of, people's shift in mindsets.

## The Case of Early Warning Indicators

In 2005, Elaine Allensworth and John Q. Easton published a report on *The On-Track Indicator as a Predictor of High School Graduation*, where they highlighted how Chicago students' course performance in ninth grade was predictive of their eventual graduation outcomes.[95] They detailed that a ninth grader who had five full course credits and had no more than one semester F in English, math, science, and social studies was "on track" to graduate high school.[96] In a 2007 paper, researchers from Philadelphia, led by Robert Balfanz, found that there were indicators as early as sixth grade that signaled reduced chances of graduating from high school.[97] In the schools they studied, they found the following factors as contributive to a reduced likelihood of graduation: having a final grade of F in mathematics or English, attending below 80 percent of the school year, or receiving an "unsatisfactory" behavior mark in at least one class.[98] In the early 2010s, these prediction systems were being used not only in Chicago and Philadelphia but also in large urban school districts, like New York City, Los Angeles, Milwaukee, Portland, Baltimore, and Houston.[99]

In 2015, just a decade since the publication of the Chicago report on EWIs, the US government surveyed a nationally representative sample of high schools and found that 52 percent of these schools had implemented some form of early warning systems. Many of these used a combination of data regarding students' attendance, behavior, and course performance to direct interventions and school services.[100] By 2017, 43 out of 50 states had also engaged in the development of EWIs.[101] By 2024, one report noted that a large majority of US school districts have adopted these early warning systems, particularly as they aim to reduce chronic absenteeism.[102] These numbers suggest a significant component of American education being transformed. While data on attendance and grades had almost always been present in schools, their use as an EWI had been initiated and institutionalized in just less than two decades.

Studies of EWIs have often been divided into three themes. One is about the predictiveness of these models. Another is about the effects, or the lack thereof, of these EWIs. The third is about how these are being employed on the ground.

*EWI Predictiveness.* Early research on EWIs had focused on how accurately they predicted dropping out and what indicators should be included for the predictors. Many have taken inspiration from what has been referred to as the ABCs of keeping students on track to graduate: attendance, behavior, and course performance.[103] In Chicago, researchers didn't just make sure that their EWIs were predictive of students in general; they also studied how these were predictive for students with disabilities and English language learners.[104] In New York City, researchers tried to see how they could make them more predictive by including an indicator for whether the student had passed a state standardized exam during their freshman year.[105] In states like Wisconsin, computer scientists have found the high accuracy of these early warning systems, including for students from marginalized backgrounds.[106]

*EWI Impact.* EWIs were not just indicators of dropping out; they were supposedly tools to prevent dropping out. The idea behind these tools was that schools could receive data on students that needed help in order for teachers and staff to intervene early enough.[107] The period of ninth grade was also crucial because this was an important period for adolescent's cognitive development, given the presence of risks and peer pressures, and an equally important period of transition to often new and larger high schools.[108] Finally, the tools and systems were created not just to direct resources but also to catalyze improvements in schools. But do these EWIs hold up to these promises?

There is evidence for positive impact on short-term outcomes but evidence for long-term outcomes is unclear and not as robust. Some rigorously designed randomized trials and promising natural experiments suggest positive effects on short-term outcomes like attendance, course passing, and grades. One Midwestern study found that schools with EWIs had reduced percentages of students who were chronically absent.[109] In New York City, a program that used data to create early warning flags and match mentors to students led to students in treatment schools being 9 percent less likely to be chronically absent.[110] In one study of Southern high schools, researchers found that being in treatment schools led to lower levels of chronic absence, but had no significant impact on the number of course credits or course failures.[111] One study in a large, urban school district in the Southeast noted that EWIs may be effective only for particular groups of students as the effects on reducing chronic absenteeism was significant only for socioeconomically advantaged students.[112] While critics and skeptics of EWIs are fearful of the misuses of data and the labeling of "at risk" students, evidence does not point to negative effects on students considered off track.[113]

Despite promising short-term outcomes, the empirical evidence on the long-term effect of EWIs on high school graduation is suggestive but remains unclear. Studies touting the positive effect of EWIs on graduation outcomes have often relied on aggregate increases in district graduation rates rather than random variations between schools that adopted or did not adopt these tools.[114] Moreover, the advent of EWIs came alongside other programs, like test-based accountability, data-driven decision-making, and professional learning communities, focused on continuous improvement.[115] One quasi-experimental study has also found no evidence of increased graduation outcomes between those just above and below the cutoff for being "on track."[116] Taken together, while proponents caution against causal attribution in the absence of more rigorous data, many researchers are optimistic about the role of EWIs in improving graduation.[117] The fact that these tools have influenced discernible changes in large urban school districts serving large minoritized populations is one cause for optimism.

*EWI Implementation.* Qualitative research on how these EWIs are implemented have noted the challenges that come with the lack of resources for interventions, mentors, and tutors.[118] Some studies have noted that teachers are not provided with the supports to interpret and take action based on the early warning reports they get.[119] Despite these challenges, some studies have highlighted positive and constructive changes, such as when teachers are able to work together not just in providing programs for students but also in creating engaging environments for students.[120] One particularly rich account is Emily Krone Phillips's *The Make-or-Break Year*, which details the story of early warning systems in one Chicago school and reveals the possibilities and challenges that come with trying to address dropping out in these environments.[121]

The present book adds to this literature not by presenting evidence of its efficacy or effectiveness but by analyzing the history of its spread across the United States. It turns the table by studying not so much the teachers and students inside classrooms but the researchers, philanthropists, and nonprofit staff who worked outside schools. In so doing, I aim to enrich how we think about the role of organizations and technologies in instituting changes. The book is an attempt at integrating emerging lines of scholarship to provide a new perspective for theorizing educational, organizational, and social changes.

## Chicago, Philadelphia, and New York City

Urban schools and urban school districts have often been characterized as failing students, particularly students of color who form the majority of students in these places.[122] Research shows that low-income, low-achieving, and non-white students in urban schools often find themselves in classes with the least skilled teachers.[123] Urban schools also often go through a rigmarole of new reforms, but with little discernible improvements to the whole system.[124] To be fair, the "problem" of urban schools is often not just about the schools. Sociologist Pedro Noguera pointed out how larger social forces like demographic change, poverty, racism, drug trafficking, violence, and social inequities contribute to outcomes often associated with schools.[125]

Although urban schools have these problems—and potentially even because of these very problems—these cities, I argue, have also become fertile grounds for innovations and creative problem-solving. On the one hand, the presence of nonprofits, research organizations, prominent universities, and philanthropic foundations based in large urban areas offers opportunities to improve the local school system. One can call this the *supply side* explanation for urban schools as sites of innovation. On the other hand, the large-scale problems of urban education make the work of these organizations more compelling and more urgent, thus fueling greater work in this field. One can call this the *demand side* explanation for urban innovation. In both cases, these opportunities challenge the often dreary picture painted about public education in large cities by showing how they can become places that go against the odds of urban education's entropic tendencies as organizations use cities as seedbeds for new initiatives and changes.

Given the focus on early warning indicators and the work of school improvement organizations, this book looks at three cities that were early pioneers of these technologies. The decision to focus on Chicago, Philadelphia, and New York City was based on a number of factors. First, the three cities had researched and created early warning systems before 2010, and this helps historically situate the development of these EWIs. Second, the development of EWIs in the three cities was not so much started by the district offices but by research and nonprofit organizations that worked with and in schools. In Chicago, it was started by a research organization. In Philadelphia and New York City, it was initiated by organizations helping with whole-school reform efforts. Third, these cities have the most extensive written documentation about EWIs, available in research studies, journal articles, annual reports, and news articles. As such, many subsequent studies have referred to the research done in these places as they created their own early warning systems. Finally, these cities did not rely on single organizations working on EWIs but had created a rich constellation of research, nonprofit, and philanthropic organizations that worked with the local school district.

Inasmuch as the three cities had considerable similarities, there were also salient differences among them. One was the size of the three school districts. In the 2020 digest from the National Center for Education Statistics, New York City was the largest school district with almost a million students, Chicago had more than 300,000 students, while Philadelphia had close to 150,000.[126] In the same digest, poverty rates for 5- to 17-year-olds in New York and Chicago were at 23.1 percent while poverty rate for Philadelphia was at 32.3 percent.[127] In a 2021 report by the Brookings Institution, which included racial demographics of students under 18 years old, the proportion of Black youth was 20.5 percent in New York City, 31.1 percent in Chicago, and 43.8 percent in Philadelphia. For Hispanic youths, it was 33.6 percent in New York City, 40.6 percent in Chicago, and 21.7 percent in Philadelphia. Taken together, these suggest large minority population in these urban school districts, but their racial ethnic proportions differ considerably.[128] Moreover, the organizations working in these three cities differ with each other as different local universities, research institutions, philanthropies, and nonprofits work with the school district.

By highlighting the similarities and differences across the school districts, I show the facility of using these cases to investigate and interrogate the role of research, philanthropic, and nonprofit organizations in educational changes. Particularly for dropout prediction systems, these three cities provide an opportune way of understanding strategies for starting and sustaining these initiatives. By highlighting the differences across the three cities, I also suggest that certain strategies may be similarly adapted despite the significant differences in population size, demographics, and organizational characteristics.

## Integrative Policy Analysis

Qualitative studies in sociology, education, and organization science often focus on a single site or a comparison between two sites. A researcher might focus on a single city, a single school, or a single nonprofit. But this book draws on *multiple sites* of study across *multiple levels* of analysis. While I write a more detailed methodological appendix at the end of this book, I share some important methodological choices toward what I call an "integrative policy analysis," which I hope can enrich the reading of the book.

The book draws on 95 in-depth interviews with schoolteachers, counselors, principals, school district officials, researchers, philanthropic managers, and nonprofit staff and leaders. To disaggregate, 73 were recent interviews with organizational actors working within and across the three cities, while 22 were past interviews of school personnel across six diverse schools in Chicago. The school interviews—which have not been used or published before—were conducted between 2015 and 2017, a time when EWIs were being introduced in Chicago schools. This makes them more appropriate to the study than present accounts when EWIs have already been institutionalized in the system and current teachers may find it harder to comment on how EWIs were initially used.[129] Aside from these interviews, I also compiled more than 2,800 pages of documents connected to EWIs, including news articles, research papers, annual reports, and journal articles.

Using the interviews and documents, I performed four different types of analysis. First, I structured a historical account of EWIs in each of the three cities. By drawing on interviews as sources of oral history and documents as primary data sources, I created a chronological account of the initiation and institutionalization of EWIs. Second, I thematically analyzed the interviews with school personnel in Chicago to understand how EWIs were operating on the ground when they were first being introduced. I show the different dynamics, challenges, and changes that happened as these "outside" interventions were being introduced inside schools. Third, I used the interviews with experts and elites in each of the three cities to understand the strategies used to support and sustain the EWI initiative. In the process of analyzing the interviews, I found that different actors focused on different parts of the system. Researchers tended to focus on the macro-level of paradigms; philanthropic, district, and nonprofit leaders concentrated on meso-level organizational networks; and school support coaches and trainers dedicated themselves to micro-level interactions in schools. Fourth, I used data on the informants' career histories and the professional connections they shared during the interviews to illustrate the intricate personal and organizational networks that span in and across the three cities. I highlight how the three cities are not independent of each other and that the consequences of change in these cities spilled over to other places as well. In this book, I kept the anonymity of schools and school informants by using pseudonyms but have kept the names of organizations and the informants in them.

This book introduces what I detail in the Methodological Appendix as an *integrative policy analysis*, a process of attending to the multiple levels, histories, and networks of a particular policy. Rather than just quantitatively understanding policy effects or qualitatively investigating policy implementation, an integrative perspective follows a policy, from its initial introduction to its eventual changes and adaptations when used in schools. It investigates the various actors working across different levels. It uses a historical perspective, showing that policies often transform because of political challenges, technological advancements, and institutional constraints. It is also attuned to coordination and competition across networked actors within sites and across sites. Such integrative analysis furthers and complements traditional policy analysis that often focuses on policies during a particular point in time.

## Overview of the Book

The book's six chapters are divided into two parts. In Part I, the chapters focus on the case of early warning indicators, with the first chapter highlighting the perspective from schools while the second highlights the perspective from outside schools. Part historical and part analytic, these two chapters describe the case in detail and highlight how the integration of these two vantage points can enrich the discussion of EWIs. In Part II, the chapters analyze the role organizations have played in spreading EWIs and the strategies they used to sustain them. Chapters 3 to 5 respectively detail the role of macro-, meso-, and micro-level perspectives on change, and Chapter 6 adds a spatial element for how these changes happened across local areas. The book's conclusion goes beyond the case of EWIs to show how similar dynamics happen with other educational changes that have been started and sustained by school improvement organizations.

Chapter 1 illustrates that EWIs were not so much just about dropout prediction; schools had adapted the available tools and technologies to suit their contexts. Drawing on interviews across six schools, the chapter presents how different schools emphasized specific parts of these dropout prediction data systems. EWIs became technologies for accountability, dropout prediction, student intervention, and systems improvement. School leaders, teachers, counselors, and staff spoke about these various perspectives and uses of EWIs—with each of these four technologies having their own tradeoffs.

Chapter 2 shifts the focus on the work of those outside schools: research, philanthropic, nonprofit, and school support organizations. This chapter focuses on the broad history of the development of EWIs across Chicago, Philadelphia, and New York City. Using documentary evidence and oral histories from more than 70 organizational actors, the chapter traces how the tool was discovered, appropriated, changed, and institutionalized. On one hand, the chapter documents a story of changes happening with the availability of new technologies, but, on the other hand, it was also a story of how powerful forces converge and diverge to sustain or threaten the initiative. More than just a history of EWIs in each of the three cities, the chapter uncovers the advantages and disadvantages of nonprofits in education, with candid ideas and opinions from the people working in these organizations.

Chapter 3 argues that one of the core reasons for the change and adoption of EWIs was because of the *creation of institutional logics* through the very form of EWI technology. As nonprofit organizations and school districts introduced new forms of EWIs, these technologies drew on specific meanings from different macro-level institutions in society. For example, EWIs used as a metric for school accountability rely on a logic of the state that privileges counting and accounting. The rest of the chapter shows how different technological forms of EWI attach to various other logics—scientific, professional, and community. The chapter illustrates how EWIs had appealed to different individuals and organizations because of the multiple logics that it took on. Such variation in logics was also often a result of the way the technology has developed throughout the years.

Chapter 4 documents the *structuring of entrepreneurial networks* in spreading or catalyzing the use of EWIs. The chapter highlights a meso-level view of organizational collaboration and division of labor. In particular, I highlight how networks were structured with particular templates in mind, spanning between a network with a clear hub and spokes, and a network with embedded connections crisscrossing each other. Using examples of inter-organizational and inter-school connections, I show how local organizations were key actors in structuring these webs that created distributive and integrative networks as well as embedded and role-differentiated networks. The networks did not just depend on the organizations' actions but more importantly emerged in response to the contexts they were in.

Chapter 5 argues that a key role of outside nonprofits is to help in *establishing webs of organizational routines* to guide the practice of EWIs on the ground. The chapter takes on a micro-level view of what happens inside schools and classrooms to show how nonprofit organizations must attend to and work with agents in schools. It documents the many forms of resistance of teachers and school leaders, and the strategies local organizations used to transform resistance into action. Core to this was the work of school improvement coaches who worked with schools to create routines that transformed not only behaviors and systems but also beliefs and mindsets. The chapter concludes with a lesson on how routines come as a precursor to, rather than a consequence of, mindset changes.

Chapter 6 emphasizes the approaches organizations used not so much to influence local districts but to transport these innovations to other places, and in so doing, transform national educational practices through inter-local changes. It argues how these organizations local to Chicago, Philadelphia, and New York City have themselves created and catalyzed a subtle web and an invisible infrastructure of organizations across the United States. In so doing, practices and ideas spread as these local examples are taken up as proofs of concept, as these organizations are linked to or contracted by other districts, and as these local initiatives gain national level supports from federal agencies and large philanthropies. The chapter theorizes institutional change not as a monolithic change but as a set of spatially specific, inter-local changes.

The conclusion moves beyond the case of EWIs by showing how local organizations have become key components in the transformation of other aspects of American education, from charter schools to alternative teacher preparation programs, from networked improvement communities to computer science education, and from anti-racist education to anti-critical race theory organizing. The book ends not just by showing the power of these organizations and the potential of this theory, but also by problematizing the role these organizations play in democracy and public life. As schools have become a battleground of political ideas and ideologies, these organizations have become embedded in education and must find ways of navigating these systems. The conclusion also suggests questions and reflections to guide the work of outside nonprofit organizations and the public institutions with which they work.

# PART I

# TRANSFORMING DATA AND DROPPING OUT

# Chapter 1
## Preventing Dropouts
### A View from Inside Schools

In the early 2000s, dropping out of high school was a problem seeking a solution. In the report *Locating the Dropout Crisis*, researchers Robert Balfanz and Nettie Legters highlighted how around 2,000 US high schools graduated less than 60 percent of their freshman class.[1] Many of these high schools were in large urban areas, disproportionately hurting students of color. More alarmingly, nearly 50 percent of African American students and 40 percent of Latino students attended high schools where graduation was not the norm.[2] Often, research had emphasized the role of the personal characteristics of individual students that increased the risk of dropping out: their race or ethnicity, gender, socioeconomic status, cognitive abilities, standardized test scores, academic engagement, and school behaviors.[3] For some, dropping out came abruptly at a pivotal moment, while for others it was a gradual disengagement from school.[4]

One of the solutions that seemed promising was a dropout prediction data system known as ninth-grade *early warning indicators* (EWIs). These were data systems that helped predict ninth graders who were at risk of dropping out in an effort to intervene before it happened.[5] To identify which students needed help, these EWIs relied on data on attendance, behavior (detentions and suspensions), and course performance during students' first year in high school. Such focus on the freshman year was motivated by researchers arguing that this period was a crucial time of transition, both *academically* as students moved into larger schools with different norms from their elementary schools and *developmentally* as adolescents experienced different risks, opportunities, and peer influences.[6] With EWIs, data were being marshalled to address a dropout problem that many had previously deemed "intractable."[7]

Sociological and organizational studies have coined the term *quantification* to refer to this contemporary tendency to use data, metrics, and numbers.[8] In K–12 schools, studies of quantification have often concentrated

*Subtle Webs*. Jose Eos Trinidad, Oxford University Press. © Oxford University Press (2025).
DOI: 10.1093/9780197786123.003.0002

on the role of test-based school accountability in transforming educational practices and influencing student outcomes.[9] Studies often investigate the intended and unintended outcomes of this process of quantification. On the one hand, evidence shows positive effects on student achievement brought about by changes in instructional practices, like lengthening class time and increasing resources for teachers.[10] On the other hand, studies have also documented how accountability pressures could influence behaviors such as teaching to the test, focusing instruction on students at the "cut off" of passing, removing students unlikely to pass, and even outright cheating.[11] In contrast to school accountability pressures that relied heavily on student test scores, there emerged a different form of quantification with EWIs that relied instead on students' grades, behavior, and attendance.

This book investigates the emergence and spread of EWIs through organizational actors—researchers, philanthropists, nonprofit leaders, and nongovernment staff—who aimed to address the problem of dropping out with new data systems. But before understanding the dynamics inside organizations and boardrooms, we must first step into schools and classrooms to understand what these EWIs were all about. Drawing on in-depth interviews with staff at six Chicago high schools, the chapter illustrates how EWIs were used, resisted, transformed, and embedded in school practices.[12] It highlights the narratives of teachers, counselors, and school leaders who were interacting with outside organizations, receiving school district mandates, and ultimately implementing EWIs.

To be accurate, an early warning indicator is not a particular policy or even a discrete program. Rather, it is more like a web of practices and support systems, with schools combining different elements. The chapter underlines four salient dimensions of EWIs and their inherent tensions. As an *accountability system*, the inclusion of on-track metrics led some schools to positively focus on improving the number of students on track but led others to negatively pressure teachers to artificially improve these numbers. As a just-in-time *data system*, these dashboards served a practical purpose of identifying students in need of support, as well as a performative purpose of being a data-driven ritual. As a *student support system*, these EWIs had become a prevention system of attendance monitoring, tutorials, and mentorships, as well as an intervention system of credit recovery for those who have already failed. As a *school improvement system*, the initiative drove tangible organizational changes for the whole school, but at the same time, buffered any radical changes from happening inside classrooms. Although

I document the many ways EWIs have been successful and limited, the evidence shows how these tools and systems have been transformative—particularly for schools that have teachers and leaders invested in this collective work, and that have resources to spur these changes.

## Accountability System

In 2003, the Chicago Public Schools (CPS) added the "on-track" rate to the district's high school accountability metric.[13] The rate was calculated as the percentage of ninth graders who were "on track"; that is, those who obtained five course credits and failed no more than one semester of a core course like English, math, science, or social studies.[14] Schools received between one to five points, with five points denoting that 90 percent or more of the ninth graders in a school were considered "on track." Officially known as the Freshman OnTrack rate, it contributed to the school's overall performance index that included other metrics like standardized test score growth rates, attendance rates, graduation rates, and school climate survey results.[15]

Schools that emphasized the accountability system of EWIs highlighted the tension between *focus* and *pressure*. On one end, Freshman OnTrack's addition to the school accountability system provided a sense of concrete direction for what to focus on; it emphasized the need to support the experience of ninth graders who were transitioning into high school. But on the other end, an over-emphasis on the metric led to resistance and resentment, particularly from teachers who felt pressured to change grades to supposedly improve their on-track numbers.

Located on the southside of Chicago, Amityville High School served a predominantly Latino community.[16] Its assistant principal shared that the accountability system was a large aspect of why Freshman OnTrack worked in their school. In 2012, the assistant principal came in with the school's new principal and noted the previous low graduation numbers in the school. Just a few years earlier, the district had begun instituting accountability metrics for Freshman OnTrack rates and high school graduation rates. What the accountability system did was not so much to suggest ways to improve but to focus discussions on the importance of freshman year for graduating. He looked back at significant changes in their school, saying:

> Prior to 2010 . . . , the accountability for turning these numbers around was not there. This is, this is horrible . . . The graduation rate was probably this

> low too . . . , and that was seen as okay. 42 [percent], 53 [percent graduation rates]. That's, it's not acceptable . . . A few years ago, it was okay to have like a 40 to 50 percent graduation rate here in the building, and now we've moved up to 60 to 70.

As with many schools in the city, these low graduation rates were previously "seen as okay" and were a normal part of neighborhood public schools in Chicago.

One of the interesting aspects of Freshman OnTrack as an accountability system was that it did not so much instruct schools how to increase on-track and graduation numbers; instead, it highlighted the importance of this goal. Like test-based accountability that had been critiqued as simply a strategy to measure and incentivize schools without any educational foundations, Freshman OnTrack could have easily been critiqued for leaving schools to figure out how to improve their numbers.[17] However, for Amityville, where the previous dismal graduation rates were concerning, the sense of focus from the accountability metric was arguably a much-needed push.

One way this focus happened concretely for the school was through meetings between teachers and administrators about their Freshman OnTrack rates. A biology teacher at Amityville said, "Our admin[istrators] really look at our grade failures and our on-track [data]. One thing that's really important about our school is we don't just look at F's, we look at D's and F's, and we also look at the other end of A's and B's." The school's arts department leader confirmed this, saying there was a "high level of accountability, like we had to, every teacher had to meet with the administration." These meetings entailed conversations with teachers about their students, the grades they gave, the on-track trends, and the interventions being done.

Such focused conversations about accountability, particularly with students' grades and on-track rates, permeated different aspects of the school. A ninth-grade English teacher who was also Amityville's Freshman OnTrack coordinator shared, "We may not throw out a number at every, you know, at every chance we get together, but we're constantly talking about who needs what, what are we doing as a team . . . , what course team is leading [a freshman intervention]." This concentrated goal of increasing on-track and graduation numbers thus became a preoccupation for the school. In this school, accountability was conceived as a necessary tool, particularly when compared to previous years when the graduation rates were below 50 percent.

But this was not necessarily the case for other schools. Some teachers in other schools had had reservations and resisted this focus on accountability because it could have been taken to a narrowly conceived extreme. Because on-track rates were computed by the number of students who had no more than one semester of a failed subject, some feared that accountability would lead to students being unscrupulously passed.

A social studies teacher from a different high school recalled how, in their previous school, there was "huge resistance, huge resentment from faculty... anytime it was getting close to the end of the semester, like teachers would be *pissed* (emphasis in the original)." The teacher continued:

> I think if you jammed [on-track rates] down teachers' throats, that "You have to pass these kids," you are going to like, you render yourself almost ineffective as a principal. You need to make sure that there isn't a sense of teacher-shaming at all.... At my old school, there was a ton of resentment around it because it was so jammed down our throats, people breathe down our neck. If we didn't follow the intervention trick, we got in trouble.

Teachers also reasoned that some students simply did not deserve to pass if they were not attending class, not submitting homework, and not showing the necessary skills.

School staff from Amityville High and other schools noted how they heard stories of teachers feeling top-down pressures when grading students. Amityville's biology teacher encapsulated the concern: "When I started teaching, my big concern was 'Okay, well if we want the Freshman OnTrack rate to look good, I feel like this could go down a really slippery slope to just passing all of these kids.'" Similarly, an assistant principal from another high school shared that "it's definitely the teachers' fear that . . . they're gonna be pressured to . . . pass students so that you get the metric."

What teachers feared had been known in the social sciences as Campbell's Law. It was named after the American social scientist Donald T. Campbell, who said, "The more any quantitative social indicator is used for social decision-making, the more subject it will be to corruption pressures and the more apt it will be to distort and corrupt the social processes it is intended to monitor."[18] In the case of EWIs as an accountability system, because on-track rates became tied with school incentives, teachers may have been pressured or inclined to artificially increase these rates by simply passing students.

Although accountability focus and pressures are often thought of as opposites, could Freshman OnTrack have led to both focus on improving systems *and* pressures on teacher behavior? Even if none of the informants experienced the explicit pressures to change grades, teachers were aware of the judgement they might have received if they gave out failing marks. A mathematics teacher mentioned that teachers had become more careful with giving out F's:

> I really explain to students, "If you get an F, it's because you chose to do absolutely nothing." So, that's my approach to it, but if I look at the bigger picture in terms of overall teachers . . . the number of students failing your class is looked at. And so, if I have a lot of students failing my class, I'm looked at. And I don't wanna be looked at. And so, some teachers tend to keep a lower failure rate.

This quote may be read in two ways. From a positive perspective, it suggests that the EWIs did not so much encourage teachers to unscrupulously pass students so much so as EWIs *prevented teachers from unscrupulously failing them*. This teacher explained to students that they only received an F if they did "absolutely nothing." If teachers could have previously easily doled out Fs to students, now teachers had to think twice when giving a failing mark.

From a negative perspective, the quote suggests that teachers changed their way of grading students in response to accountability pressures. The same math teacher mentioned that even if she did not see this happen in her school, she had "heard stories from other teachers . . . across the district, y'know, 'Your failure rate should be less than this number.' I've heard that." In these schools, the administration was actively influencing how students were graded—something teachers resisted because of its threat to their autonomy. But even for this math teacher, pressure was there to lower failure rates.

As Amityville High School has shown, the accountability system could lead to productive gains, particularly as the Freshman OnTrack rate emphasized a key lever for change. While "pressures" have often been thought to be counter-productive, pressures may interestingly change behaviors toward productive ends, such as when it prevented teachers from unscrupulously failing students. But this accountability system was just one aspect of EWIs. Productive gains may have also been driven by, and occurred in concert with, other dimensions.

## Data System

In 2008, Chicago's central district office started releasing just-in-time "on-track" data, detailing the performance of each student and flagging students based on high absences, low course grades, or course failures.[19] Provided every five weeks, it was designed to help schools intervene with students who were chronically absent, those who were failing their classes, or those who needed targeted interventions. Chicago also had other forms of data like the Freshman Watchlist, which was a report of incoming high school students who struggled during eighth grade, and the D/Fs report that grouped students in need of supports. Such data systems were crucial in the story of EWIs because several researchers argued that concrete changes in on-track and graduation rates came not with the advent of the on-track accountability in 2003 but with the introduction of just-in-time data in 2008.[20]

Similar to the accountability system, the EWI data system also moved between two poles; that is, between *practical* changes and *performative* alterations. On one end, this new technology creating intuitive color-coded lists of students was practically useful to identify students in need of help and intervene early enough to prevent failure from happening.[21] In this sense, data were discussed and used to transform practices and relationships. On the other end, such a data system may have taken on ceremonial purposes—used less for organizational efficiency and more for institutional legitimacy.[22] In other words, using the data tool was simply a performative routine to create confidence for what was already happening in schools.

Located on the northside of Chicago and serving both Latino and African American students, Seaford High School had teachers and administrators regularly pulling data from their student information and grading systems. Data came from different places: the teachers' own *Gradebook*, where they saw each student's real-time performance; the *Dashboard*, which the district provided every five weeks to detail students' real-time "on-track" or "off-track" status; and the *Watchlist*, which showed incoming freshman students' status at the beginning of the school year. One science teacher from Seaford High shared what was the most relevant data that helped with this work:

> The most important [data] is what I see myself, just in terms of looking at their work at my Gradebook. I do this thing where I will periodically print [students'] grades for all of their classes and we may spend five minutes, you know, once a month, looking at it and talking about it.

But the teacher's own online Gradebook was not the only source of information. This science teacher also mentioned that they received monthly statements on their students' attendance and biweekly messages from their assistant principal on the number of students who were off track.

Because data came from different places, these were often compared with each other. At Seaford, the resident principal said that the school pulled out a "failure report" of students who had a grade below 60 percent in any freshman course; this was from the teachers' Gradebook. They also pulled out an "off-track report" of students who the district thought were currently off track; this was from the district's Dashboard. The data were then used to monitor and identify students in need of help. The resident principal added, "I go through and I highlight the students that are off track and I'm also looking for their progress. Did they slip? Did they improve?" In this way, they were using these just-in-time indicators to identify students to make concrete plans for them.

While the school's staff acknowledged that some struggling students can be easily identified without these quantitative data, they still felt that the quantitative metrics helped them focus and catch students to whom they would have otherwise failed to attend. Seaford's principal said, "I think it'd be really difficult [without the data]. We'd focus on the kids that were in trouble, always got written up . . . So maybe the ones that have maybe one F or two F's . . . would fall through the cracks because maybe they didn't have a discipline problem [or] an attendance problem." For this school, data both confirmed which students they thought were failing and actually helped them identify the students they would have otherwise thought of as doing fine.

But the data were not always practical. At times, data have taken on a performative function.

While schools had used data to identify students and improve systems, schools were often limited by the data put into the system. Because of problems with inaccurate data at Seaford, the principal had instituted a policy for teachers to enter two grades per week to their Gradebook, saying, "I have now had to put it in very official language that it is two learning task grades, that could be formative or summative." However, in other schools that did not have this clear expectation, the effectiveness of Freshman OnTrack was limited by the data teachers entered or did not enter. One social worker from a different school said, "I think that some teachers don't [enter grades on time], you know, 'cause I get a lot of complaints from the kids, and those who are interested in their grades will check their student portal almost daily." Another social studies teacher from a different school confirmed that they did not necessarily enter grades every week. In this way, the effectiveness of the data was limited by the actions and inactions of teachers—leading to merely ceremonial use of data.

Another way that data took on a more performative role was not necessarily when data weren't used but when data were still used even when no longer useful. An arts teacher from Amityville High detailed how their school had continued with these data-focused processes even when it no longer seemed necessary:

> One thing that is like a little bit frustrating now is we've gotten so good at Freshman OnTrack that I feel like now, when we're in these meetings, it's kind of like beating our heads against the wall, like we feel we already have a lot of strategies that work.

Yes, the teachers used the data. But they used the data the same way they did when on-track rates were low. The arts teacher said that their Freshman OnTrack rate was already 97 percent, and that sweating over the remaining three percent felt like "beating our heads against the wall." Data-focused practices then became so institutionalized that they took on a performative function, even if they started out as having a real practical function.

Having just-in-time data was crucial to Freshman OnTrack, particularly as the various types of data were used to identify students that would have otherwise fallen through the cracks.[23] At Seaford High School, as well as in other Chicago schools, these data were used to identify students in need of supports like tutoring, mentorship, and credit recovery. Data confirmed what some teachers already knew about the students who were struggling. Data also added to their knowledge of the students who didn't have tell-tale signs of struggles. But data-focused practices could be limited in contexts of performative function, like when data were not input in time and when data were used in similar ways even as contexts had already changed.

## Support System

Data are only as good as how they are used. What mattered was not necessarily the accountability metric or the data dashboard, but *how* these tools were used to prevent failure and intervene when failure was imminent.

Interestingly, data on students' attendance and grades have almost always been present in schools. But what was different about EWIs was how new and intuitive information technologies were combined with good old personal relationships to create new systems of support. Supposedly, the data tools could help identify students or groups of students that needed support, and resources could be directed in the form of programs to improve students' skills, attendance, academic performance, and credit recovery.[24] In reality, however, various schools faced resource constraints in providing tailored support for different groups of students—particularly when more than 20 percent of a freshman class were marked as at risk of being off-track.[25]

As a student support system, EWIs had been used for both *prevention* and *intervention*. The support system's theory of change was that freshman year was an early enough time to identify students in need of support, prevent them from disengaging in school, and address challenging behaviors.[26] While the goal of EWIs was to prevent failure through supports during the school year, some students still experienced some form of challenge, whether because of chronic absenteeism, course failure, or social emotional difficulties. In these cases, Freshman OnTrack provided the data for interventions for specific individuals who needed to catch up.

Catering to a largely Latino community in Chicago's southside, Merrick High School had instituted a number of processes for dropout prevention and intervention. The focus was not simply on providing supports to specific groups. Before detailing the programs the school had in place for students identified as being off track, the school's principal spoke about general programs like *Freshman Connection*—an orientation to know the school, teachers, other students, and programs in the school—and *Freshman Seminars*, where staff talked about school expectations, on-track status, Grade Point Averages, college-going, and so on. The principal shared that:

> The freshman seminar class . . . in the past was just strictly reading, just support with the reading . . . [This year] we have a counselor go in there and talk to the freshmen about, you know, where they're at in their education and what they could do in order to make sure that they're ready for college when they go out.

Merrick's principal emphasized the importance of these programs being "built into the schedule" and making sure "kids are aware of what they need in order to succeed." The programs were set up to provide a baseline understanding to help all students.

But the school knew that a regular class on available supports was not going to be enough, particularly when one of the school's biggest challenges was attendance. A class with these topics would be futile if the students it was designed for did not attend. Merrick's counselor detailed several ways they addressed attendance to prevent students from failing. After receiving information from teachers, the counselor contacted students who were chronically absent to "figure out why they're not in school, . . . and I contact, have meetings with the parents, . . . and with the teachers, to see if we can come up with a plan to help this person stay on-track." The counselor added that they had a program providing incentives if students consistently got teachers to sign-off that they were on time and did their assignments.

At Merrick High School and in other places in the United States, these were often called *multi-tiered systems of support.*[27] Tier 1 supports were applied to everyone, Tier 2 programs were for specific groups of students, and Tier 3 supports were individualized and intensive interventions for particular students. In the context of EWIs, this may involve tutoring, mentoring, and counseling.

Tutoring was one of the key programs the school used to prevent students falling off track. The school's counseling department chair said, "We have all kinds of tutoring throughout the building, tutoring before [classes], during lunch periods, and after school, tutoring in the library, there's always tutoring that's accessible." At Merrick, and at other schools, tutoring was sometimes the work of teachers who volunteered their time while at other times the task of tutors was outsourced from outside the school.

Other schools had a variety of resources. Freeport High School was one of the places that had some outside partners like GEAR UP (Gaining Early Awareness and Readiness for Undergraduate Programs) and SAGA tutoring—both of which provided schools with additional tutors. The school's math teacher talked about these organizations:

> We have GEAR UP, which is not a class, but it's additional tutoring, and they do college visits. We also have [what is] called SAGA but it's a Math Lab . . . I had two students who went from being like a C, D-performing [student] in the assessments, to the end of the year, two of the students were getting 18 out of 20 [and] 19 out of 20 on the last three tests. So, having the Math Lab is amazing.

GEAR UP was in Freeport High, Seaford High, and Wantagh High. City Year was an organization working with Bellmore High School to provide in-school tutors and mentors to students. SAGA had math tutors at Freeport High, and while Sylvan Tutoring had theirs during the freshman seminar time at Wantagh High School. Merrick High School had Metropolitan Family Services, which had a social worker doing "one-on-ones" with students and working with the school's counselors. These collaborations highlight how the ecosystem of public schools has expanded with new organizations that support keeping freshmen on track.

Despite the various preventive programs, some students still failed their courses. Because of this, a number of schools also had credit recovery programs for students who failed a particular course. Merrick's principal said, "We have a credit recovery [night school] here and we're gonna have summer school, and [students] would cover those credits as soon as possible." In other schools in the city, they did not just have evening classes but also provided online classes to help students catch up. One may read this as a school's strategy to artificially increase "on-track" numbers; however, it was also an honest attempt to get students the credits they needed to pass their freshman year and to keep them on track to graduate high school.

Such credit recovery programs—available in five of the six schools interviewed—were often viewed as a last resort intervention for those who had already failed. One principal said, "Credit recovery, that's the last-ditch effort, but what I'm more focused on is again preventative. When we get to, you know, the twelfth week and we have not seen improvement, we will pull the kids down in batches and try and isolate the problem based on what they're telling us." It was at that point that schools would recommend credit recovery.

Merrick High School highlighted the use of EWIs as a student support system. Data were used to both identify students at risk of being off track and to also create supports in the form of counselors reaching out to chronically absent students, teachers mentoring students struggling behaviorally, and tutors helping students struggling academically. Although most of the efforts were preventive, credit recovery interventions were necessary for students who failed courses during the school year. A key element that emerged was the role of mentoring and tutoring organizations that provided additional human resources to the schools.

## School Improvement System

Chicago's early warning indicator, Freshman OnTrack, had multiple dimensions. It was an accountability system that helped schools and educators focus on improving graduation rates and freshman students' experiences. It was a just-in-time data system that helped identify students or groups of students that needed support. It was a multi-tiered student support system that schools used to prevent students from failing courses or to provide opportunities for students to make up for failed courses. Not everything went as planned, however, and schools experienced accountability pressures, incomplete data, performative data rituals, and resistance to changing practices. But overall, narratives across different schools highlighted how EWIs were influencing various significant changes in schools. These changes were not only about the identification and intervention for students at risk of dropping out, but also changes in the systems and processes in schools.

Arguably, these EWIs became a catalyst in improving school systems. On one end, the system affected *organizational changes* in schools. It entailed teachers in the same grade level meeting with each other when they previously worked siloed in their departments; it entailed creating clear systems for supporting students when support was previously random at best; and it entailed a shift to being responsible for the success of students when it was previously thought to be outside their control. But, on the other end, some have also highlighted how it *buffered radical changes* inside classrooms and with teachers' instruction. Concentrating on systems changes had, in some ways, absolved them from instituting changes to the instructional core of schools.[28]

Freeport High School in Chicago's southside served a majority African American student population. One of the ways EWIs influenced systems improvement was through changes in the ways teachers met. At Freeport, teachers had grade-level meetings on Mondays (i.e., meetings with teachers teaching the same grade-level students) and had course-team meetings on Wednesdays. At the grade-level meeting for freshman teachers, one math teacher detailed what they did:

> We just pulled out on-track data from the Dashboard and looked at, "These are the students that are showing like a zero. Why are they zero?" . . . And

> so, our task between now and the next week or two is to figure out what is happening to those students. So, some of the students we were able to talk about, and [we] say, "They just aren't doing anything in this class."

The math teacher continued that they would list these students and talk about reasons for a particular student failing the class, either because of absence, non-submission, or weak submissions. From there, they would "look at what else can happen, or what's our next step." Although teachers talked about some of the culpability of students for not doing well in classes, they also noted their own efforts to reduce students' odds of failing. This meeting was a remarkable shift in two ways. First, teachers of the same grade were now talking with each other about their shared students. Second, they were thinking about their role in helping students rather than merely discussing the students' deficits.

Because of the system of meetings and interventions, the school would have exhausted various efforts before failing a student. Even after a student failed, the school still felt responsible to get the student back on track. Freeport High's principal said, "Before a kid fails a class, we'll have done several things with that kid. But after the kid fails the class, the counselor follows up with them to make sure that they get re-enrolled into another class. GEAR UP [an outside organization] follows up with them to make sure that they're getting tutoring, and the teachers try to proactively prevent them from failing the next semester." This preoccupation with preventing failure was palpable in all schools interviewed but, as in an earlier discussion, this was far from the case before the early 2000s.

Changes were not merely structural improvements of dropout systems and interventions; they were cultural advances in terms of renewed relationships and collective responsibility. A social studies teacher at Freeport noted how much the school had changed, not only with students being on-track but with the school's general learning climate:

> I know with this school, it definitely had, you know, a bad reputation . . . I believe that the principal definitely changed the culture of the school . . . . [The principal] set up that culture and then improvements . . . trickled on to, you know, students completing their assignments, knowing how important it is to stay on-track, how important it is to pass.

In this way, EWIs were leveraged by the principal to create opportunities for educators to collaborate with each other and improve relationships with students.

Although teachers and school leaders highlighted changes happening in the social organization of schools, rarely did they describe instructional practices and strategies used during class time. Many had emphasized case management strategies that were often happening outside the classrooms: tutoring outside class hours, credit recovery, and attendance monitoring.

One of the few things related to instructional change was curriculum. When asked about the school's goals beyond increasing on-track rates, Freeport's assistant principal primarily shared about their goals for improving attendance and school climate. After mentioning these two, she followed up saying, "I would say the third thing is then that academic part, you know, do we have a curriculum that addresses student needs?" This quote highlights how the emphasis of EWIs had been primarily on improving organizational systems rather than instituting instructional changes.

As a school improvement system, EWIs succeeded in influencing organizational processes but were less successful in affecting instructional changes. However, perhaps the most consequential change was in terms of challenging the mindsets of educators. When asked about the most salient changes at Freeport, a school that catered to a highly disadvantaged population, the assistant principal answered that teachers now understood the implications of failing a student. She added, "[EWIs] made the difference in how they looked at, 'Oh, this student isn't doing any work, they're gonna fail [my class]' to 'They're failing a grade too.'" The insight that failure at ninth grade was extremely consequential down the line had helped emphasize that teachers actually had something they could do to prevent students from dropping out. Teachers slowly shifted their mindsets in terms of their role and responsibility—both personal and collective—in keeping students in school.

Freeport High School saw EWIs as a catalyst for school improvement. The initiative helped in changing their routines of meeting with each other, in creating systems for collective responsibility, in attempting to transform their school climate, and in shifting individuals' mindsets. However, much of the effort—at Freeport and elsewhere—had concentrated on organizational improvements rather than core instructional changes. In this arrangement, schools were able to flexibly transform systems while still promoting autonomy within individual classrooms.

## Lessons for Education Policy

This chapter sets the stage to understand the technology, tensions, and transformations that came with EWIs. The view from inside schools highlighted how the technology was more than just a data system, how different dimensions of EWIs entailed tensions and tradeoffs, and how schools were transformed through structural and cultural changes catalyzed by this initiative. Although this qualitative investigation cannot answer whether the policy increased students' grades or supported graduation outcomes, it does enrich and provide nuance to quantitative evidence regarding EWIs' effects on chronic absenteeism, course performance, and potential graduation.[29]

In this section, I use the case of EWIs to highlight some lessons for the study of education policies. Inasmuch as it is central to understand the quantitative impact of a policy, several other aspects must also be interrogated. One is to historically account how policies and technologies can often adapt with and be adapted by actors inside and outside the school system. Another is to clarify the potential tradeoffs with policies and how this can change our judgement of the policy impact. Finally, policy researchers need to understand how the change in one small technology can catalyze transformation for the larger system. Lessons below apply not just to EWIs but also to policies, both educational and organizational.

First, EWIs were *technologies* that changed through time, had different dimensions, and were variably used in different contexts. In Chicago schools, EWIs started out as an addition to the district's school accountability metric and subsequently were used as a data tool to identify and intervene for students at risk of dropping out. Rather than a policy that had to be faithfully adopted, EWIs were a set of technological systems that were adapted to specific contexts—particularly as the schools were in socioeconomically disadvantaged and racially minoritized communities often cautious with new reforms and technologies. Such adaptations entailed schools learning how best to use the various dimensions of the technology.

Applied to the broader study of education policies, this lesson highlights how policies often change and often in unexpected ways. More broadly, technical and social technologies for school improvement often meet constraints and opportunities while implemented on the ground. As it is important for studies to document the immediate impact of programs, it is equally important to show how these policies and technologies change through time. Unfortunately, the demands of scholarly publication and program evaluation can often restrict researchers' time horizons to specific cross-sections of policies. But one can remember the counsel from political scientist Paul Pierson who noted:

> Most important social processes take a long time—sometimes an extremely long time—to unfold. This is a problematic fact for contemporary social science [where] the time horizons for most analysts have become increasingly restricted.[30]

By attending to the adaptations of policies, researchers and policymakers may understand what exactly about the program is key. The story of EWIs' changes highlights how various school actors saw that what mattered was not technical and sophisticated identification, but an improvement of the social systems to support students transitioning to high school.

Second, organizational learning involves *tensions* and *tradeoffs*. Every one of the different dimensions of EWIs had their own advantages and disadvantages. The accountability system was a tool for both focusing efforts and exerting pressures on educators. The data system aided the practical identification of students in need of help and functioned as a performative ritual to legitimize schools as being data driven. The support system created opportunities to prevent failures and to intervene when failure was certain. The improvement system supported organizational changes but buffered large transformations in the instructional core of classrooms. While many individuals would like a simple answer of whether the policy worked or not, the story of EWIs illustrates that alongside substantial changes are ceremonial changes, unintended consequences, or no changes at all. It thus becomes difficult to adjudicate policies when tradeoffs are present.

One thing policy scholars can do is to clarify what these tradeoffs and unintended consequences are. Here, qualitative research focused on those leading and implementing policies can shine a light on often hidden processes when we rely solely on quantitative information on test scores, attendance, graduation rates, and so on. While some may argue that a policy's unintended consequences can be a cause for halting a policy, I argue that careful discernment be made regarding whether the right course of action is to give up on the policy or to improve certain systems that reduce these negative consequences. In the case of EWIs, a relatively inexpensive set of tools and practices, the evidence points to important changes (particularly during times and places where graduation rates were concerningly low). While EWIs were not without unanticipated consequences, on balance the initiative was an important step in the right direction.

Third, technologies can lead to *transformations* when organizations engage both structural processes and cultural mindsets. In the case of EWIs, the technology of on-track indicators had shifted not only data use, relational dynamics, and collegial meetings, but more importantly the beliefs of teachers regarding students' course failure and dropping out and educators' feelings of collective responsibility to support students. (Chapter 5 will explore this more fully.) The core concept of Freshman OnTrack was not that it was a random set of structures with data tools and interventions but that it was a coherent set of principles that directed the work and focus of school staff.

While a specific technology can spur transformations in particular structures and cultures in a system, such change may have a shelf life. This opens a point of reflection for education policy about whether the transformations we see are contingent on particular contexts and historical periods. Of course, this does not mean that policies are ineffective. Rather, it means that policies are effective for a particular period—at which point, they can be so institutionalized that they become taken for granted, or they may be so part of the system that they have little added value. (In the same sense, when one takes it out of the system, the removal may lead to negative consequences.) This opens up questions regarding when and how policies lose the advantage they provide to students as these policies become institutionalized. For example, one efficacy study of EWIs saw no significant differences between treatment and control schools. Its authors noted:

> Analyses of interview data with control-school leaders indicated that although the control schools did not have externally funded [coaches and programs], some were implementing similar interventions to help their struggling ninth graders, which included the allocation of human resources to ensure students received these interventions . . . . In short, because of widespread dissemination of early warning system ideas and the importance of intervening to keep ninth graders on track, the practices at treatment and control groups did not appear to differ significantly.[31]

In this example, EWI principles were applied to both treatment and control schools, which may have potentially helped both groups, but which also made it harder to see any effects. In these types of scenarios, researchers must analyze how transformations are possible but the effects contingent to specific times and contexts.

Lessons from this qualitative investigation of EWIs in six schools concentrate on the importance of the technical and social technology of the policy, the tensions and tradeoffs inherent in it, and the transformations that can be catalyzed from it. A qualitative understanding of policies does not just reveal the mechanisms for impacts. Qualitative studies also reveal how policies change through time. They reveal how negative and positive outcomes can happen at the same time, and they uncover larger transformations in the system as well as in the limits of those transformations.

# Chapter 2
## Predicting Dropouts
### A View from Outside Schools

Chicago, 1987. US Secretary of Education William Bennett said the Chicago Public Schools (CPS) system was the nation's worst school district.[1] He added that, "If it's not the last, I don't know who is. There can't be very many cities that are worse. Chicago is pretty much it." As if to save the windy city's face, Bennett shared that "a spokesman from the mayor's office responded immediately and said, 'We're not the worst. Detroit is the worst.'"

It was a race to the bottom. The dropout rate in the city was high, with 43 percent of the entering freshman class unable to finish high school, and among those who graduated, few performed well in exams like the American College Test (ACT). An article in the Chicago Tribune during the same year highlighted how more than half of the city's public high schools were in the bottom one percent of schools nationwide.[2] All this was happening in the context of a greater push for school accountability, pressures for the creation of a school voucher program, large bureaucratic inefficiencies, and a record 19-day teachers strike in September 1987.[3] Yet this was not unique to Chicago. Urban school districts like Philadelphia, New York City, and Los Angeles experienced similar high levels of dropouts and low levels of student achievement.[4]

Change was needed, but it was not clear where the change would originate. While teachers and school leaders were important in implementing changes, their influence can be limited at best. While the federal education department can critique the nation's worst school district, the effects can be nothing more than bad press. Although research on education has often interrogated the role of actors within the system, this chapter studies the role of actors outside schools: researchers, philanthropists, nonprofit leaders, and school support staff who saw an opportunity in the late 1990s and early 2000s to work with large urban school districts. In the process, they created a field of organizations that worked with schools and school districts. It was a subtle web of people and organizations that created

*Subtle Webs*. Jose Eos Trinidad, Oxford University Press. © Oxford University Press (2025).
DOI: 10.1093/9780197786123.003.0003

connections with each other—often in ways that were discreet, complex, and, at times, imperceptible to individuals inside the system. This chapter details the historical formation of these webs in three cities in their attempt to address dropping out and to promote early warning indicators (EWIs). The chapter also includes a discussion of the advantages and risks related to how organizations influence change, stability, and spread.

## The Cast of Organizations

One of the challenges with an account of organizational history (or, in this case, interorganizational histories) is the danger of readers being overwhelmed by the multitude of organizations, personalities, and events. To provide a loose structure to this chronicle, I illustrate how the local organizations can be categorized into three groups of research, school support, and philanthropic organizations, which are then connected to their respective central district offices (see Table 2.1).

Collectively, I refer to these organizations as "school improvement organizations," taking inspiration from Brian Rowan's discussion of the school improvement industry.[5] While these organizations can be both nonprofit and for-profit, many of these organizations are nonprofits, which is why I at times refer to them with the shorthand, "nonprofits." Scholars have also referred to them as intermediary organizations, supplementary education service organizations, and external actors in education.[6]

While *school district offices* and officials are part of the education system, they figure prominently as an important actor because of how organizations become connected to the school system through these district offices and officials. Across Chicago, Philadelphia, and New York City, I was able to interview many individuals, including a district superintendent, a research director, a school coach, a high school graduation program director, and a school district consultant.

*Research organizations* were another important group because the initial discoveries regarding dropping out and dropout prediction emerged from these organizations. In Chicago, the University of Chicago Consortium on School Research provided insights into what factors were predictive of high school graduation during the early 2000s. In Philadelphia around the same time, a group from Johns Hopkins University (JHU) saw how sixth-grade performance was also predictive of likely graduation. Later, another

**Table 2.1** Organizations and Early Warning Indicators

| | **Chicago** | **Philadelphia** | **New York City** |
|---|---|---|---|
| *School District* | Chicago Public Schools (CPS) | School District of Philadelphia | New York City Department of Education (NYC DOE) |
| *Research Organizations* | University of Chicago Consortium on School Research (Consortium) | Johns Hopkins University (JHU) Center for the Social Organization of Schools (CSOS) | Research Alliance for New York City Schools (Research Alliance) |
| | | Research for Action/Philadelphia Education Research Consortium (PERC) | |
| *School Support Organizations* | Network for College Success (NCS) | Talent Development Secondary (TDS) | New Visions for Public Schools |
| | To&Through Project | United Way | #DegreesNYC |
| | | Philadelphia Academies, Inc. | |
| *Philanthropies* | Lewis–Sebring Family Foundation | Philadelphia Education Fund | Gates Foundation |
| | Kaplan Family Foundation | Neubauer Family Foundation | |
| | | William Penn Foundation | |

organization emerged in the city when Research for Action began working with the school district to create the Philadelphia Education Research Consortium. In New York City, the Research Alliance for NYC Schools was an organization patterned after Chicago's, working closely with the district to analyze its data.

*School support organizations* often worked directly with schools to provide professional learning, coaching, data support, and community resources for school leaders, teachers, and students. Chicago's Network for College Success initially provided a space for principals to connect for collective problem-solving and then subsequently provided coaching and professional learning opportunities. The city also had an organization focused on sharing data with schools in the form of the To&Through Project. In Philadelphia, one of the early adopters of EWIs was a whole-school reform organization called Talent Development Secondary, which worked with specific high schools to improve graduation outcomes. The city later had other organizations working with Philadelphia schools, including United Way, the To&Through Project (yes, the same one from Chicago), and Philadelphia Academies, Inc. In New York City, one prominent organization instrumental in the use of EWIs was New Visions for Public Schools, a school support organization providing data tools and professional learning in more than 70 schools. While these do not exhaust the various school support organizations in the three cities, they illustrate the general cast of organizations and the roles they play.

Finally, *philanthropic organizations* play various roles, such as financially supporting these nonprofits, connecting them to other organizations, or influencing their organizational priorities. In Chicago, large philanthropies and small family foundations support the work of research and school support nonprofits in the city. In Philadelphia, funding for EWIs came significantly from three places: the Philadelphia Education Fund, the Neubauer Family Foundation, and the William Penn Foundation. In New York City, various philanthropies supported the work with the Gates Foundation playing a large role.

In the previous paragraphs, I sketched out the cast of organizations and the roles they played. The rest of this chapter details people and events crucial to the start, spread, and sustenance of EWIs. These stories reveal the broad trajectories of these early warning technologies, which I analyze in depth in later chapters.

## Chicago

Researchers were key to the story of Chicago's EWIs. Many of them were based at the University of Chicago, which, in 1990, started what many consider to be the first place-based education research–practice partnership in the United States: the Consortium on Chicago School Research (herein referred to as the Consortium).[7] The period saw great activity among education researchers in the university. Anthony Bryk was a professor of sociology and the founding director of the Consortium. Melissa Roderick was a professor at the university's School of Social Service Administration. John Q.

Easton joined the Consortium as the deputy director after his previous post as research director of the Chicago Public Schools. Elaine Allensworth and Shazia Miller were researchers at the Consortium during the early 2000s, a time of discovery regarding what predicted high school graduation.[8]

*Early failure often translates into poorer later performance.* A 1999 study undertaken by Roderick and collaborator Eric Camburn noted the importance of the year of transition into high schools.[9] They noted how their analysis "highlights the importance of students' early adjustment to high school, in part because early academic difficulty is often the beginning of a downward spiral in school performance."[10] In the same year that their paper was published, Easton worked on reports for elementary schools, showing how many of each school's alumni were on track and off track to graduating, how many dropped out, and how many graduated.

Easton affectionately called these documents sent to elementary schools as "Little People Reports," mainly because of the colored stick figures

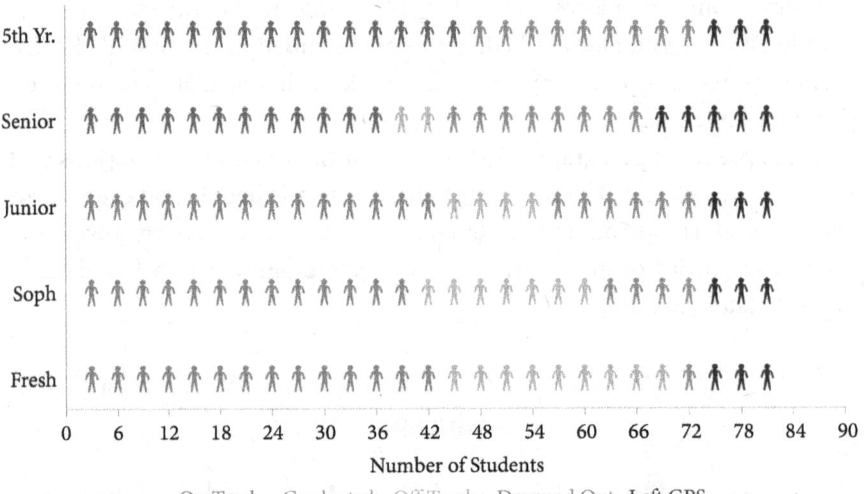


**Figure 2.1** Illustration of "Little People Reports"

*Note*: This graph followed students who graduated in 1993 at Barton Elementary School across five years of high school. Each stick figure is equivalent to three people. A student was considered "on track" if they received no more than one F in a core course (English, math, science, and social science) and considered "off track" if they received more than one F in a core course. Dropouts were recorded as no longer enrolled in CPS and had a leave code designating them as dropouts. Those who left CPS were no longer enrolled in CPS and had a leave code designating them as leaving for another school district, private school, or home school.

Reproduced with permission from: Miller, Shazia et al. (1999). *How Do Barton Graduates Perform in CPS High Schools?* Chicago: Consortium on Chicago School Research.

(see Figure 2.1). He said, "We put the ones on-track in green, the ones off-track in red, the ones who dropped out in purple, the ones who left the system as something else." In creating these reports, they needed to know how to distinguish students who were "on track" from those who were "off track." He explained that they created an indicator that followed the CPS policy for promoting students based on the number of accrued course credits (e.g., five course credits to be promoted to sophomore year). With guidance from the work of Roderick, they added that to be "on track," a student should have no more than one semester failure in a core subject—English, science, math, or social studies. Easton continued, "The person responsible for creating the indicator was a woman named Shazia Miller."

In 2002, Miller and Allensworth wrote a chapter on students' high school performance for the book *Reforming Chicago's High Schools.*[11] In it, they noted that:

> Students' performance in their first year of high school is critical to the overall success of their high school careers . . . . Being on or off track is highly correlated with long-term performance; students who are off track after their first year have tremendous difficulty catching up and graduating within four years. In the 1996–97 school year, 78% of high school eligible students who were on track one year after elementary school [i.e., ninth grade] graduated within four years. Only 15.6% of students who were off track graduated within the same period.[12]

Work by Roderick, Easton, Miller, and Allensworth all pointed in various ways the importance of students' experiences in the freshman year of high school. While they were hopeful people could do something with this new information, Shazia Miller, in our interview, noted that "that was an overly optimistic approach."

Two other organizations would take the insights from these researchers and influence the course of Chicago schools. One was the district itself, the CPS. The district's chief executive officer, Arne Duncan, had included the Freshman OnTrack metric in the high school accountability system in 2003. Duncan saw the research as an opportunity "of really understanding that if we could improve the transition from eighth to ninth grade, and then make sure that ninth grade went well, then we could put our kids on a whole different ball game and give them an entirely different trajectory." He then detailed the work of the district to create summer bridge programs for those moving to high schools, new data systems to support early identification of students at risk of dropping out, and new support structures for teachers. New offices were created, and new district officials were hired to support freshman success and graduation pathways. (Chapters 4 and 5 will detail these initiatives and interconnections.)

The other organization to take on this insight was the Network for College Success (NCS), which was also based at the University of Chicago. Set up by Roderick with Sarah Duncan in 2006, the NCS was initially a voluntary group of principals working together to collectively problem-solve. Duncan—Sarah, not her brother Arne—noted the contrast between the approach of the NCS from traditional researchers. She mentioned their approach "was in contrast to what a lot of professors would do, which would be to diagnose [the problem], to create a program, to sell it to the district, and then have the district try to implement it with fidelity." In subsequent years, the organization provided services like coaching and the setting up of professional learning communities. Some of these learning communities were focused on the ninth-grade transition because of the research coming out of the Consortium at the same time. Through connections with the Consortium, the NCS became a key actor in spreading and sustaining EWI initiatives in the city.

In 2014, the To&Through Project was set up to provide education stakeholders with public data on students' educational outcomes and trajectories. Its executive director, Alex Seeskin, described the organization as, "providing schools with both early warning indicator data and outcome data . . . and then . . . bringing the sort of larger education ecosystem together to make meaning of the indicators that we're seeing." Day-to-day operations include working on research with the Consortium, creating public-facing data tools, working with schools on the ground, and creating seminars to inform the public of EWI and graduation trends.

Discovering the predictiveness of ninth-grade performance on eventual high school graduation was a key part of Chicago's story. But a compelling set of studies was admittedly not enough to change the whole system. It took other organizations to further this insight and make it actionable for schools on the ground. The district had to provide structures to bring it about, a school support organization like the NCS had to provide professional support to spread it, and a public data organization like To&Through had to continue publishing data and reports to sustain the momentum the initiative has gained. While schools can often be silent or even ignorant about the role of these school improvement organizations, there are clear traces of their influence. Chicago's story is one consisting of the same organizations sustaining the work through the years. But what happens when organizations shift and change?

## Philadelphia

Instead of a constant constellation of organizations, Philadelphia has had various organizations initiate and lead EWIs. In the 1990s, there was Talent Development Secondary (TDS), which worked with researchers from JHU's Center for the Social Organization of Schools (CSOS). In 2014, when TDS concentrated on its national work, the EWI initiative was taken up by United Way and the Philadelphia Education Fund. In 2017, two philanthropic organizations funded research and implementation of EWIs, with Research for Action leading the new studies and the To&Through Project from Chicago leading the implementation of new data systems. Although organizations have shifted and digital technologies have changed, the initiatives have relied on similar principles that became clear during the early 2000s. One of these principles, similar to Chicago, was the importance of transitions in schools.

The first group of organizations in the city were those connected with JHU. TDS was initiated in 1994 as a school support organization working with Philadelphia middle schools and high schools to comprehensively transform these schools to enhance student attendance, improve learning, and support high school graduation.[13] In a report in 2001, TDS high schools had their own "Ninth Grade Success Academy," where teachers were organized to support ninth graders in their transition.[14] The same report showed TDS supporting increases in attendance and test score gains in reading and math, as well as contributing to significant drops in arrests and suspensions.[15] Like researchers at the University of Chicago, they were placing their bets on school transitions.

Yet their work did not emerge from an explicit study of who was "on track" or "off track." It instead came from an unlikely study of the school-to-prison pipeline. Robert Balfanz was one of the researchers from JHU who explained that their work with the district led them to build and gather data to evaluate the TDS model. In the early 2000s, they had longitudinal data on students from middle grades onward—a "relatively rare occurrence at that time," Balfanz noted. They were then asked to create a study of the predictors of students who got arrested. He described the results of the study:

> We basically found out that all the kids getting arrested in ninth grade, many of them had a very common pattern . . . they were only going to school two-thirds of the time and failing half of their classes, and on the surveys, they were indicating that their friends were starting to ask them to engage in illegal activities.

Balfanz noted that these students who were arrested had a seven percent graduation rate. But what was surprising for him was not this group, but a similar group that did not get arrested. He said:

> We also noticed that there was actually a *larger* group of kids who in their eighth grade were only going to school two-thirds of the time, were failing half their classes, their friends were not asking them to be involved in illegal activities, and they did not get arrested in ninth grade, but they still had essentially a seven percent graduation rate!

This research led to various other studies on what predicted high school graduation.

Balfanz and his colleagues at JHU worked on studies focused on "early identification and effective interventions."[16] One study saw that dropping out of high school was more likely if a sixth grader had even one of the following "signals": a final grade of F in mathematics or English, attendance below 80 percent of the year, or a final unsatisfactory behavior mark in at least one class.[17] Another study found that course failure and school absence in ninth grade predicted a student's eventual dropping out of high school—even after controlling for factors that precede ninth grade.[18] These studies were shared with the district, teachers, and researchers, while also animating the work of TDS.

In 2010, the organization concentrated on its national work, which did not just include TDS. Balfanz described the new model as the "Diplomas Now model," where they combined early warning systems and insights from TDS with increased ability to have mentors from City Year and increased ability to support high-needs students through case managers from Communities in Schools. Balfanz described it as "a $30 million award with $10 million in private funds [where] we did this massive 12-district,

60-school RCT [randomized controlled trial]." One researcher described this period not only as the expansion of the national work of JHU and TDS, but also the contraction of the work in Philadelphia. As Ruth Curran Neild mentioned, "It became really clear that the district wasn't as supportive of Talent Development as before . . . . I felt like it was becoming difficult to get work done in the school district." Thus came a time when organizational vigor for EWIs in Philadelphia was limited. She added, "Maybe it continued in some sort of quarters of the district but was largely forgotten."

Indeed, some of the work had continued. Using insights from the JHU research, the Philadelphia Education Fund and the United Way of Greater Philadelphia and Southern New Jersey launched an "Early Warning Response System" that worked in 12 underserved schools in Philadelphia. The initiative provided training, tools, and professional development for teachers and administrators to match students at risk of dropping out with resources like tutoring, mentoring, and counseling.[19] Even as some of the work continued, it did not have the same vitality.

After leaving in 2011, Neild came back to Philadelphia in 2017, no longer as a research scientist at JHU but as the director of the Philadelphia Education Research Consortium. Upon returning, she noticed that EWIs were resurrected. She added, "[EWIs] kind of came back again and they started doing work on Freshman OnTrack and actually incorporated it into a kind of performance measure and got a tracker for the district. But it's kinda funny, like everything is new again!" Part of why it felt new was because it *was* new.

Joseph Neubauer was a Philadelphia businessman and was chair of the board of trustees of the University of Chicago. In 2017, his philanthropic organization, the Neubauer Family Foundation, worked with the new administration of the School District of Philadelphia to bring EWIs (back) into the city. The foundation brought the To&Through Project from Chicago to lead the efforts. Seeskin, the director of To&Through, described their work as a combination of building data tools for the school system, having a Ninth Grade Success Network of high schools that received professional development, and providing resources for the Ninth Grade OnTrack program. To&Through worked with other groups, like the Philadelphia Academies, Inc., which interacted directly with schools and teacher teams to support their use of EWIs, and Revolution Impact, which was the project manager for this Philadelphia initiative. One other important player in the

EWI space in Philadelphia was the William Penn Foundation, which funded the research on Ninth Grade OnTrack together with the Neubauer Family Foundation.[20]

The changing constellation of actors and organizations was brought about by the changing contexts and district administration in the city. Despite the changes in these networks, a number of aspects remained the same throughout the years. As early as 1999, TDS high schools had Ninth Grade Academies focused on supporting ninth graders. In this resurrection, EWIs in the city had these academies that were "essentially a school within a school, where freshmen have a dedicated group of specially selected teachers and extra supports."[21] The different organizations also employed similar strategies in terms of working directly with schools to support their use of EWIs and working with various other organizations to increase resources for students at risk of dropping out. Although Chicago and Philadelphia initiated their research on EWIs almost independently of each other, New York City's EWIs had explicitly taken inspiration from these two cities. What happens when organizations try to adapt strategies into a widely new context?

## New York City

Two organizations stand out in the story of EWIs in the largest school district in the United States. One was a research organization that took inspiration from the Consortium in Chicago and the other was a school support organization that provided data systems and professional development to New York City schools. In both cases, they adopted and adapted ideas from Chicago and Philadelphia to the work in New York City.

In 2008, the Research Alliance for New York City Schools started as a research–practice partnership conducting studies with the New York City Department of Education (NYC DOE). Research Alliance's director, James Kemple, spoke about the genesis of the organization, noting the connection with Chicago:

> Our basic operating model is very similar to the Consortium on Chicago School Research . . . . in large part because when the organization started in 2008 there was a very high degree of collaboration with John Easton and Melissa Roderick at the time, and Elaine Allensworth, about how you would start a similar organization in a New York City context.

One of the early studies of the Research Alliance was the analysis of factors that predicted students' prospects for graduating high school. NYC DOE's high school accountability system included a school-level indicator of the percentage of students who earned a minimum of 10 credits in ninth grade—an early indicator of being "on track."[22] The group from Research Alliance wanted to understand if there were other predictors that could increase the predictiveness of New York City's own version of an early warning indicator.

Using a sample of 576,000 students across more than 350 high schools and 10 cohorts, Kemple and his colleagues found that a relatively simple measure of being "on track"—earning 10 or more credits—predicted graduation with a Regents diploma.[23] Their 2013 study showed that adding an indicator of passing at least one Regents examination by the end of ninth grade can improve the EWI prediction rate. Aside from the link to Chicago, Kemple was also familiar with the EWI work in Philadelphia because he and his previous colleagues at the research center MDRC wrote the evaluation reports for TDS middle schools and high schools in the city.

Although Research Alliance studied EWIs, they did not necessarily create the data tools. Nonetheless, Kemple pointed out, "We haven't created [a] tool . . . but honestly, the very best of those tools has been developed by New Visions for Public Schools." Here, he refers to the tool used to predict individual students from dropping out, which can then be aggregated to provide an analysis of schools and historical trends.

In 2008, New Visions for Public Schools (New Visions) worked with 63 public schools in the city and developed an on-track metric for use in these high schools. The organization created color-coded categories to describe each student's status, with blue denoting those who were on track to college, green denoting those on track to high school graduation, yellow denoting those who were almost on track, and red denoting those who were off track for graduation. The organization then used these categories to help both schools and individual students. One report noted:

> New Visions analyzes the data for each school and provides administrators with a schoolwide report on student performance based on the metric. It also creates snapshots that can show an individual student's progress toward graduation and college readiness, and encourages students to create a plan to get (or stay) on track.[24]

The report further noted how the on-track metric was adopted from the research done in Chicago and how schools convened teams of school leaders, teachers, and counselors to analyze the data and develop tailored strategies for groups of students, similar in principle to Philadelphia's Ninth Grade Academies.

In subsequent years, the team from New Visions created their own research analyzing students' progress to graduation, with sophisticated visualization regarding how students move in and out of different categories of being "on track."[25] For example, at the start of high school, a student may be in green (on track to high school graduation) but may move across to yellow (almost on track) at different points on high school. The organization also created public-facing materials, such as Ninth Grade Trackers, to help students track their course grades, credits, and Regents exams.[26]

Over time, New Visions improved its data tools, particularly those used by schools to track students' progress to graduation. Nikki Giunta, the organization's chief-of-staff, spoke about the changes in their tracker from what they previously called the "Student Sorter" to what is currently referred to as "the Portal by New Visions":

> It started out as what we called a Student Sorter. It was one spreadsheet that was 276 columns long that was updated, I think it started monthly and then we went biweekly, and then had seven or eight spreadsheets that spun off of that . . . [Then,] we developed what we now call the Portal, which is a full stack web application that's developed in-house at New Visions . . . It gets updated on a daily basis and allows [educators] to do student-level planning alongside the data.

While the tool started with the 81 schools they were directly partnered with, the tool was scaled to be available to all New York City high schools in 2020, the year the COVID-19 pandemic hit. In subsequent years, the tracker was expanded to elementary and middle schools in the city. The Portal has data on individual students' demographics, course passing, Regents exams results, real-time course grades, and attendance. Data were also aggregated to classrooms and schools so that teachers and school leaders could understand trends with their students.

In New York City, the organizations did more than just adopt the technologies. They learned to scale these technologies. Partnerships with the NYC DOE was, of course, important; however, equally important were the partnerships with large philanthropies, like the Gates Foundation and the Carnegie Corporation, as well as small community-based organizations that collaborated to create a data cooperative with Research Alliance. In a district with almost a million students, organizations cannot just transpose policies and technologies. They often need to find a way to make it scale.

## Outsider Advantage

These narratives about the influence and power of outside research, school support, philanthropic, and nonprofit organizations beg the question regarding the advantages afforded by being outsiders to the system. Researchers have often argued the role nonprofits play in providing additional financial, human, political, and professional resources to school systems.[27] Conversations with individuals immersed in the nonprofit sphere note how the sector is able to bear risks, provide stability, and influence spread (see Table 2.2).

*Risk Capital.* Dave Ferrero was a senior program officer at the Gates Foundation between 2000 and 2013, and he helped fund the work of Roderick and Easton on EWIs in Chicago. When asked about what was advantageous about outside organizations in schools, he spoke about philanthropic organizations' "risk capital". He explained that philanthropies can take on risks that the government is unwilling to make because it doesn't want to fund untested programs. Further, philanthropies can also take on risks that for-profit firms are unable to make because these bets may create little revenue. He continued, "The risk capital should be coming from philanthropy, which doesn't need to turn a profit, and which doesn't have any accountability to taxpayers." Here, the lack of accountability was not seen as a danger but as a potential advantage of having the ability to try new projects with the flexibility afforded by philanthropic dollars.

**Table 2.2** Outsider Advantages and Risks

| Advantages | Risks |
|---|---|
| Positive change through risk capital | Negative change through perverse incentives |
| Stabilizing presence | Inertial presence |
| Spread of innovation | State contraction |

This risk capital, however, is an initial investment into a promising program, not a substitute for a structural change. Ferrero explained that the best-case scenario is when outside organizations are able "to come in and tinker, and figure out solutions, which then it can hand off to the market and/or to the government." Outside organizations do not function as replacements but as catalysts for change. Of course, the education system is dotted with examples of how philanthropies and nonprofits became challengers and substitutes to public institutions rather than catalysts for collective growth.[28]

*Stabilizing Presence.* If one side of nonprofits is about change, the other side is about stability. Rebecca Cornejo was the executive director of the Neubauer Family Foundation, which funded the work on Ninth Grade OnTrack in Philadelphia. Reflecting on the work of the foundation with the School District of Philadelphia, she noted how "philanthropy is the one place that can take a truly long-term view on this [initiative] because mayors and superintendents cycle in and out." Her reference to school districts often changing administrators and introducing new reforms is explained as arising from political incentives for new district leaders to demonstrate their ability to make a difference through new programs that displace the old with the new.[29] In an environment of constant transformation, stability may be more important than change.

One factor that contributed to stability was the constellation of individuals inside and outside school districts, whose collective work on EWIs rallied support for the work. Cornejo was aware that Philadelphia's education superintendent could change. She added, however, that they have "the opportunity to advocate and sort of energize and build a coalition around this work [of EWIs because] we have everything from a principal supervisor to a teacher, from the data team of the school district over to the curriculum group—everyone understands the value of this." Such stability, then, is not so much a goal of an organization, but a consequence of the webs created across various levels of organizations inside and outside the school system.

*Spread and Expansion.* References to change and stability offered by nonprofits and philanthropies can often be limited to particular locales where these organizations are based. However, an informant from New York City spoke about the power of organizations in spreading ideas, programs, and initiatives—a theme this book takes up. William Corrin was the director of K–12 education at MDRC, a national research organization that had evaluated a whole-school reform model that used EWIs. When describing the education ecosystem in the United States, he noted the lack of influence of national agencies to bring about changes in schools:

> As you go higher in the governmental or agency structure, there's ever more limits on how much you influence, right? So, the federal government can't really do a lot of stuff, but they can incentivize through funding certain kinds of activities. The state may have a little bit more jurisdiction depending on your state to require certain kinds of things but can't control everything.

He noticed the structural barriers for widespread change in a decentralized system.

But Corrin also observed how nonprofit organizations that work nationally can challenge the status quo. He explained, "I think what some of the national education intermediaries offer is a way to try to standardize best practice in disparate local areas." As states and local school districts can do their own work, insights and ideas from nonprofits can be adapted to bring about more equitable changes across various places.

However, Corrin noted that some initiatives may be more useful in some contexts and less useful in others. He thus cautioned against spreading practices for spreading's sake: "I think one of the potential pitfalls [is an organization] could push too hard on something it thinks is really good without being sensitive enough to its applicability in a particular context." Discretion then is key to this potential advantage.

In sum, outsiders saw their role as offering some advantages to initiate change, provide stability, and influence spread. I argue that these advantages are structural in nature, given the current state of US education. In an environment where taxpayer dollars are often earmarked for particular purposes, the ability of nonprofits to bear certain financial risks for new initiatives can be a welcome resource for the district. In an environment where district leaders constantly change and create a spinning wheel of new reforms, the power of nonprofits to provide focus and stability for initiatives can ensure continuity with certain efforts. In an environment where national influence can be limited by local control, nonprofits emerge as actors for the potential standardization of educational practices. Thus, the outsider advantage is less about nonprofits' inherent power and more about the structural conditions of schools that make nonprofits a key actor to plug certain holes.

## Outsider Risks

In the book *Private Action and the Public Good*, a robust group of sociologists, political scientists, economists, and historians turned their attention to the growing work of private and charitable organizations in the provision of public services.[30] In its introduction, sociologists Walter W. Powell and Elisabeth S. Clemens questioned the assumption of whether nonprofits represented "a more authentic and independent alternative to the market or the state."[31] Implicit in this questioning was an interrogation into the potential risks that come with private influence on public institutions. In the field of education, studies critical of these outside organizations highlight the risks of unaccountable and undemocratic processes that can exacerbate racial and socioeconomic inequities.[32] Interestingly, individuals in these organizations were aware of these risks and noted how some of the risks come alongside the advantages previously noted (see Table 2.2).

*Perverse incentives.* As Ferrero, from the Gates Foundation, noted the ability of nonprofits and philanthropies to provide expertise and assume risk capital, he was also candid about the ways his work was susceptible to creating perverse incentives. He explained that initiatives from large funding organizations can shift resources and "shift the center of gravity" in support of particular strategies—which may not be supported by communities or may work only under limited contexts.

Ferrero was acutely aware of the power the organization wielded, even as it had no public mandate to do the work. He said decisions on public education were being made by "a bunch of anonymous nobodies like me calling the shots . . . we're unelected and unaccountable, and we are sitting there with consultants from McKinsey, dreaming things up on whiteboards and then foisting them on the country." He was particularly critical of the market-oriented mindset that has changed philanthropy, which he argued was "not necessarily aligned with the messy political nature of a public institution like education." The favoring of particular strategies and mindsets can lead to substantial changes, but not with the consequences originally thought.

*Inertial Presence.* Stability can at times be seen as inertia. Inasmuch as organizations can shield against change in a positive way, the flipside is that organizations and organizational processes can prevent radical change from taking root. Starting in Philadelphia and expanding his work on EWIs nationally, Balfanz is a widely respected expert who has not just pioneered studies on EWIs, but has also collaborated with and brought together various other organizations working to support high school graduation. However, when asked about risks with his work, Balfanz spoke candidly about organizational work potentially preventing more radical changes:

> Is this [initiative] a band-aid on a broken system? So, you could marginally, or even modestly, or even moderately improve the number of kids that aren't dropping out . . . , but are schools really going to take it that far? Are they really going to see changes for the kids struggling most? And instead of making the deep systematic improvements we need to really change the system . . . *we have a technological solution to a structural problem.* (emphasis added)

His last sentence is haunting, making reformers reflect about how deeply the change should be.

Balfanz reflected on the question of EWIs as a technical fix to a deeper systemic issue of inequality and injustice—a band-aid to a serious wound. In contrast to the stability that buffers education from unnecessary changes, inertia shields education from much needed radical changes. But Balfanz was also a pragmatist, saying, "Structures aren't going to change overnight . . . In the meantime, kids are waving their hands that they need help. And schools should organize themselves to be able to provide it while we're figuring out the bigger solutions." His concern for practical action may be seen as an inertial force preventing more radical changes, but his deep attention to it provides a glimpse of his concern for such change.

*State Contraction.* As nonprofits arguably gain an ability to spread programs and expand their influence, how does government respond to such expansion? Kristin Black, a postdoctoral research associate at the Research Alliance for New York City Schools, commented about the downsides of nonprofit intervention. She highlighted the possibility of the state retreating from its responsibility. She said having private actors in public institutions "sort of forces things that should be citywide structural improvements out [and] so you've got this kind of bizarre marketization of a public good." By relying on outside organizations, the state can handover the responsibility of larger scale systems changes to organizations that often provide more gradual and piecemeal improvements.

In sum, behind the advantages of nonprofits are complementary risks on public institutions. Although nonprofits can catalyze changes, these changes may lead to perverse incentives and unintended consequences. Although they can be a stabilizing presence to a district beset by constant changes, they may also become an inertial presence buffering the institution from more radical changes. Although nonprofits can spread and standardize practices, this expanding private sector can lead to a contracting public sector. Individuals working in the sector know very well the risks and challenges that come with the work, but many are also pragmatists who know that radical changes take time, and, in the meantime, there are practical challenges *now* that need creative solutions.

## Lessons for Education Politics

The story of EWIs in Chicago, Philadelphia, and New York City reveals the importance of context in the emergence of organizations outside schools. In Chicago, the stigma of being called the worst school district in the nation revealed that *change* may need to come from outside the school system. In Philadelphia, the rigmarole of superintendents and new reforms highlight the need for *stability*, which can also be elusive for the set of organizations that transitioned in and out of the EWI space. In New York City, the size of the district necessitated partners that could *scale and spread* initiatives with discretion and without the strong arm of the state.

Studies in the politics of education have documented many of the themes presented in this chapter. Scholars have noted the importance of organizations and interests outside schools, and how these can impact school board elections, research use, district policies, racial inequalities, and potential school improvements.[33] Studies have also shown how networks of communication, information, and power can support and constrain changes, like the adoption of new technology, the implementation of new curricula, and the creation of new state education policies.[34] Like the themes in the chapter, many other studies have also highlighted the ambiguity and tensions emerging from private action in public education, particularly questions on outsiders' influence, accountability, financial interests, and giving voice to the community.[35] The accounts of EWIs in these three cities provide depth and description regarding processes that contribute to the politics of education.

But many of these previous accounts highlight the movement *from* nonprofits and philanthropies *to* educational institutions, state agencies, school districts, and schools. Yet a second look at EWI organizations illustrates how organizations *emerged from the context.* In some ways, the early emergence of outside organizations is less intentional and sometimes more serendipitous. The idea of being "on track" in Chicago emerged from reports conducted not for high schools, but for elementary school principals. Organizations like the NCS in Chicago emerged in response to a simple need for school leaders to collectively problem solve. The research on predicting dropouts in Philadelphia emerged from an interesting discovery in a study originally about the school-to-prison pipeline. The adaptation of EWIs by New Visions was not originally intended to be used across the city; however, over time, it has scaled to become one of the most sophisticated tools for early identification. In this way, the context provides the ground from which organizations and initiatives emerge.

The politics of education can often emphasize powerful agents while downplaying the role of context, randomness, and luck. And while many organizations and individuals play God by asserting power and influence over educational processes and institutions, perhaps one lesson to take from EWIs is how the most potentially transformative initiatives are those that emerge from the context rather than those imposed from without. In this way, organizations' success depends not so much on planning ahead, but on being sensitive to the current needs and gaps in the system.

# PART II

# LOCAL ORGANIZATIONS AND THE TRANSFORMATION OF US EDUCATION

# Chapter 3
# How Technologies Shape Institutional Logics

EWIs is work about relationships
that's kind of packaged and disguised as data.

—Dominique McKoy,
*Associate Director, To&Through Project*

Early warning indicators (EWIs) had different uses. They were yearly accountability metrics, where schools received points for the percentage of students who were "on track" to graduate. They were just-in-time data tools that helped in identifying students at risk of dropping out. They were intervention mechanisms, which helped teachers provide support through tutoring, mentoring, and credit recovery. Finally, they were school improvement systems that influenced larger structures and cultures to transform through changes in the relationships between students and staff, as well as the relationships among teachers themselves. The first chapter documented how these various uses were evident in schools; the present chapter illustrates how local organizations have influenced these various uses. In a sense, EWIs had a flexibility about them that drew on different ways of thinking.

Sociological studies of organizations have often studied how broader belief systems can influence and shape people's cognition and behavior.[1] In this view, society is made up of different *institutions*, like the bureaucratic state, the capitalist market, the professional world, the immediate community, the large corporation, the nuclear family, the scientific enterprise, and the religious establishment. Each of these institutions is guided by a "logic," or a system of beliefs and expectations by which people and organizations make sense of their everyday actions and activities.[2] These *institutional logics* guide and constrain behavior, meaning making, and decision-making as individuals draw on particular ways of thinking from the set of institutions

*Subtle Webs*. Jose Eos Trinidad, Oxford University Press. © Oxford University Press (2025).
DOI: 10.1093/9780197786123.003.0004

in a society.[3] For example, biological and physical scientists may view their work from the "logic of science," where doing research is fundamentally about the pursuit of knowledge for its own sake. But it may also be viewed from the "logic of the market," where scientific research is seen as affecting the world and having value in the marketplace.[4] Each institution (e.g., state, sciences, professions, community) has a set of organizing principles that can influence how individuals and organizations act and make sense.[5]

In the case of EWIs, different individuals drew on differing institutional logics to make sense of data and dropping out. Government leaders thought of EWIs as accountability metrics rooted in the logic of the *state*, which emphasized bureaucratic processes and audits to support public goods. Researchers and data analysts highlighted the logic of *science*, which privileged efficiency and data-driven processes. Coaches and teachers focused on EWI interventions and the logic of the *profession* to highlight the creation of new experts and the development of expertise. School leaders saw in EWIs' school improvement systems the logic of the *community* that emphasized trust, reciprocity, and shared responsibility among school staff. Thus, various ways of making sense of EWIs emerged across the various actors that instituted these practices (see Table 3.1). Although different actors initially had different ways of thinking about EWIs, many of these institutional logics have pollinated across each other for logics to converge and complement one another.

An important question that arises is what has driven these institutional logics. Organizational studies highlight the role of individuals and organizations in the governance of institutional logics. At the individual level, people's positions as managers or as street-level workers can influence how logics are leveraged and how they compete with each other (e.g., managerial vs. community logic) or complement each other.[6] At the organizational level, firms can influence change by displacing old logics with new ways of thinking, as in the case of the rise of the market logic in healthcare displacing the previous dominance of a professional logic.[7] In many cases, the emphasis is on the role of powerful organizations, bureaucratic elites, and professional experts directly using their resources to shape and maintain the logic.[8] In the case of EWIs, organizations and individuals outside schools contributed to the various logics at play, but less by directly shaping of logics and more by devising the technologies aligned with particular logics.

**Table 3.1** Early Warning Indicators and Institutional Logics

| Logic of... | Key Ideas/ Concepts | Focal Actors | Technology |
|---|---|---|---|
| State | Bureaucratic processes and rational audits | Government leaders | EWI as an accountability metric |
| Science | Data, evidence, and efficient organizational systems | Researchers and data analysts | EWI as a just-in-time identification tool |
| Profession | Division of labor, expertise, and specialization | Coaches and teachers | EWI as a social technology |
| Community | Relationships, culture, collective responsibility | School leaders and teachers | EWI as a catalyst for systems change |

Institutional logics rely on technologies, both digital and social. However, few studies have explicitly investigated the role of *technology* in influencing how institutional logics are shaped, maintained, and sustained. This chapter documents how the various uses and logics of EWIs emerged from the technologies created by individuals and organizations outside schools yet were buttressed by how they were used by people inside schools. Rather than the power of direct intervention to create an institutional logic, it illustrates the power of subtle changes in technology to generate new logics. It also connects the first two chapters to highlight the connection between EWIs inside schools, and the people and organizations outside schools.

The chapter discusses each of the state, scientific, professional, and community logics of EWIs through the respective examples in Chicago, Philadelphia, New York City, and a national program. Although the various institutional logics were present in different locations, I use specific examples in each context to show the power of particular technologies in shaping and transforming how EWIs were viewed. The chapter ends with a discussion of the role local organizations have played in shaping institutional logics through digital and social technologies.

## Freshman OnTrack and the State Logic

In 1997, John Q. Easton shifted from his role as Chicago Public Schools' (CPS) director of research and evaluation to a new role as the University of Chicago Consortium on School Research's deputy director. As a research director at the CPS, he regularly received requests from elementary school principals to know what happened to their graduates who went on to high school and how they progressed. Thus, in his new role at the Consortium, they started, in 1999, to create reports tracking students graduating from eighth grade and following their performance in high schools around the city.[9] These became the "Little People Reports" (named after the stick figures that tracked students; see Chapter 2), which had a metric for what makes a student "on track" to graduation.

The metric was the technology. Freshman OnTrack was a simple metric, determined by the number of courses accumulated and the number of semester course failures in ninth grade. To be more accurate, a student was on track if the student accumulated five full course credits and had no more than one semester F in English, math, science, or social studies.[10] Research from the Consortium showed that 81 percent of on-track freshmen in 1999 eventually graduated high school four years after. However, only 22 percent of off-track students graduated within the same time.[11]

Freshman OnTrack—Chicago's version of an EWI—was used as an accountability tool by the district in 2003. It was a time when accountability was central in everyone's minds, particularly with the recent introduction in 2002 of the federal test-based accountability system called *No Child Left Behind* (NCLB).[12] Chicago was no stranger to standardized tests and accountability regimes, particularly because it had had high-stakes testing in place since 1996. CPS was the first large urban school district to implement an accountability system consisting of testing students, placing schools under probation if standards were not met, and reassigning or dismissing staff if the school did not improve.[13] Aside from test scores, high schools now also had to account for the number of freshman students on track.

CPS Chief Executive Officer Arne Duncan was key in getting this new technology into the school accountability system. He described a presentation by Easton with the district's management team, where he showed the correlation between passing classes as a freshman and students graduating high school. Duncan noted, "This data . . . in hindsight seems really common sense, but at the time, it was pretty revolutionary." With much of the focus on objective test scores and much of the common wisdom downplaying the role of subjective course grades, the insight took on a novelty for leaders in the system. In a 2005 report, researchers at the Consortium explained, "The importance of course performance in high schools is often overlooked, especially in the current era of accountability, when test results often take predominance over students' actual classroom experiences."[14]

At this point, the technology of knowing the percentage of ninth graders on track had become an important metric for individual schools and the whole school district. But it was not enough to know just the trends, as the district wanted EWIs to influence behavior. Duncan mentioned, "People think of accountability as like a punitive thing; I just never sort of thought of it that way. It's just that if something's really important, you wanna measure it, you wanna share best practices, you wanna help people get better." Thus, the Freshman OnTrack metric was added to the set of measures upon which high schools were evaluated.

Duncan was drawing on the *logic of the bureaucratic state*. With this logic, government bodies use methods of counting and accounting, not only to influence technical changes in the system but also to convince audiences of the legitimacy of the enterprise. In this way, Freshman OnTrack had a *rational* function and a *rhetorical* function.[15] The logic of the state privileges systematic ways for changing organizations and influencing people's behaviors. Accountability—which comprises measurement, incentives, and consequences—is a key tool for the state to influence its organizations.[16] In the case of Chicago, Freshman OnTrack was a technology used for measurement, in addition to other measures like schools' graduation rates, attendance rates, and standardized test scores.[17]

Any measurement system is, of course, open to corruption. In the case of EWIs, teachers may pass students unscrupulously to reach a certain Freshman OnTrack percentage. District leaders and university researchers were not oblivious to potential unintended consequences of EWIs. Easton noted that they had fears that teachers would simply move students receiving an F to a D. Another district official feared that test results would go down as a result. In a way, they knew that there were risks to the logic of the state and to the method of accountability.

But district leaders also believed that in the absence of accountability, changes could not take root. Paige Ponder was the director of Graduation Pathways at the Chicago Public Schools and was tasked with supporting programs for Freshman OnTrack. Like Easton, Ponder was also conscious of the potential drawbacks of adding EWIs to the school accountability report card. But in her work of supporting programs, she realized how important the accountability aspect was. Ponder said, "It was so critical for [Freshman OnTrack] to be in the accountability system because that was the only chance it had to cut through that fatigue and the cynicism." She was referring to so many other initiatives coming and going because schools could easily do away with them. And while accountability was imperfect, it was almost necessary for her so that the school could be attentive to the importance of ninth grade.

The logic of the state was implicit in the technology of accountability. District leaders saw the potential for Freshman OnTrack to influence behavior as school leaders and teachers could focus on and create changes in ninth-graders' experiences. However, researchers and some of these leaders were also aware of the potential risks that come with measures that could easily be gamed. While the district relied on the state logic as it started to include the metric into the school accountability system, they subsequently created other technologies that relied on other logics.

The technology of the Freshman OnTrack metric has persisted for more than 20 years, and it has changed little—it is still calculated with the number of course credits and semester failures at the end of ninth grade. But the logic of the state has not been the only one to take root. As new technologies emerged, new logics were attached to these new technologies.

## Grades Monitoring Tool and the Scientific Logic

New technologies offered new institutional logics. The original EWIs were yearly indicators of whether a ninth grader was on track or off track. But with new information technologies came real-time data systems that were updated monthly, weekly, or even daily—providing teachers with an opportunity to see their students' present course performance. While the yearly indicators were used with a state logic of accountability, the just-in-time measures of individual students' performance were used with a new logic. It was a logic that relied on data-driven identification and evidence-based planning, a focus on the effective use of digital tools to support students.

In Philadelphia, researchers and nonprofit staff at the To&Through Project created a tool that provided a summary of students' average performance at a particular point in time. The Grades Monitoring Tool was a spreadsheet that had a tab where a school leader or teacher could input a comma separated value (CSV) file from the student information system—essentially a table of rows and columns—and then receive an output that showed a color-coded student roster with students' performance record (see Figure 3.1). The tool had students' names, demographic characteristics, attendance percentages, average grades for core subjects, projected grades for each subject, and a trend indicator denoting if grades were improving, staying the same, or declining.

Emily Kulick was the consultant hired to help design, create, and develop this data tool in the district. In describing the genesis of the Grades Monitoring Tool, she first talked about the tool the district was already using that provided aggregate dashboards to schools. Kulick said the district "was sharing a lot of tables and charts with high school leaders on things like grades, attendance, standardized tests—all of which were being presented to them in some really pretty select tools." In this way, the school district's emphasis was less on strict accountability and more on the use of data. Inasmuch as the school leaders were appreciative of this aggregate tool, they pointed out, "This looks great, [but] how do I find out who those students are?" They were

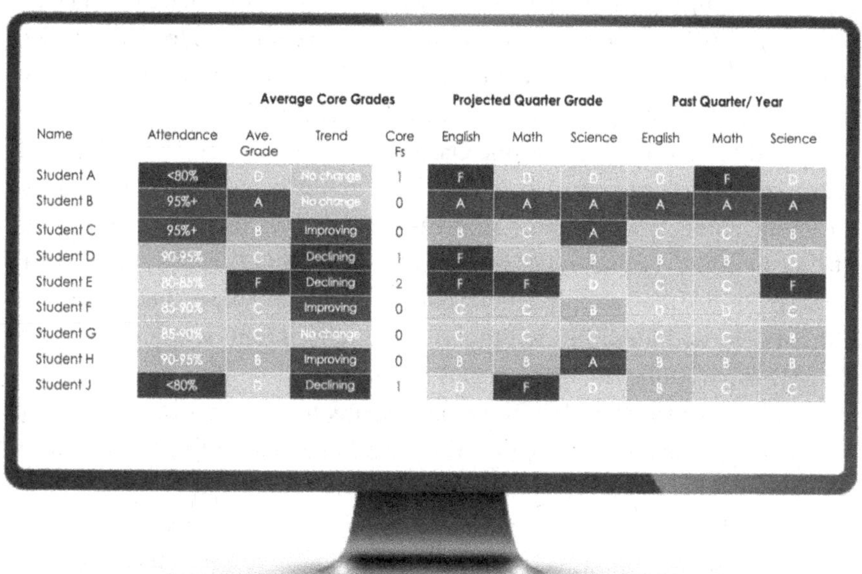

| | | Average Core Grades | | | Projected Quarter Grade | | | Past Quarter/ Year | | |
|---|---|---|---|---|---|---|---|---|---|---|
| Name | Attendance | Ave. Grade | Trend | Core Fs | English | Math | Science | English | Math | Science |
| Student A | <80% | D | No change | 1 | F | D | D | D | F | D |
| Student B | 95%+ | A | No change | 0 | A | A | A | A | A | A |
| Student C | 95%+ | B | Improving | 0 | B | C | A | C | C | B |
| Student D | 90-95% | C | Declining | 1 | F | C | B | B | B | C |
| Student E | 80-85% | F | Declining | 2 | F | F | D | C | C | F |
| Student F | 85-90% | C | Improving | 0 | C | C | B | D | D | C |
| Student G | 85-90% | C | No change | 0 | C | C | C | C | C | B |
| Student H | 90-95% | B | Improving | 0 | B | B | A | B | B | B |
| Student J | <80% | D | Declining | 1 | D | F | D | B | C | C |

**Figure 3.1** Grades Monitoring Tool (Philadelphia)
Rendering by the author.

referring to parts of the graphs for students who were chronically absent or had low grades. After a number of consultations with school leaders, Kulick and her colleagues came up with the Grades Monitoring Tool to provide a way of identifying students or groups of students in need of help.

The emphasis on data and identification hinted at the *logic of science*. This logic emphasizes the role of data and efficient organizational systems. In the case of EWIs, the Grades Monitoring Tool provided the data that teachers and school leaders used to identify students at risk of dropping out. Researchers saw this as a way of providing more information to teachers. By gaining more information about their students, teachers can supposedly work on practices that improve students' performance, leading to improvements in the school's on-track rates and graduation numbers. Taken together, the motivation for the new technology was less about bureaucratic accountability and more about evidence-based improvements.

Doesn't the new technology simply confirm what teachers already know? In spaces where teachers are in close contact with students almost every day, it seems redundant to have these early warning systems. More importantly, this scientific focus on data might simply take on a ceremonial function to create a sense of legitimacy in schools being "data driven."[18]

But two nonprofit staff members provided examples of when the data were actually helpful and even necessary. One is in the context of teachers understanding their students *holistically*. Kulick explained that teachers often only know their students' performance in their own class. Thus, a student may be judged to be doing fine in one class but not in another. She elaborated, "From a teacher's perspective, if you think about it, they're so focused on their own subjects . . . on how students are doing in their class. So, to put that in the context of how *that* student is doing in *other* classes can be really helpful." Rather than simply a redundant confirmation of teachers' intuition, this data-focused identification tool could catch students who may perform variably across different teachers and courses.

Another way for the early warning systems to function in schools was by catching students who might otherwise have *fallen through the cracks*. Nadia Schafer was a director at the Philadelphia Academies, Inc., and lead for the Ninth Grade Success Network, working with ninth-grade assistant principals on incorporating these data tools. In talking about the data tools, she mentioned that, in some cases, the teachers already knew even before looking at the data who was off track. However, she noted that the tool was particularly important in one context—large high schools. She said:

> The smaller schools, they're not as surprised by the data, like "Yeah, I know Jimmy, I know Shivan. I know they're not doing well." Like, they don't need a spreadsheet to show them that. I think in some of the bigger schools where kids are in different hallways and classes, it is more helpful that they're like, "Oh, I thought that was just me," or "They're doing fine over here. I didn't know they weren't doing fine over there."

In a sense, the data tools could be benign when teachers already know their students. But they could be enormously informative and transformative when students did not show the tell-tale signs of disengagement and distress.

The technology of just-in-time identification relied on a logic that privileged data-driven processes and evidence-based empiricism. In the case of EWIs in Philadelphia, the Grades Monitoring Tool was an intuitive tool for identification, and the process of identifying students in need of help opened ways for teachers to focus resources on those that really needed them. The scientific logic came alongside researchers and the new technology of just-in-time identification. The entrance of this digital technology in schools encouraged an addition to the state logic of accountability. However, technologies are not just digital; they are also social.

## Data Portal and the Professional Logic

While EWIs were digital technologies for yearly accountability and just-in-time identification, these EWIs were also social technologies affecting the division of labor in schools. One of the social technologies was the reorganization of work in schools as teachers attended to students' course performance, counselors managed students' profiles, tutors provided resources for students, and data and school improvement coaches worked with leaders and staff in schools. The technology of getting students on track for graduation incorporated an understanding of new professional roles—both inside and outside schools—to support student success.

In New York City, the school improvement organization New Visions for Public Schools (New Visions) introduced the *Portal by New Visions*. It was a web-based tool which the organization argued "centralizes critical information and organizes views so educators can focus on their students . . . [and] enables staff to collaborate around a shared picture of students and create a plan for every student to succeed."[19] In contrast to traditional EWIs that provided parsimonious metrics showing whether a student was on track or off track, the Portal had various other data on credits earned and on schedule, current course performance, projected GPA, and performance on Regents exams (see Figure 3.2). The technology was less about answering whether the student was on or off track, and more about answering what the current gaps were for the student.

As the technology shifted from a single metric of students' on-track status to multiple indicators of students' performance, more individuals became involved in EWIs. Aside from teachers and school leaders, two other roles became prominent: counselors and coaches. In the context of the Portal, coaches from outside the schools often worked with counselors and assistant principals inside schools.

Jamie Esperon was a continuous improvement coach with New Visions, working with a set of 11 schools to develop supports for ninth graders and to incorporate the use of the Portal in their work. She described her work with counselors as constituting *strategic data check-ins*, where the organization has a calendar of when to look at students' grades and exam performance to prevent failure, provide opportunities for credit recovery, and promote on-time graduation. She described the work, saying:

> I will go through each kid with counselors, or whoever the lead is . . . . If I'm looking at credit gaps, it's already telling me where I might potentially

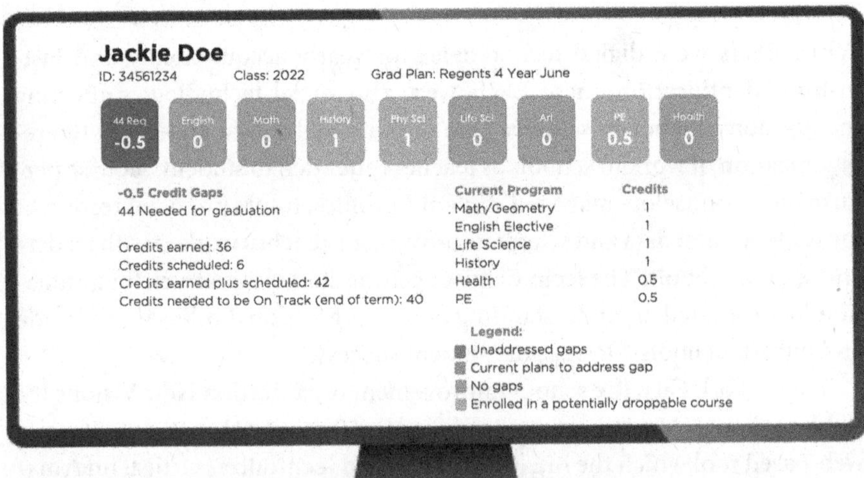


**Figure 3.2** The Portal by New Visions (New York City)
Rendering by the author.

> have a gap [for a student]. And when you click on tiles, it'll bring up their transcript record right here.

She further talked about the various uses of the Portal, with its roster of students' current performance, its in-depth account of each student's credits and gaps (see Figure 3.2), or its attendance trends for the past days. Data were presented to counselors, teachers, and school leaders to spur conversations.

Esperon emphasized the importance of professional development opportunities. When we met, she had just finished one professional development session with a New York City school. She described the goals as "for teachers to be aware of student progress in the current term, and two, to have an action to support the data that we're presenting." She further noted how the individuals in her session had different capacities for understanding data, with some teachers being comfortable with the Portal and others relying on their personal spreadsheets. In either case, she noted, "my role as coach is to make [data] meaningful, and like I said, actionable." She then detailed strategies of grouping students into projected grade bands to see how they could support those failing a course.

Technologies create opportunities for new sets of professional roles to emerge. In the case of EWIs, data and continuous improvement coaches emerged to support school staff in making sense of their schools' data. Outside organizations, like New Visions, also had professionals, like software developers, data analysts, and managers, working on these tools in the background. The technology also increased the professional expectations for teachers to use and interpret data.

The *logic of professions* highlights not just the expertise of professionals but also the division of labor among them. The social technology of EWIs created an interdependent system. As sociologist Andrew Abbott noted in *The System of Professions*, "each profession has its activities under various kinds of jurisdiction."[20] The advent of more sophisticated data tools and the emergence of new professionals contributed to a system where specific individuals had their own jurisdictions. Teachers had a role. Counselors had a role. And the motley crew of tutors, social workers, and coaches each had their roles to play as well. By creating digital and social technologies that emphasized this division of labor, outside organizations were able to highlight the logic of professions, emphasizing the work of professionals inside and outside the school system.

## Student Success Systems and the Community Logic

The technologies of EWIs included an accountability metric, an identification tool for students at risk of dropping out, and a social technology for dividing labor and providing interventions. Many of these technologies relied on particular tools. In Chicago, the tool was an "on-track" metric at the end of the year that categorized whether a student was on track or off track. In Philadelphia, it was a color-coded roster of students that showed their real-time performance. In New York City, it was a sophisticated data system with various ways of aggregating and disaggregating. But the technologies were not just material or technical. Technology can also be a set of principles for how things are done.

In 2022, nine organizations across the United States started a collaborative initiative to partner with schools, districts, and local community organizations to support work that took inspiration from EWIs. *The GRAD Partnership* was a group composed of organizations that had worked in Chicago and Philadelphia, like the Network for College Success (NCS) and Talent Development Secondary (TDS), as well as new organizations, like the Rural Schools Collaborative and the Carnegie Foundation for the Advancement of Teaching.[21] Their goal was to partner so that schools can "use high-quality student success systems."[22]

There was a conscious shift from EWIs to student success systems. Part of it was a move away from the deficit language inherent in words like "early warning," "dropout prediction," "off track," and "at-risk." Part of it was a new emphasis on successful postsecondary pathways, rather than simply high school dropout prevention. The technology of the GRAD Partnership was not about particular tools; instead, it was about a set of principles for supportive student success systems. Kelly McMahon from the Carnegie Foundation, one of the partner organizations, highlighted how research and experience about EWIs helped distill some aspects core to this new initiative:

> There's an unambiguous research base that tells us that graduating from high school really matters for lots of things . . . . But we also [have] a very strong research base that predicting dropouts was possible and you can do that as early as ninth grade . . . . And we also know that there are ways in which people have been using this research in schools.

Using the experiences of the different organizations and the research base of EWIs, the GRAD Partnership underscored four "essential elements" in creating student success systems: (1) strong, supportive relationships;

(2) real-time, actionable, holistic data; (3) strategic improvement actions; and (4) student-centered mindsets.[23] More than technological and data tools, the collaborative initiative put an emphasis on the relational work of teachers working with each other.

McMahon mentioned how important teams were in EWIs and how structures provided by nonprofits could help schools. She said, "We know good teams . . . They rarely happen by accident. They're intentional efforts to build structures that support people to, you know, do this kind of complex work." One of the ways teams and relationships were important in EWIs was through the ninth-grade teacher teams. In many places, these teams worked to catalyze systematic improvements in the schools in a way that was more than just the routine dynamic of identifying and intervening for specific students.

The technology was partly the reorganization of schools. Across different interviews in Chicago, Philadelphia, and New York City, many emphasized how teachers were previously grouped by the courses they taught such that ninth-grade math teachers often collaborated only with math teachers from tenth to twelfth grades. However, EWIs highlighted the importance of teachers in the same grade level connecting with each other to provide a more holistic assessment of students. By being organized this way, teachers could talk about common or shared students.

This change in the organization of teachers influenced and drew on a *logic of the community*, in which trust and relationships are privileged, rather than instrumental and goal-oriented processes. By influencing how teachers interacted and connected with one another, outside organizations were able to push for a perspective on EWIs that emphasized them being used to foster community. The digital technology was a gateway to new forms of social organization. Among teachers and school staff, the technology fostered a new logic that emphasized collective responsibility and community culture.

Dominique McKoy, associate director at the To&Through Project, noted the importance of community and relationships, more than data and interventions. He said, "Fundamentally, this is relationship work. This is work about relationships that's kind of packaged and disguised as data." He noted that, for policymakers, EWIs were helpful because they were concrete indicators of success—something that leverages both the state and scientific logics. But McKoy was emphatic that at the school level, "working with that data is fundamentally about having conversations about kids." The technology was about shifting perspectives about the shared responsibility for the students.

In certain places, EWIs may have been less about individually identifying students at risk and more about fundamentally changing systems and processes in the school community. In this way, the logic necessary was not so much a scientific logic of gaining evidence or a professional logic of individual intervention. Rather, what was needed was the community logic emphasizing relational trust and collective responsibility.[24]

## Why Technology Matters for Institutional Logics

From the perspective of the schools, EWIs were an accountability metric, a just-in-time data tool, a sophisticated intervention system, and a catalyst for school improvement. From the perspective of outside school improvement organizations, these EWIs were made sense of by different people using various institutional logics. The accountability metric drew on a state logic of bureaucratic power and centralized accounting. The just-in-time data tool drew on a scientific logic that emphasized data, evidence, and efficiency. The sophisticated intervention system drew on a professional logic that highlighted the emergence of new experts and the division of their labor. The school improvement system drew on a community logic of relational improvement and collective responsibility.

This chapter contributes to a different way of studying EWIs, a different way of understanding nonprofit influence in schools, and a different way of theorizing institutional logics.

Studies of EWIs have often focused on the use of specific tools and processes. Most of the time, researchers look at how teachers and school staff monitor ninth-grade course and attendance indicators to provide timely interventions.[25] The theory of the problem was that there was imperfect identification of students in need of help, and thus, change needed to include identification and intervention. However, as I show in this chapter, EWIs were not *one* thing. While in some schools, the problem may indeed have been about identification. In other times and places, the problem may have been a resource allocation problem that required both the district's support and the school's collective investment. With this type of problem, dropout prediction alone may seem imperfect and incomplete. Thus, in implementing and studying EWIs, researchers and policymakers needed to be clear about the logic being used to motivate the program, which often depended on the context of districts and schools. In places with very high chronic absenteeism and very low on-track rates, identifying that 50 percent of the students needed intervention was not very informative nor was it very helpful. In such schools, EWIs and other policies needed to focus on systematic improvements—drawing potentially on state and community logics—rather than on data-driven logics of individual identification. By separating the various logics of EWIs, I show that EWIs may or may not work in particular schools, depending on the congruence between the needs of the school and the logics being employed.

Studies on the influence of research, philanthropic, and nonprofit organizations in schools have often focused on the active work of policy advocacy and material support. On the one hand, organizations work at the federal, state, and local levels to influence policies, such as affirmative action, school voucher programs, and school segregation and desegregation.[26] On other hand, these organizations can themselves directly impact and influence what happens in schools and districts by providing financial and professional resources in the form of free educational materials, school improvement coaches, research studies about the district, and networked improvement communities.[27] The case of EWIs illustrates how outside school improvement organizations were able to influence *paradigms* about dropping out and schools' ability to prevent it, more than just direct influence on school policies and resources. Organizations influenced paradigms through the development of technologies that drew on various institutional logics. By drawing on different institutional logics, EWIs could appeal to various individuals. To the zealous district official, it was a tool for state accountability. To the data-driven researcher, it was a scientific tool for efficient identification. To the school where students could have fallen through the cracks, it was a professional tool for expert interventions. To the school where systemic changes needed to happen, it was a catalyst for community building. Here I highlight the power of an idea, and its related technologies, to shape our understanding of change and improvement.

More broadly, studies of institutional logics have focused little on the role of technology in shaping the ways individuals and organizations make sense of their actions and activities. However, I show here how technology is a constitutive element in the creation of institutional logics. The form and the use of the technology are crucial in how people make sense of their work and their initiatives. Thus, if organizational actors and policymakers intend to influence people's cognition and behavior, it is best to think about how the technology structures and is coherent with particular institutional arrangements. While many of these processes can be unconscious to the individuals pushing for changes and those receiving these changes, knowledge of this subtle process reveals a macro-level perspective for how change happens through shaping paradigms and logics.

# Chapter 4
# How Templates Structure Entrepreneurial Networks

> Institutional entrepreneurs are actors who have interests in particular institutional arrangements and who mobilize resources to create new institutions or transform the existing ones.
>
> —Julie Battilana[1]

Ninth-grade early warning indicators (EWIs) created changes in schools. The change was not just about having new data systems in schools; it was also about shifting the conversation toward how high schools can prevent dropping out, how students can exhibit predictive signs as early as the ninth grade, and how teacher teams can be organized to support students' graduation. All these were in contrast to previous practices that emphasized dropping out as the result of out-of-school factors and schools being able to do very little to prevent this from happening.[2] These new systems influenced changes in predicting, identifying, and intervening for students at risk as well as in improving school systems in general.[3] The change was not simply an addition of a new data tool but a consequential educational transformation.

Individuals and organizations were key in bringing about these changes and they had vested interests in bringing them about as well. In the case of EWIs, individuals from research, philanthropic, and nonprofit organizations had interests in initiating, implementing, and institutionalizing these transformations. Organizational theorists have often referred to such individuals as *institutional entrepreneurs*, who challenge current systems and structures by mobilizing their resources and allies.[4] In different fields, these actors would also be called policy entrepreneurs or educational entrepreneurs to emphasize how their enterprising actions were directed in particular domains.[5]

In studies of organizational and institutional changes, scholars highlight two aspects of institutional entrepreneurs: their social position and their social skills. Social position enables action for change. A person's location in

*Subtle Webs*. Jose Eos Trinidad, Oxford University Press. © Oxford University Press (2025).
DOI: 10.1093/9780197786123.003.0005

a formal hierarchy or informal network can provide them with legitimacy, new perspectives, the ability to bridge allies, and the capacity to leverage resources.[6] Social skill is an institutional entrepreneur's ability to engage and motivate others to cooperate with their intended change.[7] This skill may come in the form of framing debates, setting agendas, making change seem necessary, recombining elements, and persuading others toward collective action.[8] In the case of EWIs, organizations had a position that was "in between" because they were outside traditional public education but embedded with actors in it—bearing advantages and disadvantages with such hybrid position.[9] Certain individuals in these organizations also possessed social skills, which they used to make salient the problem of dropping out and to enlist public and philanthropic champions to bring about changes.

Theories of institutional entrepreneurs can often focus on individuals and individual characteristics, leaving out the larger social structure and context. In this chapter, I explore how institutional entrepreneurs structured connections with schools, organizations, and funders. Using examples in the three cities, I illustrate the different types of network structures that functioned as templates in starting and spreading EWIs. On one end of the continuum is a more organized network with clear central and peripheral organizations, while on the other end is a more organic network with organizational connections crisscrossing various nodes. I highlight these types of network structures to document the contexts and circumstances that bring forth and match with specific webs of institutional entrepreneurs.

More than simply documenting the rise of these networks, I also theorize how they have become templates, or models, for structuring networks of institutional entrepreneurs. Instead of thinking of these networks as random collections of individuals and organizations, researchers can think of these networks as being structured in specific ways and being useful in specific circumstances. In this chapter, the figures and graphs function as general representations of abstract concepts rather than empirical illustrations of concrete ties. I use them to suggest the various templates institutional entrepreneurs draw on when connecting across individuals and organizations.

## Interorganizational Webs and Network Templates

Institutional entrepreneurs do not just have to be skillful in framing problems and pushing solutions; they also need to be skilled in spinning webs that bring about change. Particularly for a transformation in a field like education, hierarchical top-down changes can often be resisted while market-based competitive forces can often be met with suspicion.[10] In a field where neither hierarchical nor market-driven approaches are optimal, *networks* become an important alternative.[11] In this situation, institutional entrepreneurs must find ways to structure these networks.

Organizations catalyze the creation of *interorganizational webs*, such as webs among schools, among different organizations, and among their funders. In the case of EWIs, local organizations influenced networks of schools to work with each other, networks of organizations to collaborate, and networks of philanthropies to champion the initiative. But more than bringing together and simply connecting different organizations, institutional entrepreneurs drew on general forms that structure these organizations. What this chapter explores is how certain network templates worked for particular contexts and were useful for particular circumstances.

On one hand is a web with a clear center and threads that branch out from it, like a hub and its spokes, or like a sunburst design with its rays. This network template has one organization as a central "source" of innovation and other organizations as the "destination." An example of this type of web is a school district. This is because a central district office forms a clear center with schools connected to that center. On the other hand is a web characterized by interconnections among various organizations, with complex threads crisscrossing one another. This network template has no clear center, even if there are powerful actors in the system. An example of this type of web is a network of friends, where connections between individuals often span in different ways and clusters can form among certain groups and connections.

Institutional entrepreneurs often initiate and spin these webs. An *orb web* occurs when a central organization has threads connecting and organizing nodes in the inner and outer circles of the structure. A *tangled web* occurs when organizations have threads running across other organizations with no clear center and with the structure emerging from the multiplicity of ties. This chapter details the story of orb webs in New York City and tangled webs in Chicago and Philadelphia (see Figure 4.1). In New York City, for example, EWIs spread through the efforts of New Visions for Public Schools (New Vision) to reach district schools in using a data portal to support students. In Chicago, on the other hand, EWIs spread as the Network for College Success (NCS) connected schools with each other in collectively working through

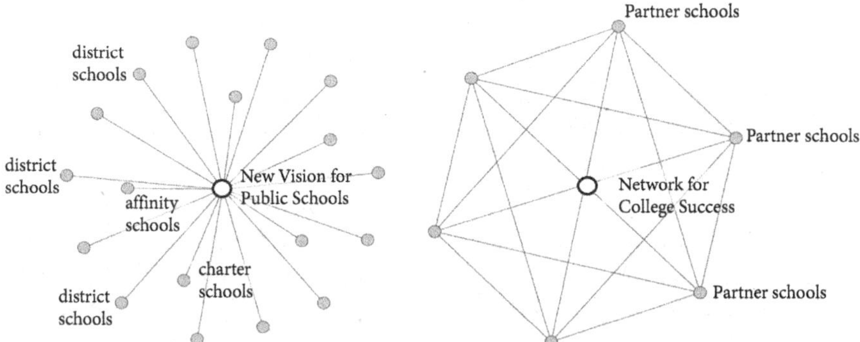


**Figure 4.1** Orb and Tangled Webs for Spreading Early Warning Indicators
*Left*: Orb web structure adopted by New York City with the spread of the Portal by New Visions for Public Schools. *Right*: Tangled web structure adopted by Chicago as various schools collaborated on early warning systems, initiated by the Network for College Success.

the problem of dropping out. The following sections provide greater detail on these webs and their role in spreading EWIs.

How do entrepreneurs choose which one to use? Or, more importantly, which of the two is more effective? This chapter tries to uncover the dynamics and consequences of institutional entrepreneurs spinning different types of webs for various purposes. It highlights how certain structures were adopted because of political processes, environmental (un)certainties, and the need for adaptation and flexibility. The chapter also proposes circumstances that prove useful for particular network arrangements. In the next sections, I will discuss New York City as structuring orb webs in an environment with powerful centers and greater certainty. Next, I discuss Chicago and Philadelphia as creating tangled webs in an environment with emerging organizations and greater uncertainty.

## Orb Web

Institutional entrepreneurs come in many forms. One of the forms they can take in education are intermediary organizations, a term which refers to school support firms, professional development organizations, coaches, consultants, and design teams that help implement changes in schools.[12] More than simply mediating between two organizations—like policymakers on one hand and implementers on another, or researchers on one hand

and practitioners on the other[13]—these "intermediaries" have taken on powerful roles with implementing change, creating networks, and transforming instructional processes in schools.[14]

One of the ways these intermediary organizations can impact schools is by working directly with them and introducing new practices. In New York City, some of these organizations are called "partnership support organizations" that work with traditional public schools around the city. These are university centers and school reform nonprofits that collaborate with high schools in the city to support their curricular, operational, data, leadership, and professional development needs.[15] In its current form, these organizations were part of the Affinity District, a group of six large nonprofits that supported 164 public schools, roughly one-third of the public high schools in the city.[16]

One of these affinity organizations is New Visions, which provided curriculum resources, teacher and leadership coaching, and professional development to the 71 public schools they were supporting and the 10 charter schools they were operating. In 2008, this New York City organization developed its own "on-track" metric, and they used the metric to map out the progress students needed to make to graduate with a high school diploma in four years. Like Chicago and Philadelphia, New Visions's metric included students' course credits and grades. However, given the requirement for the city's students to pass end-of-course exams in New York state, the organization added passing these Regents exams in calculating whether students were on track. Describing how these were used before, Lyndsay Pinkus wrote:

> Using this metric, each student's status is described through the use of color-coded categories: on track to college readiness (blue); on track to graduation (green); almost on track to graduation (yellow); or off track to graduation (red). New Visions analyzes the data for each school and provides administrators with a schoolwide report on student performance based on the metric. It also creates snapshots that can show an individual student's progress toward graduation and college readiness, and encourages students to create a plan to get (or stay) on track.[17]

The organization had these on-track systems initially used by the schools with which they were partnered.

New Visions's chief-of-staff, Nikki Giunta, highlighted the various changes their early warning systems had gone through. She mentioned that it used to be a spreadsheet called the Student Sorter, with 276 columns, updated monthly and then biweekly. The *Portal by New Visions* was a comprehensive web-based data tool that teachers and school staff could enter to view the performance of students, classes, and schools. Giunta mentioned it had "demographic data, attendance data, course credits, Regents [exams passing], marking period grades—the full range of data." It also had ways of focusing on specific students and aggregating to different clusters and subpopulations in a school.

Initially, the tool spread to New Visions's charter schools and partner public schools as the organization had coaches working with these schools to introduce *strategic data check-ins*, which were conversations with teachers and administrators at particular points in time to help with student-level planning. The organization created time for *graduation planning*, which helped students strategize for the diploma type they should get; they instituted *credit gaps analysis*, which helped teachers catch students with missing credits for graduation; and they established *periodic reviews*, during which teachers would consider students' grades and attendance to identify the academic supports students needed. Across all these systems, the organization was a core and centralizing force driving the initiatives.

For a technical tool like the Portal, spread happened from the center to the peripheries (see Figure 4.1, left panel). Similar to an orb web, certain nodes were closer to the center than others. At the organization's 10 charter schools, Giunta said New Visions was able to "figure out what are some strategies or things that can be learned." At the 71 public high schools they partnered with, the organization had coaches to work with schools to test, implement, and revise these data tools, protocols, and processes. Later, the Portal became available to a number of public community schools, and then in 2019, to all public high schools in New York City. By 2021, the tool had even expanded to be used in elementary and middle schools in the city.[18]

Coaches like Jamie Esperon worked to coach teams of teachers or mentor specific point persons in schools to use data in actionable ways. Her work entailed her being the central node and this work further branched out to the individuals in the school. As a central node, she assembled data on attendance, credit accumulation, marking period grades, and the Regents exams passing rate. She collaborated with the schools to create focal groups for students who needed closer attention. She mentioned how the school used the data to assist "an advisor program, an advisory structure, where there's a point person for each kid . . . and [teachers discuss] next steps." In her role as coach, Esperon functioned as a central source for the set of schools with which she worked.

More than just New Visions's coaches in New York City, this type of orb web is common in many coaching, professional development, and early warning systems work. Coaches help individual teachers or groups of educators to identify goals, sequence activities, and foster new interventions.[19] Professional development providers train teachers on instructional routines and help implement specific policies—making them central actors that influence schools' actions.[20] In the case of EWIs, schools often had coaches that ensured they would use their "on-track" data, hold teacher team meetings, and create appropriate interventions for students exhibiting off-track signals.[21] By creating this webbed structure with a central node, organizations were able to institute practices that were strikingly similar across different contexts. In such a web, most initiatives emanate from the center, and many of the outside nodes are only weakly connected to other nodes in the periphery.

Such orb webs need a powerful center, receptive nodes, and an environment with greater certainty. Although New Visions had the power and expertise to develop the Portal, the initiative further scaled because of the powerful support of champions in the city's educational bureaucracy. One such champion was Meisha Ross Porter, executive superintendent of the Bronx between 2018 and 2021, and subsequently the city's chancellor in 2021.[22] Giunta shared how Porter "had [the Portal] for all of the schools in her portfolio and she knew the value, so she wanted to provide that value to all executive superintendents, and that's when we just recently scaled to every school in New York City." In the absence of such powerful support, it is doubtful that this centralized structure would be sustained in America's largest school district. Such structure also had variable effectiveness, as Giunta acknowledged: "It's one thing to provide them with the tool, [but] very few people are going to be able to just drive right in." In this way, the tool might be accessible but not necessarily used or only variably used.

But this centralized structure did lend itself well to a context in which there was greater certainty of EWIs' theory of change. The structure was helpful in spreading a tool with clear applications and uses. An example of this is not only the web-based tool but also the strategic check-ins that had become part and parcel of using these tools in schools. For schools closer to the center, which had access to coaches from New Visions, these tools and practices became embedded. For schools farther away from the web's hub, the impact was more varied. A teacher from a public high school in Brooklyn shared that, "I use New Visions a lot; we use their curriculum a lot. But that particular Portal, I've never accessed or seen. But we do have a lot of different ways of looking at data." This hinted at the variety with how things were used depending on the access with experts from outside organizations—a clear limitation of an orb web.

## Distributive and Integrative Networks

An orb web has a clear center or source. Many times, the central organization dispenses information or technologies to the peripheral organizations. However, at other times, this center also incorporates information and technologies from constituent organizations. In detailing the use of an orb web in New York City, I illustrate two templates associated with it. One is a *distributive network*, where the center provides various materials, resources, and services to the peripheral organizations. The other is an *integrative network*, where the center functions to incorporate these materials, resources, and services.

In spreading technical tools and data systems, New York City adopted an orb web with a clear center and peripheral nodes. To spread these tools to schools, New Visions distributed and made these accessible to public schools around the city. Something similar happened for community-based organizations (CBOs) as two organizations became convenors for CBOs to receive data on the youths with whom they worked. One organization was a group led by education professionals and youth advocates called #DegreesNYC, while the other was a research organization based at New York University, the Research Alliance for New York City Schools. Both organizations worked together in establishing the *Data Co-op and Learning Network*, which brought together CBOs focused on youths' college, career, and postsecondary trajectories.

Judith Lorimer was the director of #DegreesNYC, the organization that aimed to increase the number of students with postsecondary credentials across all racial/ethnic and income groups.[23] One of the dimensions of the organization's work was measured in terms of data and accountability, which had led to the Data Co-op initiative. Lorimer detailed:

> The Data Co-op is what we've worked on in close partnership with the Research Alliance. Originally, it was a group of 14 community-based organizations that were joining their data at the student level with the Research Alliance's longitudinal educational database . . . And so, these community-based organizations were sharing data and then getting reports back not at the individual level but at the group level.

The group started in 2018 with different New York City nonprofits coming together in working groups to understand how to make college more accessible to students and how to help students become more successful in college. One of these working groups was concentrated on how data were being used.

Lisa Merrill, an associate at the Research Alliance, shared about the genesis of the Data Co-op when #DegreesNYC convened a number of working groups, one of which was tasked with data and accountability. The group was composed of large organizations, like the NYC Department of Education (NYC DOE), City University of New York (CUNY), and the Research Alliance, which had student-level achievement data as well as community-based organizations that had personal and qualitative data on their respective youths. Merrill noted how there were "obvious complementary datasets, where the Research Alliance and the district had institutional longitudinal data . . . and community-based organizations had a whole host of other information and perspective on young people but they weren't able to connect it to their academics." She went on detailing how they were "connecting individual organizations' data to the Department of Education data, and then running some analyses and sharing those results."

The example of the Data Co-op highlights an orb web template, but with two unique dynamics. One dynamic moves inside-out while the other moves outside-in. One is a distributive network while the other is an integrative network (see Figure 4.2).

Similar to the school web that made data accessible through the Portal, the Data Co-op infrastructure distributed data to nonprofit organizations that were part of the Data Co-op (see Figure 4.2, left panel). Given Research Alliance's ability to draw on data from the NYC DOE, CUNY, and the national student clearinghouse, the organization was able to function as a hub for sharing data across different groups. On its website, the Research Alliance noted that CBOs "use the resulting information to improve their practices and to engage policymakers and others in data-driven conversations about how all NYC students can be academically successful and college and career ready."[24] On the one hand, the network structure highlights a

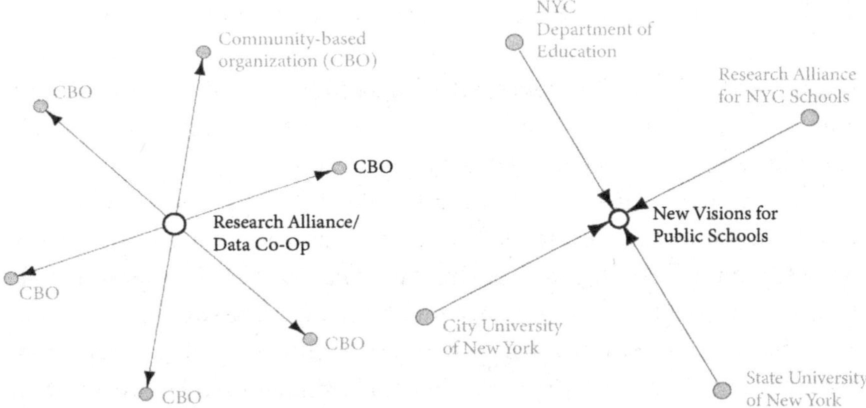


**Figure 4.2** Distributive and Integrative Aspects of an Orb Web

*Left*: Distributive web with the Research Alliance for New York City Schools providing aggregate data reports for participating community-based organizations (CBOs). *Right*: Integrative web with New Visions for Public Schools bringing together information from various sources.

distributive network where the Research Alliance provides data to CBOs. On the other hand, the dynamics also included an integrative network as the Research Alliance combined data from various sources like the NYC DOE, CUNY, and the national student clearinghouse.

In an earlier section, I noted the distributive network of New Visions as they distributed the Portal to their charter schools, their partner district schools, and the larger set of schools in the city. However, New Visions was only able to create the Portal by bringing together data from various systems and organizations. For example, much of the data relied on the Automate the Schools (ATS) administrative system and STARS Classroom tool for entering grades—both of which were under the purview of the NYC DOE.[25] More than a distributing organization, New Visions was also an integrating organization (see Figure 4.2, right panel).

Jeremy Greenfield was the deputy director of college access and success at New Visions and spoke about the organization's role in New York's education ecosystem:

> In many ways, we [at New Visions] see ourselves as an intermediary between the Department of Education and CUNY; that's where two-thirds of our students go. So, one organization we work deeply with is the Department of Education, and the other organization we work deeply with is CUNY. We work with SUNY. Increasingly, we're working with other entities in the college access and success space.

The NYC DOE and CUNY were among the largest public institutions in the United States, collectively with a million and a half students. New Visions worked with them to incorporate their data to the Portal because the data tool aimed to be a convenient place to access critical information to help students remain on track to graduate high schools.

In this scenario, what mattered was less the distributive power of organizations to influence others to use the tool and more the convening power of organizations to bring together others' data. The web-based Portal accessible to schools throughout the city started because of a data-sharing agreement with the NYC DOE. But it had subsequently grown to include data from the city's urban university system. Greenfield shared that the organization "completed a data sharing agreement with CUNY that puts all of the college application data for all New York City public school [students] into the Data Portal, and so in that way, we're connecting the DOE and CUNY." Such data sharing agreements were crucial in bringing together data to initiate these dropout prevention systems.

The structure of an orb web can be both distributive and integrative. In New York City, I have shown how these hubs functioned to share data and to integrate data. Interestingly, in all these cases, the focus was on technical systems that needed centralized structures to be brought about and distributed. Such distributive and integrative webs also needed powerful outside organizations, like New Visions and the Research Alliance, which were capable of influencing and integrating large public institutions and smaller community-based organizations.

Institutional entrepreneurs in New York City created distributive and integrative networks to spread and sustain their EWI initiatives. This template of an orb web—that is, a network structure with a clear center—made sense for technical changes where data needed to be consolidated and it made sense in environments with powerful organizations with the capacity to bring it about. But the spread of ideas does not just happen through a single powerful source that integrates and distributes to others. It can also happen through diffused agents creating robust networks across each other.

## Tangled Web

In contrast to the orb structure of New York City's networks for early warning indicators, Chicago's schools can be characterized as tangled connections that were facilitated by outside organizations (see Figure 4.1, right panel). Like New Visions, the NCS in Chicago was a school support organization that provided professional learning, coaching, and capacity-building to several public high schools in the city.[26] However, the organization did not start as a provider of these services, but rather as a convenor of school leaders trying to improve their high schools.

Melissa Roderick and Sarah Duncan were co-founders of the NCS. Roderick was a professor at the University of Chicago while Duncan led the university's leadership in community schools program. In 2005, a number of principals reached out, noting that they needed help solving problems, not simply understanding them. Duncan spoke about the genesis of this *network* of schools as arising from Roderick's idea as "the answers are in the field. Let's get some principals together and talk about what's working." Here the co-founders emphasized not an orb web with a central source and peripheral destinations, but a tangled web of schools working with and learning from each other. The organization was not primarily the source of ideas; Duncan highlighted that the ideas came from principals who were connected with each other.

Mary Ann Pitcher joined the two co-founders in 2006 and became the NCS co-director. Previously a director of a charter school in the southside of Chicago and an English teacher in a southwest public high school, she was deeply embedded and connected with schools and leaders in the district. She noted that the NCS originally started with the goal of being a "peer community . . . of principals who are interested in engaging in this [school improvement] work." Her new role entailed bringing this network of school leaders together, and creating a space for a group of 10 principals who were interested in learning both from research and from each other.

The principals had convenings organized by the NCS. For her part, Pitcher worked with particular schools to design school visits, where "the principal would identify a problem of practice, we [at NCS] design a school visit around it, and then invite the newly forming network at that time to be part of the visit process and help the school leader think through the problem of practice." In the process, the network of school leaders identified three central priorities: transition into high school, student learning experiences in classrooms, and post-secondary planning and success.

Over time, different schools would come in and out of the NCS because of changes in school principals. Pitcher noted how principals who were part of the NCS would speak to other principals, informing them about what they were doing with the NCS. One example was Elizabeth Kirby, who was the principal at Kenwood Academy and who informed other principals about the NCS, both in her district-structured network and in her own informal network of principal friends. Pitcher noted how Kirby "would share with people what she was doing, what we were learning, and then, that would spark interest in others." It was through this process of informal sharing that the tangled webs of schools were learning more about emerging EWIs and dropout prevention systems.

In subsequent years, the NCS started to have different types of coaches, like freshman success coaches, as well as leadership, instructional, equity, and postsecondary coaches. This variety of coaches focused on specific aspects that supported the high schools with which they were working. In a way, the coaches started to function similarly as the school support organizations in New York City, particularly as Chicago's coaches were also meeting individually with school leaders and instructional teams. One can argue that the advent of coaches mimicked the distributive network of central organizations providing resources and services to schools.

In 2012, Amy Torres joined the NCS as a leadership coach. Aside from working with principals, she also worked with different schools' *instructional leadership teams* composed of assistant principals and other teacher leaders. Initially, she thought that her role was to spread and disseminate to the schools early warning indicators and processes. After all, she was the one who knew more about the research and being in an intermediary organization was a mark of her ability to translate research into practice. But she had a shift in thinking as she began working with these schools:

> When I started Network for College Success, I thought my role was to convince the principal and the people in the school that this [early warning indicator system] is important work and teach them how to do it the right way. And *what I've learned since is that I'm there to help and support the leaders and our network*. When they meet together as principals . . . , that in and of itself, the sharing of ideas, spotlighting schools to have practices that are really helping them around attendance, [helped schools]. (emphasis added)

She recounted how a principal had initially resisted her idea about bringing data to the school's ninth-grade teacher team meetings. The principal justified that this was a controversial move to which the teachers were sensitive, and he was scared to bring this up for fear of opposition.

But Torres shared that change happened when school leaders went into the principal network meetings and heard other principals speak about the same issues they were experiencing, particularly "what they did, what the results and the impacts were, what were the pitfalls, what wisdom they shared, and then we had principals collaborate around these ideas." Torres explained that the principal's initial resistance went away with the assurance of colleagues who had already practiced what the coach had initially suggested.

During the next coaching session, the principal said, "Oh yeah, I definitely wanna bring data to my freshman team meetings now." Torres explained this as the power of the network. It was more effective for principals and schools to receive new ideas from principals that were working and at times struggling with that same new initiative. While Torres still had a coaching role with individual schools, she highlighted that what the principal needed "was the dialogue and conversation and the examples to make this change, number one, possible, and number two, concrete." It was the tangled web of schools, not the central position of a coach, that made the difference in ideas being taken up by the school principal.

Such a tangled web entails a network of school leaders intentionally coming together as a community to collectively problem solve with each other. The role of the "outside" organization is less about being a source and more about being as a *convenor*. The success of innovations diffusing through this network is less a matter of the power of the convening organization and more a consequence of the interaction of the whole group. As hinted at by institutional entrepreneurs like Roderick, Duncan, and Pitcher, the success depended on the group that they were able to assemble. Compared to an orb structure in which innovations are clear, a tangled structure entails innovations as emerging from the individuals convened. This did not mean, however, that school support organizations did not have power. As Torres had shown, there was power in suggesting ideas and focusing conversations that aligned with early warning systems' theory of change. But power ultimately arose from the group coming together.

Thus, educational change happened not only through the work of a central hub organization but also through the creation of what scholars have called networked improvement communities.[27] In these communities, the focus was less on expert-driven innovation and fidelity of implementation, and more on the collective practice of discussing problems, crafting solutions, and testing practices.[28] Such tangled webs lend themselves to institutional entrepreneurs when there is greater uncertainty of the change and when the shift is about a change in practice rather than a change in technology. In this ecosystem, outside school improvement organizations will function differently than when they are sources of innovation.

## Embedded and Role-Differentiated Networks

Unlike an orb web, in which the form is often set with clear central and peripheral nodes, a tangled web can often come in different forms. Rather than describe the different possible forms, I illustrate how organizations can be deeply *embedded* with different ties that cross each other, or how organizations can be formally *differentiated* as each organization relates to other organizations through more formal division of labor. Like the schools in Chicago, whose connections were often informal, the city's philanthropies and nonprofits have also created informal ties that characterize an embedded network. In contrast, organizations in Philadelphia created clear connections across various organizations and district offices, hinting at a formal division of labor and illustrating a role-differentiated network.

### Embedded Network

Philanthropies are often seen—perhaps, even feared—as directly influencing the direction of the organizations they fund. Studies on venture philanthropy, in particular, have described how this relatively new form of philanthropy has poured large sums of funding for particular education reforms, like those that support school choice and charter schools.[29] Some scholars contend that this type of entrepreneurial philanthropy can be problematic because public institutions and public goods like education are being directed by private actors that are often unaccountable to the general public and whose practices are also often opaque to outsiders.[30] However, other scholars suggest the potential good in these philanthropic investments as they provide "a vehicle for identifying and supporting promising individuals and ideas that may be an uncomfortable fit for education bureaucracies and routines."[31] Nonetheless, in both cases scholars have focused on the power of philanthropies to directly intervene and shape the trajectories of educational initiatives.

While large philanthropies do play powerful roles in the direction of organizations, less attention is given to smaller place-based family philanthropies—often networks of local elites in particular cities that try to support and fund various initiatives and nonprofits.

In Chicago, in particular, the work of the three school improvement organizations did not just rely on large sources of funding, like the Gates Foundation, the US Department of Education, or the Institute of Education Sciences. There were often smaller foundations that provided operational and project-based support. The network was an embedded group of local elites who were supporting these organizations (see Figure 4.3) and challenging the idea that philanthropies directly impact the direction of organizations.

Penny Bender Sebring was a co-founder of the University of Chicago Consortium on School Research and spoke about the various ways the research organization looked for funding. Initially, their operations were supported with grants from the Joyce Foundation, the MacArthur Foundation, and the Spencer Foundation—large philanthropies with their base in the city. However, she noted the shift in funding, saying, "they started moving to a

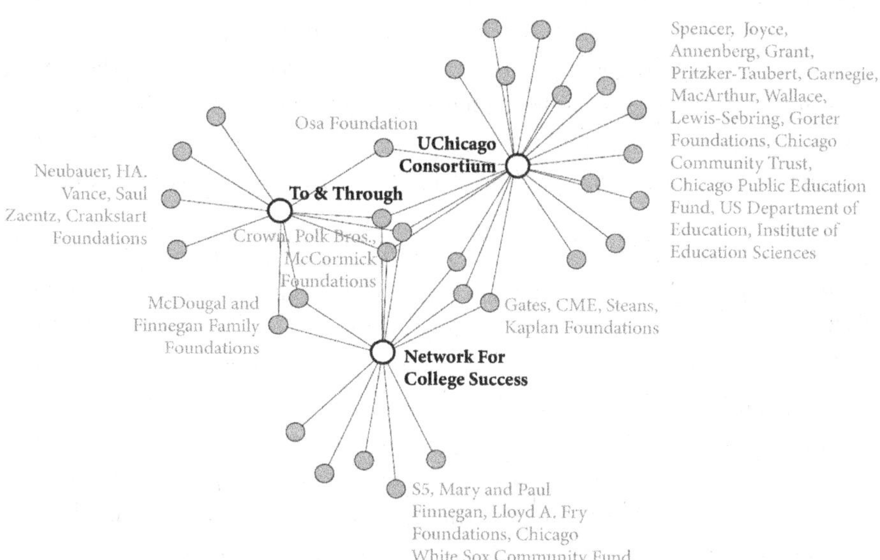


**Figure 4.3** Embedded Philanthropic Network for Chicago Organizations Working on EWIs

*Note*: Hollow circles denote organizations that initiated early warning systems in Chicago while shaded circles are philanthropies and foundations funding them. Some philanthropies funded more than one organization, thus, showing the interconnections among organizations.

*Source*: The network map was created with information on funders from the three organizations' websites.

project-by-project funding model, and that was very hard for us because research is only part of what we do." Sebring talked about the need for greater flexibility, which was difficult when funds were restricted to research. Because of this, the organization had to be creative in seeking funds:

> In 2016 and 2017, we started the Consortium Investor Council, which is a group of about fifteen family and larger foundations that provide flexible funding for us. And so, when we went out and started talking to funders, we argued that the Consortium was a civic asset . . . They stepped up and said, "We'll help you." So, the agreement we have with them is that they provide anywhere from 10,000 to 100,000 dollars every year for five years.

Since that time, the Consortium was able to raise more than $600,000 for different projects—from replicating previous studies and seeding new ones to translating their research into practice and refreshing their data archives.

By having such flexible funding, the Consortium was able to be nimble with their research because it could take up to a year before grants were approved. Sebring argued that, by that time, a research question may have become irrelevant. But such flexible funding had emerged from networks that knew the work of the Consortium and the fact that members of the Consortium were themselves embedded in Chicago's philanthropic community. The tangle of relationships in the city—formal and informal connections among philanthropies, nonprofits, and public officials—contributed to such structure.

Philanthropies did not just function as sources of funds but as gateways to connections. The Mayer and Morris Kaplan Family Foundation had funded the NCS and the Consortium, with yearly grants of less than $100,000. Although the grants were not as large as project-based grants, the foundation's executive director, Dinaz Mansuri, spoke about how their work was about "bringing funders together and ensuring that people are working off of the same information." Their role was not so much to direct the work of these organizations but to support the creation of a network of individuals.

The focus was less on initiatives and more on relationships. Mansuri shared the example of Sarah Duncan, who was the co-founder and co-director of the NCS, and had been invited to speak to the foundation's board. She said about Duncan that "we're obviously very impressed with her and had a good relationship with her." Mansuri also added the connection of the family with Melissa Roderick, the other founder of the NCS. The Kaplan Family Foundation had also supported Roderick and her work because she was "really instrumental obviously in this research and in a lot of the Chicago-based education research, and it is sort of, like, [if] Melissa has her hands on something, you would say it's probably really important and it's probably really good work." These praises highlight how some foundations can be motivated less by organizational initiatives and more by organizational initiators; that is, by the institutional entrepreneurs that start these initiatives.

In contrast to studies highlighting the role of philanthropies to direct organizations, smaller family foundations often facilitate ecosystems for connections and embeddedness. In this environment, support comes from various places rather than from singular sources. Often, these local philanthropies are connected with each other and are able to provide collective support for local nonprofits, particularly those that work on similar initiatives like EWIs. The embeddedness of these organizations with similar organizations and similar initiatives contributes to an ecosystem in which institutional entrepreneurs structure networks in informal ways.

## Role-Differentiated Network

In contrast to the organic and informal nature of embedded networks, a role-differentiated network is formally created through the assignment of specific roles and the division of expert labor. When the Neubauer Family Foundation started to support the work of Ninth Grade On-Track in Philadelphia in 2017, it employed the services of a Chicago organization that had been working on Chicago's public interfacing data tool to understand students' graduation and postsecondary patterns. The To&Through Project—named this way because it aimed to get students to and through college—was not the only institutional entrepreneur in Philadelphia. The organization collaborated with the Philadelphia Academies, Inc. because they were already working with a number of school-interfacing projects in the city. They also worked with Research For Action (RFA), which had already established a research-practice partnership with the district's research office, creating the Philadelphia Education Research Consortium (PERC). Finally, they contracted with Revolution Impact, which acted as a project manager handling various data aspects of the on-track initiative.

All these organizations connected with each other in a tangled web of institutional entrepreneurs trying to move the needle on improving the city's on-track and graduation rates. They did this not just by collaborating with

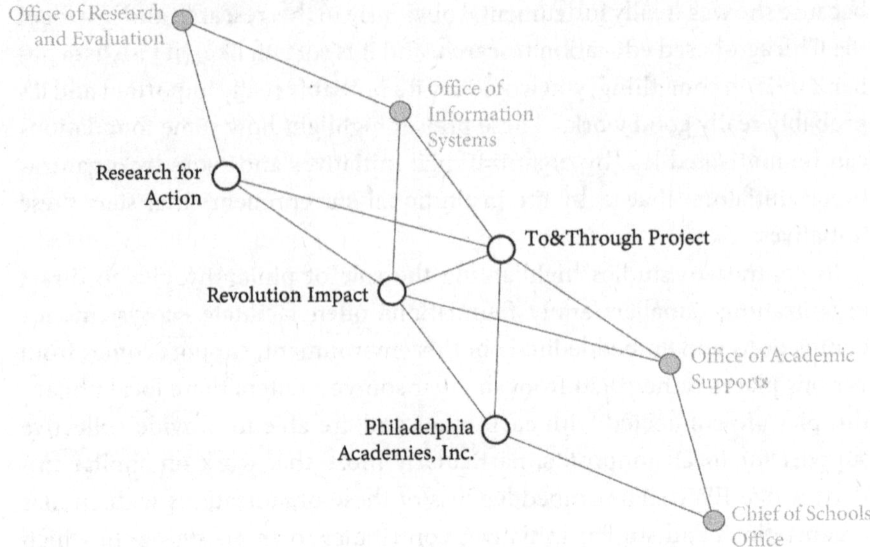


**Figure 4.4** Role-Differentiated Organizational Network in Philadelphia

*Note*: Hollow circles denote non-school organizations working on Ninth Grade On-Track system while shaded circles denote counterpart offices with the School District of Philadelphia. Connections/ties were created with mentions from interviews of organizational connections.

each other but also by coordinating with their public counterparts in the School District of Philadelphia (see Figure 4.4).

Each organization had a role in this tangled web. Although the organizations worked collectively to spread EWIs, they also had specific roles. To&Through and Revolution Impact collaborated to build data tools and provide professional development for the city's high schools. Philadelphia Academies Inc. led the Ninth Grade Success Network—a group of more than 10 schools collaborating to support ninth-grade students. RFA led research to understand attendance, on-track, and credit accumulation patterns of Philadelphia ninth graders to support on-time graduation.

Because of the role of each particular organization, they at times worked more closely with specific district offices than others. For example, RFA worked closely with the district's office of research and evaluation. Alyn Turner, who was RFA's director of quantitative research and also the co-director of PERC, detailed this collaboration between individuals from her team at RFA and individuals like Theodore Wills from the district's research office. Revolution Impact's CEO, Pranav Kothari, also characterized it as a tangle with a "cross-organizational, cross-functional team that meets weekly online to help develop the data tools, develop the professional learning around the data tools, and then also inform how the district is implementing Ninth Grade On-Track." While the network remained a tangle with overlapping ties, each organization had a niche and its own specific role.

In such a tangle of organizational collaborations and configurations, entities may experience conflicts, particularly when the division of labor is unclear. However, from interviews, the organizations seemed to have adapted in taking on their specific niches. Nadia Schafer was the director of data supports and evaluation at Philadelphia Academies, Inc., and she mentioned how her organization was able to delineate its work with their partners from Chicago—both the To&Through Project and Revolution Impact:

> [There are] two main streams of professional development . . . The UChicago folks [To&Through] take the lead on the *district-wide* trainings for high school leaders; we support that. And then there's also the *school-level* professional development that Philadelphia Academies leads for like the 13 schools in our network that will do trainings with teachers, weekly coaching with assistant principals—more kinda on-the-ground hands-on support at the school level. (emphasis added)

In this way, the organizations were aware of who was leading initiatives directed to specific audiences. The web was a tangle of organizations, but it was also often formally set.

In this tangled web, institutional entrepreneurs organize networks not by creating hub-and-spokes but by clarifying organizational roles. In a situation where no clear center is driving changes, the challenge comes with organizations understanding how they fit with each other and how they can complement each other.

At times, though, this clarification of niches happens by making mistakes and resolving conflicts. One such example is the To&Through Project, which was initially part of the University of Chicago Consortium on School Research. However, the data-reporting organization became independent of, but still affiliated with, the Consortium. In an interview, a philanthropic manager shared that "there was this big fight between us and the Consortium . . . because essentially, some people in the Consortium felt like this wasn't their job; their job was not regular data reporting."[32] In this example, the two organizations' roles became clarified as conflicts arose regarding the proper role of each organization. In networks where roles are differentiated, the tangle of institutional entrepreneurs needs to clarify each one's specific role and contribution.

## How Structures Inform Institutional Entrepreneurs

Organizations can structure networks for the spread of innovations and practices. Institutional entrepreneurs do not just leverage their social position and do not just employ their social skills. They often need to be attentive to their contexts and the structures necessary to bring about specific types of changes. In the case of EWIs, institutional entrepreneurs in Chicago, Philadelphia, and New York City structured networks not just by random connections with each other but through intentional templates. On one end is an orb web with a clear hub and its component spokes. Such hubs can also function as distributive or integrative centers. On the other end is a tangled web of organizations connected with each other. Connections emerge through organizations being informally embedded with each other or through organizations being formally differentiated according to their roles in the network.

Studies of social networks in education have often highlighted the importance of these networks of individuals and organizations.[33] Whether these are networks of teachers inside schools or networks of advocates and politicians crafting new policies, relationships across individuals and organizations are key to changes.[34] In addition to the dyadic relationships among actors, an equally important factor is the structure of connections—whether they are an orb or tangled web, a distributive or integrative network, or an embedded or role-differentiated network. An analysis of the whole network of actors can provide a sense of which conditions and circumstances support the networks created.

What I have shown in this chapter is how institutional entrepreneurs create templates or models to structure these networks, and how they draw on these templates as they attempt to spread ideas and practices related to EWIs. In contexts that require technical changes and where there is greater certainty in the theory of change, an orb web can lead to significant changes. In contexts that require nimble changes in practice and where there is less coherence in the theory of change, a tangled web of emerging initiatives and efforts can lead to more sustained changes. In influencing change, it's not just what you know. It's also not just who you know. Instead, it is what network structure supports the change needed.

# Chapter 5
## How Routines Change Organizational Resistance

I have to work on their actions to change their beliefs.

—Krystal Payne,
*Co-director, Network for College Success*

Krystal Payne started out as a school coach with the Network for College Success (NCS) in 2009, working with Chicago high schools to initiate and implement ninth-grade early warning indicators (EWIs). More than 10 years later, she became the co-executive director of the organization but still remembered when she was directly working with schools. Like other school improvement coaches, she also worked with school leaders and teams of ninth-grade teachers to help them look at data on attendance, behavior, and course performance, as well as to be "more attentive to what's going on with the ninth graders that were transitioning into their schools." Her organization in Chicago, as well as similar organizations in Philadelphia and New York City, was key in spreading EWI practices in schools, although change was not without challenges, resistance, and skepticism to their introduction of these new practices.

Sociologists have often noted how urban schools are characterized as experiencing "so much reform, but so little change." A book of a similar title illustrates how teachers are inundated with constant reform efforts and how they consequently challenge such efforts, not just through pragmatic strategies of resistance but also through cultural schemas (i.e., shared ways of thinking) that further the status quo.[1] These strategies span active and passive forms of behavior, with some ignoring new policies, others creating work-arounds through them, and still others intentionally disrupting new initiatives.[2] As "outsiders" expect to experience resistance from "insiders" like school teachers and leaders, how do these organizations address it?

When attempting to change practices, these organizations could have focused either on motivating a cultural change or on initiating organizational practices. On one side, some scholars have argued for the importance

*Subtle Webs*. Jose Eos Trinidad, Oxford University Press. © Oxford University Press (2025).
DOI: 10.1093/9780197786123.003.0006

of changing cultural schemas or the learning climate in the school.[3] In this sense, change happens from the *inside out* as schools must first create a culture of openness to bring about external behavioral transformations. On the other side, some have emphasized the significance of changing organizational processes and concrete systems first.[4] In this sense, change happens from the *outside in*, as schools institute practical routines and pragmatic changes that can subsequently be embedded in the school culture.

Organizational sociologists in general, and institutional theorists in particular, have often highlighted the role of social interactions and everyday practices in influencing organizational changes and institutional transformations. Using the theory of inhabited institutions, theorists suggest that change is explained not just through new meanings (i.e., institutional logics) or through new resources (from institutional entrepreneurs), but also through changes in people's interactions.[5] Such interactions can be powerfully set up through *organizational routines*, or repetitive patterns of interdependent activities and actions that are carried out by multiple actors and are fundamental in accomplishing the work of an organization.[6] Often, these routines are established by, or emerge from, people inside the organizations. However, what happens when individuals outside the organization try to establish these routines and meet resistance?

This chapter details how nonprofit staff in Chicago, Philadelphia, and New York City initiated changes in schools, not by directly challenging people's thinking, but by forming *relationships*, revising school *practices*, and sustaining specific *routines*. Rather than coming in with specific change ideas, these outside organizations worked with schools to incorporate data systems, test out communal practices, and adapt already existing school routines. This chapter also documents the tensions that came between outside organizations, which had particular interests in changing school practices, and school staff, who had legitimate reasons to resist and be skeptical of these changes. Yet, with time and with sustained relationships, organizations were able to integrate ideas, principles, and routines from EWIs into the everyday practices in schools. Schools, too, were able to adapt and contextualize these. Changes were also layered onto the routines already established in schools. The present chapter, then, is an analysis of how conflict and collaboration figure in the spread of school practices and in the implementation of new ones.

In understanding educational change as it happens in schools, I document how outside organizations have functioned not so much just to provide information and expertise, as if one pours water from a pitcher to a glass, but more so for these organizations to spin webs of school routines—adapting previous school practices, embedding new habits into old ones, and connecting new routines into a coherent whole. These organizations did not necessarily know from the start what shape this web would take. Rather, they learned to spin such practices by interacting with individuals on the ground and, arguably, even by facing resistance from them. In contrast to more distant district officials and academic researchers, these coaches were immersed in schools and formed connections that enabled them to spin webs of routines that had greater odds of being sustained and permeating school practices.

The chapter is divided into three sections. The first section documents the experiences of resistance to EWIs and the justifications for it. This resistance included skepticism, fear, and foot-dragging. The second section highlights how local organizations addressed the resistance by establishing relationships and introducing routines. These webs of routines included the introduction of new data systems, relational practices, and tiered community interventions. The third section connects these practical changes in routines to cultural changes in beliefs. As I quote from Payne at the start of the chapter, change may come not when one focuses on influencing belief but when one focuses on influencing action instead.

## Resistance

Resistance to new school policies and practices is neither surprising nor unusual. Teachers' resistance can take active and passive forms as some ignore, misinterpret, or misuse policies while others actively protest or pursue litigation.[7] For example, studies have documented resistance to school accountability regimes as teachers argue that "accountability systems are destructive to teaching."[8] However, far fewer studies have documented the reception of predictive data tools that would become less a form of accountability and more an instrument of student identification. Yet even with this explicit shift in the theory of change, these EWIs still faced considerable challenges from teachers.

Coaches noted three ways resistance emerged. First, teachers were initially skeptical of the data—whether they were truly accurate, objective, or predictive. Second, school staff had fears about the unintended consequences of EWIs being used to game systems or threaten their autonomy. Third, teachers turned to practical ignorance of the tools, justifying that they were too busy or too jaded to turn to these data systems. Rather than simply view these as reactions to EWIs specifically, I argue that such examples of *skepticism*, *fear*, and *foot-dragging* suggest more general strategies of resistance to new practices.

But the resistance was from the perspective of coaches who viewed such reception as obstacles to their work of spreading new routines, practices, and innovations. For teachers, they were legitimate responses to threats to their professional autonomy and pressures from outside organizations. Across various contexts in the three cities, outside coaches and coordinators spoke about similar concerns teachers had. Although there was a sense of frustration as they spoke about these challenges to their efforts, many of them also sympathized with teachers. They were, after all, former teachers and school leaders who themselves had to navigate the hassle of new school practices and had to allocate time for all sorts of new demands on top of their already busy day. With one foot in and another one out, nonprofit staff were able to speak about the resistance they received and the empathy they had for it.

## Skepticism

Data are products of social processes.[9] What gets counted and what counts as countable are influenced by people who have the power to ordain the data to be used. In the case of EWIs, researchers suggested focusing on attendance, behavior, and course performance—the ABCs of staying on track to graduate.[10] Districts used the percentage of students "on track" as an accountability metric. Coaches had lists of students with Ds and Fs to help teachers focus conversations on these students.

Because data are social, their origin is open to critique. Are the grades in teachers' records really accurate? Can we really predict who will drop out at ninth grade? Aren't grades subjective and so we should just rely on test scores? These were among the questions school support coaches and data strategists heard as they worked with teachers in the schools. These were questions of the data's *accuracy*, *predictiveness*, and *objectivity*. But behind such queries was a reasonable skepticism for how different these data systems were from previous forms of quantification.

*Are the data accurate?* Amy Torres had worked as an instructional coach with the NCS, the organization that supported a number of Chicago high schools with the district's Freshman OnTrack program. She primarily coached teacher teams as they received and used the five-week data on students on track or at risk of being off track. But before she and the teacher team could work with the data, she felt that teachers were already resistant:

> Any time we would bring in data, you know what their detour was? They did not even want to think about student outcomes. They would challenge the accuracy of the data, which is not a bad point, but literally every time. [They would say,] "This isn't accurate because it was pulled on this date, and I've entered grades since."

Although she acknowledged that a healthy skepticism of data was not necessarily a bad point, her frustration came from this dynamic happening so often.

A similar observation was made by Lakecia Whimper, who was a senior data analyst at the Chicago Public Schools (CPS) and worked to provide the five-week data to schools. She mentioned, "I think the biggest resistance sometimes would be like, 'Oh, it's old data,' or 'That's not accurate. All our data is not in there.'" Her interactions with teachers mimicked that of Torres's as teachers questioned the accuracy of the data. While school changes were eventually made, such as requiring grades to be inputted at certain times, these examples show a predisposition to question and criticize new metrics before they are given a hearing.

*Are the data predictive?* Dropping out is not one event. It is a process that culminates in the student being out of school.[11] Such a process—many argue—is driven by various reasons, from family challenges to academic disengagement to socioeconomic problems.[12] Because many factors predict dropping out, the argument that one can reasonably predict those at risk of dropping out with just their grades in ninth grade seems rather suspicious. When students can be driven to dropout because of so many reasons outside schools, how can we ever predict this occurrence with just data inside schools? Here, skeptics argue, school data was doing a lot of heavy lifting.

Yet underneath this suspicion of data's predictiveness was a question regarding what this predictiveness meant for teachers and staff in schools. If schools could predict who were likely to drop out with in-school factors, then things happening in schools may actually matter for dropping out—or at least, catching those at risk of dropping out. Research director Elaine Allensworth noted how this did not sit well with some teachers, saying, "there was resistance at first from this idea of, 'It's not us, it's not our practices; it's the students we get and there's nothing we can do.'" On the one side, teachers had good reason to defend themselves from culpability of something widely documented to be affected by processes outside their control. Yet on the other side, organizations were trying to change and challenge this narrative.

EWIs entailed a change. There was a shift from thinking that dropping out could not be predicted to it being predicted with data as early as ninth grade. There was a shift from thinking that dropping out was mainly from outside-school factors to it being also influenced by inside-school factors. There was a shift from schools not having control of who dropped out to them having the power to make a difference. And so, teachers questioned if the data were truly predictive. But Allensworth pointed out, "there were all these evidence that, no, it's really important that students pass their classes in ninth grade, and that really sets the stage for the rest of high school."

*Are the data objective?* If dropping out can be predicted then why would it be predicted by such subjective data as grades? Shouldn't it be predicted by something more "objective," or by something less mediated by human actors? These were questions Allensworth received when she spoke about EWIs, particularly when individuals remarked, "Oh, grades are variable; they're subjective!"

In 2003, during the early years of No Child Left Behind, the federal policy that pushed national test-based accountability regimes, standardized tests were on everyone's minds, particularly as they seemed to be a more legitimate and less biased measure of student achievement.[13] Course grades had taken the backseat, being thought of as too dependent on human subjectivity.

But Allensworth and her colleagues at the University of Chicago showed that a student who was at the bottom quartile of a standardized test but was on track in ninth grade had higher odds of graduating than a student who was at the top quartile of a standardized test but was off track in ninth grade (see Figure 5.1, comparing the first bar of the 68 percent graduation rate and the last bar of the 37 percent graduation rate). The compelling data pointed to the fact that the on-track indicator at the ninth grade was far more predictive of graduating high school than standardized test scores in the eighth grade—a surprising finding that challenged those who thought that grades were subjective and less valid a measure.

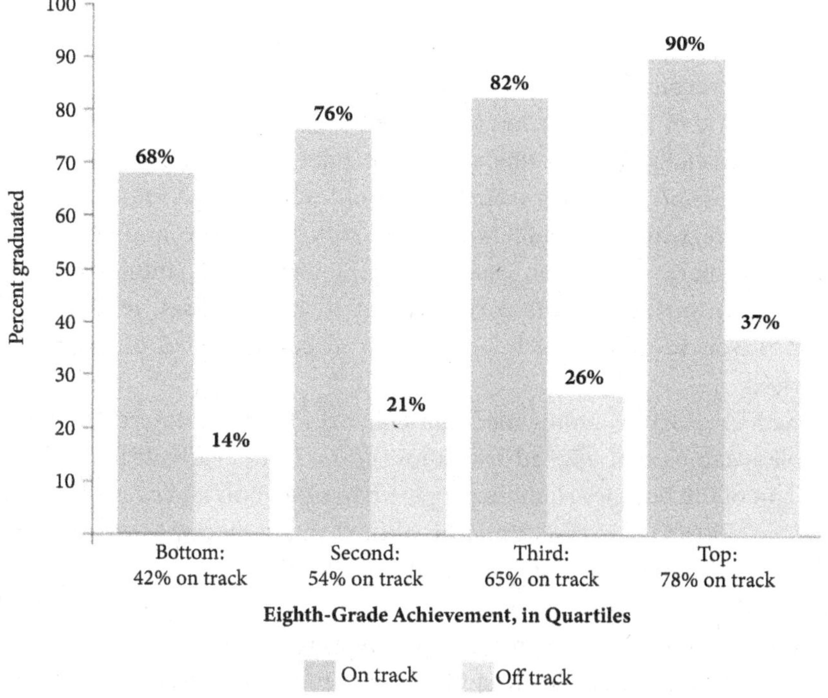


**Figure 5.1** Four-Year Graduation Rate by Eighth Grade Test Score Quartile and On-Track Status.

*Note:* The bars show the percentage of CPS freshman in 2000 who graduated in 2004, grouped by their on-track status and their eighth-grade test scores. Students who dropped or transferred out of CPS before the end of the school year were not included.

Reproduced with permission from Allensworth, E. M., & Easton, J. Q. (2005). *The On-Track Indicator as a Predictor of High School Graduation.* Chicago: Consortium on Chicago School Research.

## Fear

Fear is a potent catalyst for action; it is also a potent justification for resistance. For EWIs, teachers were fearful of potential misuses of data. This is understandable because another form of quantification, test-based accountability, had opened the door to all sorts of strategies to artificially game this system. Some schools concentrated on teaching students at the middle of the proficiency cutoff, disadvantaging both high- and low-achieving students.[14] Some schools moved students who were going to pull down the test score average to special education so that they could be "excused" from taking the test.[15] More egregiously, some schools had performed outright cheating by changing students incorrect answers or providing answers in advance of a test.[16] No surprise, then, that teachers were fearful of the pitfalls of this new form of quantification. When measures become the goal, they distort the social process being measured.

In the case of EWIs, coaches understood teachers as fearful that schools would artificially increase their on-track rates by passing as many students as possible. One fear was that school leaders would pressure teachers to fiddle with their students' grades such that those undeserving of a passing mark were given one. With past forms of quantification and research on quantification's corruption of social processes, teachers had good reason to preemptively assume the ill consequences of these new metrics.

The fear of EWIs' unintended consequences led to an interpretation of people's actions that aligned with those fears. In the early 2010s, Adelric McCain of the NCS was handling a portfolio of schools and coaching them in using EWIs. One of the schools he worked with was trying to turn things around and was accused of "gaming the system [by] just changing grades." In his interview, he continued, saying that there were accusations that "some teachers . . . translated the pressure that we were putting on them to justify the F's that they were giving to students as changing grades, but [they] were never asked to change any grades." While the fears of forced grade changes did not hold water in the school McCain was coaching, this sense of fear was common.

Schools were not the only ones who feared this possibility. Even the very researchers who promoted EWIs were quite fearful of EWIs' potential to be misused in accountability systems. John Q. Easton, the previous director of the University of Chicago's education research consortium, said, "There were lots of fears in the beginning where teachers are just gonna move kids from F's to D's, they're gonna be on-track [in freshman year], but then they'll flunk out in sophomore year." But Easton was quick to point out, "Well, that didn't happen!"

A number of people provided evidence suggesting these fears were more imagined than real. Easton showed that graduation rates mapped out very closely to the freshman on-track rates four years prior, suggesting that improvements in on-track rates had contributed to substantive changes in graduation outcomes. The district's previous chief leadership officer, Steve Gering, also pointed out that standardized high school test scores did not decrease, even as more students were taking the test. He spoke about the district's fears regarding Chicago's American College Test (ACT) scores for their high school students because "we had literally 2,000 or 3,000 additional kids who hung around and that would've dropped out previously." He explained that they were convinced that their scores were going to dip because of these additional students but what they saw surprised them:

> We were convinced that it was gonna tank, our ACT scores, but it didn't. In fact, I think our ACT scores went up like 0.2 or 0.3 that year, and we all looked at each other like, "What the hell just happened?" That shouldn't have happened!

Skeptical of this claim, I reviewed published research regarding ACT scores in Chicago and there have indeed been significant increases in ACT scores. One report emphasized not just the increase in scores in the standardized test but also the increase of the number of students who took the test. It mentioned, "As over 5,000 more CPS students took the ACT and graduated from high school in 2015 compared to 2006, the percentage of students that scored at least a composite ACT score of 21 increased from 23% to 33%."[17] These figures hinted at significant, rather than merely symbolic, changes that came with EWIs and systems.

## Foot-dragging

Resistance to EWIs came in many forms. One of them was just good old foot-dragging, or simply ignoring tools and resources related to these ninth-grade early warning systems. For example, one way staff resisted was when they made clear that they did not want to be contacted. Chicago coach Torres recalled an incident both distressingly familiar but also patently humorous. Talking about her work with schools, she recounted:

> I experienced a lot of resistance, and what that looked like was a lot of meeting cancellations. We had appointments and I would show up and be in the lobby, and [the principal] would not show up. Security would say like, "He's in a classroom, blah, blah, blah." [But I saw him and] literally chased him down the hall one time.

Because of this, she just settled with working with the school's instructional leadership team that had more enthusiastic teacher leaders who were willing to institute changes in their schools. These two teacher leaders then brought together their ninth-grade colleagues to form a teacher team.

However, even with the enthusiasm of some teachers, many others were not as elated. Torres said the teachers thought EWIs were just another reform coming into their school. These teachers figuratively (and perhaps literally) dragged their feet into meetings, saying, "How do we know it's gonna work? We're just tired and we don't want anything else to do. Just tell us what to do." Now stepping into the shoes of these teachers, they make a good point. Almost every new policy, every "innovative" practice, and every "effective" program would have to be done by the teachers in one way or another. Here with EWIs was yet another program that teachers specifically and school staff more generally had to work on.

Just tell us what to do. This was the way they thought initially about EWIs and teacher team meetings. My conversations with other coaches highlighted the shared interpretation of teachers feeling defeated and just wanting to know what the district wants. Such resistance came variably as some teachers remarked that they had little time to speak with their colleagues and some that they would just rather have coaches "tell me the thing you want me to go back in my class and do."

This sense of time—or more accurately, the lack of it—was a critical aspect. Nadia Schafer, a coach in Philadelphia, spoke about this as a common challenge she encountered in schools:

> I guess another pushback is always around time. Like, teachers will be like, "Okay, when do you want me to do all this intervention work? When am I supposed to call home? When am I supposed to meet with the kids? . . . I already am teaching. I'm already going to this meeting and that meeting. These are my hours. When do you want me to do this extra work?" It can feel that way, I think, sometimes.

Schafer was sympathetic. Many coaches actually were. Many of these coaches were previous teachers and school leaders, and so they knew the demands of new programs. Using EWIs was indeed an additional ask from teachers, which was why Schafer emphasized the need for school leaders and administrators to create the space and allocate the time for these things to happen.

Most new practices are met with some form of resistance. With the example of EWIs, I suggest that resistance manifested in *skepticism*, *fear*, and *foot-dragging*. I have detailed these resistances not to paint school staff as antagonists and outside organizations as protagonists in the drama of EWIs. If anything, I have endeavored to show how teachers had good reasons to resist and how organizations had their own interests to further and protect. My aim in detailing the reception of EWIs as recounted by outside organizations is to show how organizations engaged these forms of resistance. To spread EWIs, coaches couldn't just provide professional development as if mere information were going to change practices. They had to address resistance, engage schools, form relationships, and adapt these practices.[18] Core to addressing resistance was the web of routines designed to change relationships and everyday activities.

## Web of Organizational Routines

How do micro-level changes in schools happen despite resistance? Various scholars highlight the role of social networks, particularly teachers and experts, in scaling educational initiatives. Education scholar Kenneth Frank and his colleagues have found that informal access to experts and peer pressures can help in diffusing practices within schools.[19] Sociologist Cynthia Coburn and her colleagues have emphasized the importance of integrating new social interactions—particularly being in contact with "experts" and coaches who come into schools—which have been consequently facilitated by specific organizational routines.[20] Core to these new relationships were organizational routines that were the focus for change. Rather than conceive of routines as contributing to bureaucratic inertia, Jennifer Sherer and James Spillane argue that "routines can serve as a mechanism to build instructional coherence, internal accountability, and professional community."[21]

*Organizational routines* are often described as behavioral and cognitive regularities that structure people's interactions, expectations, responses, and procedures within an organization.[22] Many studies highlight how important these routines are to promote stability, or viewed negatively, to further organizational inertia.[23] However, management studies have also suggested how such practices can create a space for flexibility and change, leading to routines that help organizational transformation and adaptation.[24] In schools, for example, these routines have been found to more tightly connect formal policy from the top with the implementation of practices on the ground.[25] But routines are started and sustained by individuals. Amidst active resistance from teachers, abstract routines from top-down policymakers and singular "how to" research briefs from academic researchers may be ignored, critiqued, or ceased.

School support organizations offered an interesting solution. Organizations like the NCS in Chicago, New Visions for Public Schools (New Visions) in New York, and the Philadelphia Academies, Inc. provided human capital to promote, adapt, and contextualize organizational routines. On one end, these organizations had the *expertise*, *time*, and *focus* to synthesize and apply EWIs in school contexts. On the other, they also had the ability for *sustained connection* with people on the ground—something district officials and academic researchers had far greater hurdles in establishing. The coach's role was not merely to promote EWI routines, but to work alongside schools in cultivating them.

Across the three cities, school support organizations collectively noted the work they did in innovating *data systems*, *relational systems*, and *intervention systems*. Although schools had always had data on grades, teacher team meetings, and supports for students—things that were all too common in schools—what was unique was that these organizations spun these practices to cohere with each other and revised certain aspects to be made sense of differently.

At the micro-level of instituting changes in schools, organizations had to create webs of routines—webs that drew on previous school routines, that were coherent with each other, and that were embedded in everyday practices. The task was part science and part art. Part of the science of school improvement coaching was knowing the innovations well enough to know what routines worked, but part of the art of it was knowing schools well enough to know what routines worked *there*. Thus, the spinning of these webs of routines could not be done by outside organizations alone; they had to be done in conversation with teachers, counselors, social workers, and school leaders.

## Data Systems amid Data Skepticism

Although schools have always maintained data on students' attendance, behavior, and course performance, what EWIs did was to create intuitive just-in-time data systems that helped identify students in need of help and classroom practices in need of change. Chicago had color-coded lists available every five weeks of students' "on-track" status predicted by their grades. Philadelphia had a similar list with its Grades Monitoring Tool that showed not only students' grades, but also their absences and grade trends. New York City's Portal had individual, list, and aggregate views of students' current grades, course credits accomplished, credit gaps, and state exam results. Although each of these data systems was unique, they all functioned as centralizing features for investigating individual students, attending to groups of students, and marking the calendar with specific practices related to using data. These data systems were, therefore, central to the organizational routines that sustained EWIs.

*Data for Identification.* Given that some teachers were skeptical of data, school improvement organizations had to address these concerns. But data were already present in schools, just often not presented in the most optimal way. What EWIs did was to create lists of students with grades from different courses rather than merely grades of individual teachers, thus creating a holistic picture of the students. Such data were then used to monitor individual students, group students into specific buckets, and help teachers reflect about their practices. More importantly, such data within schools—rather than in peer-reviewed research papers—addressed some of the suspicions school staff held about data's accuracy.

Instead of just indicating student performance, the grades were used to identify and monitor students. Having just-in-time data meant that teachers could supposedly identify specific students with whom to take action before things were too late. Some scholars called these "foot-in-the-door interventions" that "equip a child with the right skills or capacities at the right time to avoid imminent risks (e.g., grade failure, teen drinking or teen childbearing) or to seize emerging opportunities (e.g., entry into honors classes, SAT prep)."[26] Although teachers often have a good sense of students' performance, data can help emerge students in need. Schafer, of Philadelphia Academies, Inc., shared how conversations ensue from data being shared. She said that EWIs "can still target the conversation and help [teachers] narrow down the conversation." The data system was an object that facilitated the routine of getting different teachers to speak about students they shared in common.

*Data for Grouping Students.* Coaches pointed out how inefficient individual identification can be. Particularly in highly disadvantaged schools, the number of students "off track" may leave teachers with little time to discuss each one. In the context of these high-need schools, it was difficult to customize responses for each student at risk. Research of EWIs beyond the three cities has also suggested that while tiered and personalized interventions were theoretically ideal, they were practically improbable given the realities of the needs on the ground.[27]

To address this, school support organizations had to adapt data systems to group students into particular performance categories. In the early 2000s, many of Chicago's high-need schools in the southside and westside of the city graduated less than half of their freshman class.[28] In these schools, monitoring every student in need of support was close to impossible. Sarah Howard from the NCS shared that they clustered students into four different categories by their first semester "on-track" status to make analysis easier:

> A group of kids who had at least a 3.0 [GPA] first semester,
> A group of kids who were on track below a 3.0 [GPA],
> A group of kids who had some failure but were still on track, and
> A group of kids who were off track.

After grouping students according to their first semester grade point averages (GPAs), they would compare their performance to their second semester performance, where teachers would discuss, "Here are students who had no failure in the first semester and had a new failure." In this example, they did not so much look at individual students as they did the larger categories to which they belonged.

Data did not only motivate what students could do to improve; data also initiated thinking about what teachers could do to help. In coaching schools, Howard would sometimes work with teachers whose students had only one F. Rather than discuss the student, they reflected with the teacher about particular pedagogical approaches. Howard explained that "this one F means [the students] generally know how to do [work], but in this class, it's not working for them." She explained that this coaching session brought attention to what individual teachers could change in their practices because the students had actually performed well in other subjects.

*Data for Organizing Routines.* In New York City, the school support organization New Visions had created strategic data check-ins to systematize and routinize how schools used data. Jamie Esperon, a continuous improvement coach working with 11 NYC schools, detailed the various routines they had around data. They had graduation planning in the summer, monitoring and credit accumulation meetings throughout the school year, marking period data meetings in the fall, and state examinations planning in the spring. She detailed this rhythm as:

> In the summer, a lot of what we're doing is we're doing grad planning. And when we're doing grad planning, we're trying to really put a plan and a path together for a student based on their accumulation of credits [and] based on their pass rates of Regents . . . And then as we go into the school year, it's still an on-going grad planning but it's also looking at programming and looking at credit accumulation and pass rates. And as we go through into the fall, it's looking again at the marking period data. Because we are a testing state, in January, it's really looking at Regents planning data. So, there's real intentional timeline and flow to our strategic data check-ins.

With a timeline of when to focus on graduation planning, credit accumulation, and test-taking data, New Visions was able to organize the way work happened in their schools.

In a way, the word "organizational" in organizational routines can mean two things. First, it can mean the organization as a noun, where the routines are created by and set inside the organization. However, a richer second meaning of "organizational" was for such routines to be an organizing principle and an organizing element to the work. As shown in Esperon's work in New Visions schools, the tempo of the school year was marked, organized, and aligned to data that were available at particular times. In Chicago and Philadelphia, regular meetings to analyze data became routinized practices as coaches integrated data with processes to make sense of them.

What outside organizations did was to work closely with schools to adapt a set of routines that made sense for the data they already had. When schools resisted data that they thought to be inaccurate or unpredictive, what turned the tide were outside organizations working with schools to show how *their* own school's data can be flexibly used. As one coach shared, "What I have learned this year [was] that schools are more interested in data that is their own, versus 'Oh, research shows. . . .'" Although data's social character could lead to suspicion, the same social character matched with outside guidance could bring about sustained routines and practices.

## Relational Systems Amid Foot-dragging

Meetings among teachers are not unique to EWIs; in fact, many schools have routines to meet. But what EWIs created was a focus on discussing common students. In Chicago, OnTrack Labs created processes to have ninth-grade teachers speak about common students. In Philadelphia, the To&Through Project introduced routines for teachers and students to keep track of their progress. In New York City, coaches highlighted the consequences of having regular teacher team meetings. Although some staff felt like they were dragging their feet with EWIs, outside organizations leveraged the power of collectivity to sustain changes.

*Initiating Routines to Foster Relations.* When the data systems were introduced in Chicago around 2008, the district had six schools that were considered OnTrack Labs. These schools had facilitators helping them institute practices to support EWIs. One of the OnTrack Lab coordinators, Rodney Thomas, was assigned to a particularly challenging high school in Chicago's southside where many of the students came from disadvantaged backgrounds and had experienced some form of emotional or physical trauma. He said:

> What we did was we brought teachers together to look at freshmen data and create interventions based on who these particular students were, because they were not doing that at the time. Teachers were not having those types of meetings to look at student data so we brought these cross-functional kind of teams together to begin to look and analyze and make sense of the data, and have targeted strategies to meet the needs of these students.

He shared that most teachers worked with their colleagues teaching the same subject (e.g., ninth-grade math teachers spoke with other math teachers in the same or other grade levels), but would not have these "cross-functional kind of teams" who were teaching students in the same grade. With the EWIs and with the help of these outside groups, grade-level teacher team meetings in high school had become much more common.

Thomas shared that one of the goals of teacher teams was to identify root causes for grade or attendance trends in the school. He shared the story of how the school had low attendance rates because students would not come to their first and second period classes. When they looked at the data, they found that those periods were usually Physical Education (PE) for the students who did not attend first or second period. Thus, their team asked what was happening in PE, and they found that "students did not want to get undressed for gym and put on uniforms because they were concerned about their hygiene." Thomas followed up and said, "We had to then bring in uniforms for these students because they could not afford to wash the uniforms that they had." This emphasized for him the importance not only of identification of students, but of teachers working as a group.

But not everyone shared this enthusiasm for teacher teams and Thomas also shared the continued resistance from veteran teachers who did not want to give up their lunch break or stay in school for yet another meeting. Although there were some that were more open to these meetings, there were others who chided Thomas saying, "Look, I've taught for years in that school. I'm tired. I just wanna go home, okay? Rodney, I just wanna go home. I don't wanna go to another meeting." The feelings were justified because these demands did weigh on teachers.

Coaches highlighted, however, that sentiments changed when school leaders embedded on-track teacher team meetings to the regular school day. Change happened in different ways. Some schools had specific days each month when teachers arrived in school early to discuss students. Some had specific periods during the week when grade-level teachers were all free to meet. While organizations pushed to embed these routines in schools, the changes were ultimately driven by school leaders who made this a priority and teachers who felt it was important to incorporate in weekly or monthly routines.

*Institutionalizing Relational Routines.* Once routines were embedded in school practices, they became a lot more difficult to take out. In some Philadelphia schools, teachers and students had a process of checking on students' current performance. The To&Through Project had introduced a tool called Check-and-Reflect, which allowed students to see their own cumulative and projected Grade Point Average, attendance record, individual grades, and behavior (see Figure 5.2). Cari Cantor, the director of the Philadelphia school district's planning and evidence-based support office, talked about how this tool had become widely used in schools. During the week I interviewed her, the tool had malfunctioned, and she spoke about how others reacted to such disruption to their routines:

> That tool is a huge benefit to my schools. And when it's not working—like, I guess there was a glitch in the system this week—schools were really mad, students were mad. You hear some of the vocalization of students saying, "I wanted to check!" And obviously, there are other ways for them to check their data, but *they're just so used to these systems* being there. (emphasis added)

**Check and Reflect**

Cumulative GPA: 2.77
Represents completed Courses

Projected GPA: 2.75
Represents cumulative GPA + projected courses

**Attendance**
Goal: 95% attendance or above

| | Term 1 In-Progress | Year-to-Date |
|---|---|---|
| Days Enrolled | 41 | 41 |
| Days Present | 40 | 40 |
| Days Absent | 1 | 1 |
| Attendence Rate | 97.6% | 97.6% |
| Days Tardy | 6 | 6 |

**Grades**
Goal: A's and B's, no D's and F's

| | Term 1 In-Progress | Projected Final |
|---|---|---|
| Biology | 88 | 88 |
| English | 79 | 79 |
| Algebra | 78 | 78 |
| Social Science | 90 | 90 |
| Phys. Education | 85 | 85 |

**Behavior**
Goal: 0 suspensions

| | Term 1 In-Progress | Year-to-Date |
|---|---|---|
| Period Cuts | 7 | 7 |
| Out-of-School Suspension | 0 | 0 |

**Figure 5.2** Check-and-Reflect Tool
*Source*: School District of Philadelphia (Rendering by the Author)

When people become "just so used" to particular systems—even ones they had initially resisted—reversion to the original often met its own set of resistance.

Routines change relationships. When previously teachers were just talking with others teaching the same subject, the routine of ninth-grade teacher team meetings led to relationships with other ninth-grade teachers. When previously students had just received grades at the end of the quarter, the routine of collectively checking and reflecting on one's performance became a ritual to see personal and collective progress. These collective and relational practices introduced by outside organizations, like grade-level teacher team meetings and Check-and-Reflect, had consequences for the relationships being built in schools.

But relationships also sustain routines. The trust built between teachers and outside coaches facilitated the continuance of teacher team meetings. The camaraderie created between teachers in the same grade-level produced a sense of collective responsibility. The closer connection between teachers and students sustained routines for showing care and attending to people's needs. Jessica Sasko, the director for Career Readiness at New Visions, detailed how important these relationships were for sustaining practice:

> The point is that even in a large school, *you could have a group of teachers who know you well* because they all have like a smaller subset of the students in the school together; kinda like a teacher team. And so, we would look at the data to see which kids were on-track by their attendance and

> course performance, and which kids were starting to slip off-track and [we] develop interventions with the teachers. So, there'd be like a point-teacher who would champion for the rest of the teachers depending on their relationship with the student and then talk through them and do case reviews and make referrals as needed to counselors or social workers. (emphasis added)

Teacher teams did not just provide important insights for teachers who shared information with each other; they gave students a way of being "seen." These relational systems and routines in a school were key to changes, not so much just the presence of data or data systems.

## Intervention Systems amid Fears

Tiered interventions happen even without EWIs, but outside organizations had appropriated some aspects of these interventions. These initiatives—spanning remedial courses, individual tutoring, and one-on-one mentoring—were not necessarily about inside-classroom instructional practices but outside-classroom intervention systems. While interventions were an important part of EWIs, some coaches felt that this emphasis on intervention over instruction was a concession to address teachers' concerns regarding EWIs' threat to their instructional autonomy.

Kareem Sayegh, a former Chicago high school teacher who came to lead their school's freshman success team, noticed that "it's a lot easier to talk about individual students and what needs to be fixed about individual students . . . than it is for teachers to think about how their instructional practices or how the instructional practices of the team influence the experiences and outcomes of students." Rather than have the locus of change inside the classroom, it was much easier for it to be shifted outside of it, when students are in remedial classes, or doing lunch-time homework sessions, or working with a mentor or social worker.

Sayegh, who in 2019 transitioned to become the NCS's national student success manager, spoke about his work with different teams from different schools, and how various school staff were core to providing supports for different "tiers" of students. He explained that:

> Tier 1 intervention is something that influences all students. A Tier 2 intervention is something that would either support an individual student or a group of students. So, a Tier 2 intervention that I've seen is like

> a check in-check out procedure, it's very common, where a student or a group of students need to check in with somebody at the beginning of the day... Tier 3 interventions are generally more intensive. These are like the wrap-around supports. Like home visits, they are definitely a Tier 3.

The use of "tiers" to describe interventions was also common across the informants in the three cities because of the literature that supported "tiered intervention models"[29] and "multi-tiered systems of support."[30] Many of these tiered interventions, though, had to rely on outside help like mentors, counselors, social workers, and volunteers who checked in on students. Although tiered interventions might have been seen as an imperfect solution, they were solutions nonetheless that changed practices and routines in the contexts they were in.

Tier 1 interventions were meant to influence practices for all students. These interventions were applied similarly to all students in an effort to address general trends. Sayegh detailed an example of teachers coming together and asking how they can get more students to complete their homework. In their teacher team meetings, they found that students were not necessarily abandoning their homework; they were merely incomplete:

> I've seen a Tier 1 intervention that all of the teachers on the team agreed [which] was to circulate and make sure that students turn in their assignments regardless of how complete those assignments were... because what they found out from their students was that students didn't feel like they had enough time and so they were just not turning in the assignment at all even though they had finished 75% of it and could've gotten a grade.

Other examples of Tier 1 interventions included changes regarding when to provide grades and changes with grading practices by not giving zeros (instead giving "50" for those who failed to submit something). Such interventions were induced by teacher teams meeting and data systems showing patterns that teachers can address.

Tier 2 interventions were for more specific groups of students who needed additional support. Schafer helped form teams of teachers and introduced an intervention for students that were more difficult to reach out to. She called it the "two-by-ten strategy," and described it as:

> essentially a sort of formula for building relationship with a student, which is to talk for two minutes about anything not related to school for ten days in a row. It's the idea of chatting and getting to know a student, sharing about yourself, asking what they're doing on the weekends, asking what they're passionate about, or talking about a movie or other pop culture reference.

By consistently speaking with certain students about non-school-related things, teachers gain their trust, an essential component in building relationships with them. Schafer noted how successful this was for many teachers who told her, "I was really stuck with this kid, but like after I did that, they came into the fold. They're much more willing to participate or they felt more engaged."

These interventions were successful in so far as they were routines. As these routines were mostly outside the classroom, they relied on the support and push of outsiders. In New York City, Esperon worked with schools to create strategic plans for certain segments of students. She spoke about her work creating *focal groups*—students in the same school with shared characteristics, like having 70 percent attendance and failing one course. By sub-setting students, teachers could find more specific ways to support these students. She further noted, "If I look at everything, it becomes too much. If I can look at an isolated focal group, I can make movement and I can make an impact." Organizations like New Visions suggested new routines, such as creating focal groups that assisted these intervention systems.

Amid fears that schools would unscrupulously pass students to artificially increase their on-track rates, outside organizations attempted to work with teachers to establish routines that supported actionable changes. Amid fears that schools would threaten teachers' professional autonomy, these routines were mainly focused on non-instructional changes that relied on outside supports, like tutors, mentors, and counselors. Coaches and nonprofit staff supported these interventions by adding them as routines to the multiplicity of behaviors that were introduced.

## Shifting Beliefs by Shifting Behaviors

To address resistance, outside organizations created webs of routines for data systems, relational practices, and tiered interventions—all incorporating previous routines and embedding them into current school practices.

The spinning and embedding of these routines to school practices were key in changing initial resistance to EWIs. By letting teachers use and understand their own school's data rather than simply general research findings, teachers lessened skepticism of data's provenance and predictiveness. By creating teams of teachers in the same grade who routinely met, schools created collective experiences that reduced defiance. By having tiered interventions to support specific groups of students, outside organizations helped reduce fears that EWIs would threaten teachers' autonomy or would be yet another ceremonial change in the sea of failed education policies.

Beneath actions of resistance are shared beliefs and mindsets—often imperceptible, often difficult to change, and often subtly shared within groups.[31] The previous sections illustrated how routines established by school support organizations addressed teachers' resistance to EWIs. But I argue that organizational routines did not just influence behavioral changes addressing practical resistance to EWIs. They also influenced shifts in beliefs that addressed more cultural resistance to these data systems. Routines do not just change people's actions; routines can change how they think about their actions.

## Shifting Beliefs about Teaching

Changing routines can change beliefs. Before the advent of EWIs, coaches noted how teachers originally held on to beliefs about their autonomy, knowledge of students, and intuition for practice. But with changes in routines, these coaches saw significant changes toward collaboration and data use.

McCain started at the NCS in 2012, initially as a transition success coach before becoming the director of the organization's equity and national impact work. In our conversation, he outlined three large shifts in culture that he saw with the introduction of new routines, saying that the focus was not so much to change the culture but to "develop the systems and structures so that [teachers] can use those as tools."

First, the introduction of tools and routines brought about tighter forms of *collaboration and interaction* among teachers and staff, particularly those in ninth grade. Because classic education theory has underscored schools as loosely coupled organizations that privilege teachers' autonomy in the core technical work of instruction, many coaches had also noted that collaborations among teachers of the same grade level were few and far between.[32]

But a core shift with EWIs was the coming together of teachers to talk about ninth graders. McCain said schools had to create structural changes first:

> Structures and systems had to be recreated to enable this adult collaboration, right? So, in partnership with the CTU [Chicago Teachers Union], principals throughout the district would negotiate to have space and time designated exclusively for adult collaboration around freshmen. That in itself was one of the most significant changes. We're getting together within a school day or after school to do professional development.

Such a shift was not just about making space and time. For McCain, the shift was about the changing perspective regarding teachers' collective responsibility. He shared that one of the most significant changes was the shift in language and tone, where "instead of *these* kids and *these* families; it was more about *our* kids, *our* families, and these people are showing up better in service of the communities they were in" (emphasis in the original). Such a change in thinking about the collective role of teachers was in some sense brought about not by challenging mindsets directly but by changing everyday routines like creating shared professional learning communities.

A second shift was about teachers' *knowledge of their students*, one brought about by how data could complement, supplement, or challenge teachers' conception of their students. Like other coaches, McCain noted the shift in how teachers saw their students who might be performing poorly in their class even as they were thriving in other classes. He mentioned that teachers "got to know [their] students . . . beyond just what they're presenting in class . . . , to start seeing kids from a strengths-based approach instead of a deficit approach." By having data on how students are performing in other classes, teachers received a more holistic picture. Other coaches in Philadelphia and New York City also detailed similar narratives for how teachers' perspectives of particular students were challenged because of information they got from outside their own individual classrooms.

A third shift for teachers and teaching was about the *use of data* in their classroom as well as data's role in decisions, interventions, and instruction. McCain said:

> The third big thing that I wanna put in there is around this idea that "I'm a professional that can look at data and can use that data to inform my practice." Before, even when I first got here [to Chicago], there was just a disbelief. There's not a lot of teacher pre-service programs that support us

> in how to look at data and how we can translate it into practice. I would actually say in the past decade, there's been a lot more of that now because of the result of our work.

Because data became readily available and easier to use in terms of color-coding students as being on track or at risk of being off track, teachers started using data and, as McCain pointed out, thought of their professional work as imbibing the use of data. However, not all teachers saw this for themselves.

Taken together, these shifts in beliefs highlight how specific routines—webs of routines spun from previous practices and embedded in school structures—were core to bringing attitudinal changes. By the repetition of routines and their integration in day-to-day practices, coaches saw discernible shifts in how teachers saw themselves and their work.

## Shifting Beliefs about Students

One principal in New York City shared that mindset changes among teachers ultimately influenced their beliefs about students. Mr. Costa,[33] a principal of a New Visions partner high school in Brooklyn, shared how he would hear teachers and school staff saying, "Oh, the kids are better, so much better." He would challenge this perspective, however, saying, "We're not getting better kids; we're just treating them differently, and so they have a chance to be better." There was a shift not so much in the school's demographics but in the beliefs the teachers had of the students.

Mr. Costa continued, pointing out that through teacher team meetings and data systems, they were able to learn more about the students they had, thereby changing their attitudes and beliefs about them. He further explained, "We know our students better. [Data] let me know what their strengths and weaknesses are, both academic and personal. And we're more invested. And so, that's the difference!" The change was not specifically about creating new cultural narratives but about employing new organizational routines that slowly brought about changes in beliefs.

However, many sociological studies have illustrated the potential dangers and risks of predictive surveillance, particularly for minoritized populations. Research on predictive policing and racially biased algorithms had become more common, alerting the public to how supposedly bias-reducing and "objective" technologies can have unintended and undesired consequences.[34] Even in schools, the supposed promised benefits of data-based accountability systems had been shown to reproduce inequalities as schools with different demographic composition employed such systems differently.[35] In their school, with a racially diverse student population, Mr. Costa noted that "we use [data] to improve; we don't use it to police." That, for him, was the core difference for why these dangers were averted for EWIs.

Many other coaches and researchers said similar things as they talked about how they saw this predictive technology as a means of supporting rather than policing. Indeed, if EWIs were not used for identification and improvement, it would be difficult to imagine where else it might be used for. Mr. Costa shared a story of when race figured into their work:

> When we looked at our social emotional data, and we started seeing that they, the ones that are labeled as "needs improvement," 15 out of 16 of the students that were labeled "needs improvement" were young men, and then not just young men. They were specifically Black and Latino young men and so that's the part for us to be able to reflect and say, "Why is this going on? What is our perception? Is our perception skewed?" And so, we see systemic issues and then we survey kids based upon [those], and then we, and then we delve into different ways of teaching, in different ways of looking at a curriculum. And then we say, "All right. Well, maybe you know [there is something wrong]." And then we got into culturally, culturally and historically relevant education.

In this example, organizational routines—in concert with meso-level relationships and macro-level meanings discussed in previous chapters—did not only challenge beliefs about students; they also provided a means for shifting actions from such changes.

As coaches in the other cities also detailed, the surveillance of EWIs did not so much change the behaviors of the surveilled as it changed the behaviors—and more importantly, the beliefs—of the ones surveilling. Such social technology thus changed not only the teachers' work routines but also their mindset regarding the students with whom they interacted.

## Why Organizational Routines Matter Amid Resistance

The micro-level perspective of EWIs highlights the dynamics between resistance and routines, as well as between behaviors and beliefs. Resistance in schools came in the form of skepticism about the data, fear for their unintended uses, and ignorance of tools and practices. But school support organizations like the NCS, Philadelphia Academies, Inc., and New Visions worked in schools to craft and spin webs of organizational routines that promoted various uses of EWIs and addressed various forms of resistance on the ground. These personal relationships with and in schools were key not just in shifting behaviors but also in challenging beliefs. By trying to influence routines and behaviors, organizations shifted beliefs about teachers and students.

The experience of EWIs in Chicago, Philadelphia, and New York City provided some lessons for EWIs, educational change, and inhabited institutions. In the case of EWIs, adaptations and relationships on the ground were key to changes. EWIs were not simply about data. EWIs were not simply about identification and interventions. Inasmuch as school support organizations introduced EWIs in schools, they also worked to connect and embed EWIs to routines already present in the places they were entering. The routines in schools and EWIs themselves were adapted together. But potentially more important than routine adaptations were the threads of relationships connecting individuals inside and outside the school. Connections and webs among principals, coaches, teachers, and staff—all happening on the ground—supported the creation of new routines. Although institutional logics that support meaning-making and the networks of institutional entrepreneurs were key components in initiating EWIs, the relational and routinary work on the ground was arguably the most important in institutionalizing them.

In the case of educational change, one key lesson was how actions can change beliefs rather than the other way around. Often, studies on the implementation of school reforms and the adoption of new educational policies emphasize the importance of teacher buy-in.[36] Without discounting this, this chapter has shown the equally powerful draw of organizational routines, actions, and behaviors. Designing organizational routines does not just affect behavior; crafting routines can also influence our beliefs about the work. In this way, researchers and policymakers must clarify what beliefs can change alongside the change in behaviors. As routines become repeated and become taken for granted, their constant repetition does not remain at the level of practice but can go deeper to the level of cognition.

In the case of inhabited institutions, EWIs illustrated how the dynamic interplay between resistance and routines at the micro-level can influence cognition and beliefs at the macro-level. Inhabited institutionalism, as a theory, often focuses on the recursive relationships between interactions and institutions.[37] The EWI example conceptualized interactions not simply as discrete relational actions. Rather, interactions were also often patterned and repetitive. The dynamics of routine introduction, resistance, and adaptation provided a helpful way of thinking about the types of micro-level interactions that are consequential for the macro-level institution. In a sense, the interactions that can change institutions are those that are dynamically patterned and repetitive.

# Chapter 6
## How Local Systems Have National Consequences

> If we had done [EWIs] in a wealthy suburb, it would have been a lot less interesting.
>
> —Sarah Duncan,
> *Co-director, Network for College Success*

This book proposes a way of theorizing educational change that looks differently at the factors contributing to it. Although many social scientific studies of education concentrate on what happens inside schools, I focus on the dynamics that happen outside the education bureaucracy. Although many studies highlight specific levels for change, either with policy elites or teachers on the ground, I thread these levels to enrich the analysis of instituting change. In this chapter, I highlight the spatial aspect of educational change. Although many studies concentrate either on the national work of federal policies or the local work of schools and school districts, I note the dynamics of inter-local changes.

The concept of *inter-local changes* takes inspiration from urban sociology, and I appropriate it to mean the changes that happen first in local spaces—often urban centers with an agglomeration of organizations and strong links between school districts and these organizations—and that subsequently have consequences spilling over to other local spaces within the context of interconnected organizations and districts.[1] In this formulation, education is not simply a local phenomenon. The links across these local spaces in the United States can be seen in the dynamics of urban, suburban, and rural migration, particularly during the COVID-19 pandemic and also through the dynamics of segregation and gentrification.[2] An urban sociological perspective sees local spaces as nodes with interconnections to other places—much like a web spun with crisscrossing airplane flights across the United States. Cities adopt changes because of the network of organizations within a city, as well as because of the connections outside of it.[3]

*Subtle Webs*. Jose Eos Trinidad, Oxford University Press. © Oxford University Press (2025).
DOI: 10.1093/9780197786123.003.0007

In the context of US K–12 education, which is often characterized as local school districts with varying degrees of independence from each other and from the state, this idea of inter-local changes may be a potent tool to describe the current dynamics of educational change. Using the case of the adoption and spread of ninth-grade early warning indicators (EWIs), this chapter highlights *how* changes happen across local spaces. It suggests three ways for inter-local change: (1) as school improvement organizations are connected across local areas and individuals move across them as well, (2) as school districts become proofs of concept for other school districts to notice, and (3) as national agencies and large philanthropies influence the systematic and broader spread of changes that started locally. Thus, change happens through interorganizational webs of nonprofits, inter-district webs of educational administrators, and national webs of federal and philanthropic initiatives. Such webs, however, are often subtly spun. This chapter attempts to make these webs more visible.

Local systems can have national consequences. What happened in Chicago, Philadelphia, and New York City did not just have repercussions for these respective school districts. Rather, what happened in these places can influence, inspire, induce, or initiate changes in other places. Patterns of macro-level changes in institutional logics, meso-level shifts in entrepreneurial networks, and micro-level transformations in school organizational routines were not just limited to the three cities; they also happened across local areas. This chapter uses examples from EWIs to trace changes from the three cities to other places, as well as to theorize this process of inter-local changes.

## Interorganizational Webs

Organizations across local areas are connected with each other, either through individuals that move across local contexts, through organizations that operate in different areas, or through organizations that are connected with each other. This section discusses the three types of interorganizational webs that emerge in transferring local changes. First, inter-local change can happen at the individual level as researchers are connected with each other and as they move across local contexts, moving, for example, from Chicago to Philadelphia to New York City. Second, change can transpire through the expansion of the network of nonprofit organizations, such as the original nonprofits in Chicago and Philadelphia being contracted in other school districts. Third, inter-local change can emerge from the creation of new networks with new nonprofits. In all three types, the focus is on the work of organizations and individuals locally based, and how these networks create ways for change to happen across local areas.

## Mobile Individuals and Networks

Chicago and Philadelphia were epicenters for research on EWIs with scholars from the University of Chicago and Johns Hopkins University (JHU). Individuals like Elaine Allensworth and John Q. Easton in Chicago and Robert Balfanz and Ruth Neild in Philadelphia were key people in spreading the discovery through their papers and their outreach. In addition to these original researchers, other researchers, like James Kemple and Vanessa Coca, show how their mobility in transferring from one context to another helped with the spread of EWIs.

Ideas spread through individuals making efforts to spread them. For EWIs, a lot of it depended on individuals who spoke to others about the initiative. Allensworth shared the efforts they made to spread EWIs when they were starting. She said, "We went on a road tour, [where] we went all over the city talking about this research. I did like a parent meeting for Kenwood High School... I went to DC [Washington, DC], I went to New York, I went to lots of different places talking about this research." Easton also did several presentations. He attributed part of EWIs' spread to all these engagements, saying, "I presented to the Council of Great City Schools, I presented to lots of these groups of leaders .... I made a presentation one year; I went back the next year." In these meetings, Allensworth and Easton met superintendents and school leaders who were interested in the research. Easton shared, "A superintendent came to me and said, 'You know, I had my research people replicate this [study] and it replicated 100 percent.'" Instead of relying on school leaders and researchers finding their way to EWI papers, they made an intentional effort to spread these ideas.

At times, the mobility was not just about individuals traveling but the very idea itself taking a life of its own. Balfanz, from Johns Hopkins, remembered that the initial spread of EWIs in Philadelphia had been unplanned. He said, "We presented the early results . . . at just a local conference in Philadelphia, and I guess the Philadelphia Education Fund put the PowerPoint up on their website. And from that, the PowerPoint went everywhere." Balfanz explained that the spread came because "this made sense to people . . . and most of our systems aren't designed to let us know early who's struggling." With researchers in Chicago and Philadelphia, individuals and ideas were crucial in bringing this about.

But these dynamics were not limited to researchers who have devoted their studies in particular contexts. Many researchers also move from one context to another. One was James Kemple, who had previously studied Talent Development schools in Philadelphia and Baltimore before becoming the director of the Research Alliance for New York City Schools. In the early 2000s, he and other researchers at MDRC did an evaluation of Talent Development middle and high schools, which pioneered the use of EWIs in Philadelphia. They wrote two reports: *The Talent Development Middle School Model* and *Making Progress Toward Graduation: Evidence from the Talent Development High School Model*.[4] Kemple and his team were connected to different researchers in Philadelphia. They mentioned that Balfanz "clarified the components and implementation of the Talent Development High School model," and Neild "provided assistance in data acquisition and in conceptualizing key issues in the analysis."[5]

In 2008, Kemple became the executive director of the Research Alliance for New York City Schools. In this role, he also collaborated with colleagues at the University of Chicago Consortium on School Research. His connections with Easton, and Allensworth were helpful in modeling this place-based research-practice partnership in the United States' largest school district. Across these connections, it is unsurprising that Research Alliance had also initiated research on EWIs in New York City.[6]

Similarly, researcher Vanessa Coca worked with Melissa Roderick and Jenny Nagaoka in Chicago before moving to pursue her doctoral degree at New York University. Her collaborative studies in Chicago on college pathways—"College Readiness for All: The Challenge for Urban High Schools" and "Potholes on the Road to College"—were related to the discussion of EWIs and postsecondary success in the city.[7] During her time in New York, she started working at the Research Alliance doing similar work. Coca shared that Kemple, the director, "initially wanted to recreate what I had done in Chicago for New York . . . to track students' college enrollment experiences." They then assembled a data archive with data from the New York City Department of Education and the City University of New York.

Movement of people—whether those based in one area or those that move from one context to another—can create webs that contribute to changes in education. In the case of EWIs, researchers like Easton, Allensworth, and Balfanz crafted intentional ways for the research to spread beyond just the places they were in. For researchers like Kemple and Coca, their personal mobility across contexts had contributed to such spread. At the individual level, then, people's personal movement can be consequential for ideas and initiatives to spread. Educational change is not merely structural because even personal decisions can affect these changes.

## Expanding Organizational Networks

As organizations initiate their work in specific places, these organizations often subsequently scale their work to other places. In the case of Chicago, for example, the Network for College Success (NCS) started with high schools in the city but has since created larger national programs related to EWIs and student success systems. In the case of Philadelphia, the Talent Development model that started in some of the city's schools has been appropriated in other schools around the United States through the Diplomas Now initiative. In both examples, organizations branch out from their original local contexts so that EWI principles and programs can be used in other local contexts.

Aside from working in Chicago schools, the NCS engaged school leaders and staff outside the city through its National Freshman Success Institute and its National Partnerships program. When asked about what motivated this expansion, NCS co-director Sarah Duncan mentioned:

> We were in a good position to say, "Here's what we've learned." We had, sort of, the pieces in place, like, "Here's the coaching model we use." We had all the pieces in place, and so we were in a good position to help them . . . We couldn't necessarily fly out to every place and do the on-ground coaching, but to have someone on the ground to do the follow-through and do the problem-solving and the thought-partnership with the schools, I think, it's an excellent model.

This concept led to the National Freshman Success Institute, where high school administrators and educators came to Chicago to learn about strategies for the successful transition of students from middle school to high school, as well as the support systems needed for collaborative action.[8] These were week-long workshops with individuals from different schools and school districts around the country.[9]

Aside from the annual workshops, the NCS also worked with particular districts and schools throughout the year. Kareem Sayegh was the organization's national student success manager and his role was specifically to support national clients in developing freshman success teams, implementing their strategies, and supporting data systems for ninth-grade on-track systems. Sayegh spoke about how the NCS worked with schools and school districts in Colorado, Wisconsin, Texas, and Illinois. Asked about how the organization initially made these connections, he answered:

> A combination of things. Some of the districts, we have previous relationships with, so . . . there are educators in those districts that used to work in CPS [Chicago Public Schools] and knew of our work when we were supporting CPS schools. Also, we have . . . something called the National Freshman Success Institute which happens every year. So, we have hundreds of districts who have come through that, and every year there's a couple of folks at the end of the year that want to move into some continued learning and partnership coaching.

In this example, the organizations that were originally just working with schools in Chicago were able to work with schools outside the city. Duncan had noted that the spread was "organic more than strategic," highlighting that they had not originally expected their work to extend this much. Nonetheless, the creation of new networks from one local place to another happened through connections developed through annual events or year-long engagements.

In Philadelphia, the group from JHU started Talent Development Secondary (TDS). While the work of TDS's whole-school improvement model started with two districts—the middle school work in Philadelphia and the high school work concentrated in Baltimore—they found that they needed more help in managing students that were on off track to graduate. Thus, they collaborated with *City Year*, which provided mentors who could check-in and help groups of students, as well as *Communities in Schools*, which provided more directed supports for highly vulnerable students. This collaboration between these three organizations became what would be known as the Diplomas Now model. Balfanz, of TDS and Johns Hopkins, spoke about this time:

> We did rapid prototyping in Philadelphia actually in around 2008 and then a couple of districts around the country in 2009. In 2010, we got one of the large [Investing in Innovation, i3] awards that came out of Obama's [American Recovery and Reinvestment Act of 2009]. It was like a $30 million award with $10 million private funds. With that, we did this massive 12-district, 60-school RCT [randomized controlled trial], and that's really what consumed us from 2009 to 2015.

The spread of EWIs from Philadelphia to other places happened with the whole-school improvement model being adopted by partner schools across the nation. The integrated Diplomas Now program initiated curriculum, teacher coaching, early warning systems, and student supports for schools in places as diverse as Boston, Denver, Los Angeles, San Antonio, Seattle, and Washington, DC.[10]

In these examples from Chicago and Philadelphia, the organizations expanded and branched out from their original local contexts. At times, the spread was organic, as it was when the NCS created opportunities for professional learning and for school leaders from outside Chicago to learn more about EWIs. At other times, the spread was intentional, such as when Diplomas Now worked with their own select group of schools across varied geographic areas. In both cases, local organizations had expanded their work to include schools and districts farther away—often with very little strategic forethought to it.

## Creating New Networks

Other organizations took inspiration from the organizations in Chicago, Philadelphia, and New York City as they created their own versions of early warning indicators and systems. One example of this on the East Coast is Connecticut RISE, while an example on the West Coast is the California CORE Districts. In both cases, their model for providing coaching and support to schools was informed by the experiences in the cities that initiated EWIs.

The Connecticut RISE Network supported a group of schools in terms of "on-track and postsecondary culture" as well as "targeted transition supports" for ninth-grade students.[11] While the organization primarily supported nine high schools across eight school districts in Connecticut, the organization also had a Freshman Focus Network with partners beyond the state, such as schools in Maine, Massachusetts, and New York state.[12] One of the pioneer members of the RISE Network was Caitlin Gallagher, and she acknowledged their organization's Chicago and New York City connections:

> We brought teachers to Chicago three times for their Freshman Success Conference . . . It was like a freshman success symposium and there would be people coming from across the country. It was like 100 people, and we brought freshman teachers and then we brought those strategies back to their high schools.

The RISE Network had a similar model to that of the NCS, especially as they created a way for educators across schools and districts to be supported in cross-school learning and data systems. Gallagher had also worked at New Visions for Public Schools (New Visions) while she obtained her MBA from Columbia University.

These connections between the NCS in Chicago, New Visions in New York, and Gallagher were important in the emergence of this new organization in Connecticut. Gallagher said, "I was connected with NCS, and then New Visions, [and] the Connecticut RISE Network actually spun off of that." It hints at the migration of individuals and how this can lead to new organizations that can spring from the original initiatives in specific local areas.

Another example of a school support organization incorporating these EWIs was the CORE Districts, an acronym for the California Office to Reform Education.[13] Composed of eight California school districts, including Fresno, Los Angeles, Long Beach, Oakland, and San Francisco, with more than a million students, the organization served as "a hub for this collaboration and supporting partnership and shared learning at the superintendent, central office, school leader, and teacher levels."[14] Like the work in Chicago and Philadelphia, this California nonprofit also had their own version of an EWI initiative through their "Ninth Grade On-Track Breakthrough Success Community."[15]

Gina Pascual, a senior improvement coach for three schools in the Oakland Unified School District, met regularly with each school's assistant principal and a set of about five teachers instructing ninth grade. She explained that while the nonprofit worked often with district leadership, they had a set of coaches that worked in schools, and they had a focus on Ninth Grade

On Track. Pascual shared, "There's a coach assigned to each school.... We are supposed to have a set of highly validated change ideas that we ask the schools to implement and run, and basically use PDSAs [Plan-Do-Study-Act improvement tools] to have high quality implementation." One of the ideas that they had was EWIs and the ninth-grade transition. Across California, however, the schools they worked with were limited to less than 50 schools.

Although the Connecticut RISE Network and the California CORE Districts were new organizations that took inspiration from what was happening in Chicago, Philadelphia, and New York City, they were only in a limited number of schools that formed part of their network. Thus, it is questionable whether the emergence of these new organizations truly had an influence on larger shifts in US education. Nonetheless, the independent development of these initiatives highlights the possibility for change to happen in places that were geographically apart from the original EWI contexts in large Northeastern and Midwestern cities.

## Inter-district Web

As organizations created webs across local areas, webs were also spun across places as other school districts became familiar with the EWI work in the three large urban school districts. Primarily, these webs were created as Chicago, Philadelphia, and New York City became important proofs of concept for these new data systems. Given the many challenges urban schools experienced during the early 2000s (see the Introduction), the fact that substantial and consistent improvements were being observed in these places was an important factor for other places to take notice.

Duncan, of the NCS, shared her observation regarding why EWIs in Chicago had the influence they had on other districts. She said, "Having Chicago as the 'worst school district in America' be able to improve stuff, I think it attracted attention. If we had done this in a wealthy suburb, it would have been a lot less interesting. But we're in the third largest school district, have a huge disproportionate poverty rate, pretty low achieving, and if we could do it, it's like, 'Well....'" In the trailing off of her voice and the pregnant pause after "well," Duncan was suggesting that change can happen almost anywhere if it can happen in Chicago. As four-year high school graduation rates in the city increased from 60 percent in 2007 to 82 percent in 2019 (see Figure 6.1), it was hard not to look for an explanation. EWIs provided

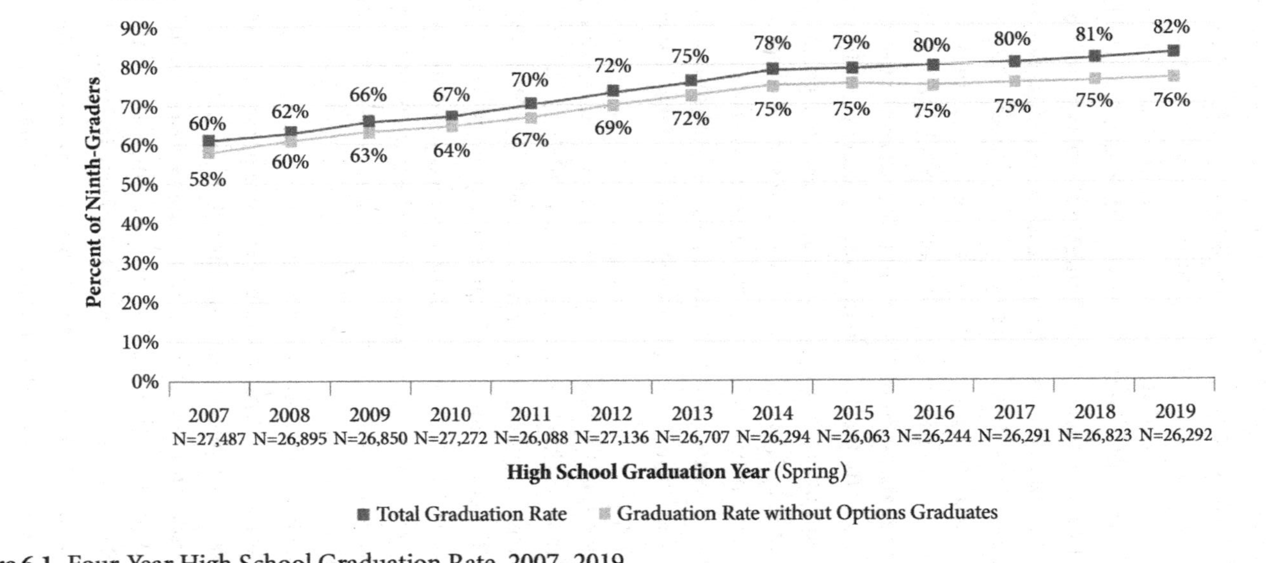


**Figure 6.1** Four-Year High School Graduation Rate, 2007–2019

*Note*: Students were defined as graduates if they earned a high school diploma within four years of their first-time ninth-grade year. Ns represent the number of students included in each ninth-grade cohort.

Reproduced with permission from Nagaoka, J. et al. (2020). *The Educational Attainment of Chicago Public Schools Students: 2019*. Chicago: University of Chicago Consortium on School Research.

at least one proximal explanation that could influence graduation, alongside other factors changing in the city.

In the years following foundational studies like Chicago's *The On-Track Indicator as a Predictor of High School Graduation* (2005) and Philadelphia's "Preventing Student Disengagement and Keeping Students on the Graduation Path in Urban Middle-Grades Schools: Early Identification and Effective Interventions" (2007), various other districts documented EWI initiatives.[16] In Los Angeles, the partnership between the LA Unified School District and a research organization called LA Education Research Institute created new EWIs that focused on college readiness—defined as completing courses required for admission to the University of California system—instead of just focusing on high school graduation.[17] In Houston, schools created teams of staff that monitored student attendance and academic performance; they called them Dropout Recovery, Intervention, and Prevention Committees.[18] In Milwaukee, a research group from the University of Wisconsin Madison worked with the school district to replicate EWI studies done in Chicago.[19] In these cities, districts and partner research organizations created similar studies and initiatives because of their knowledge of the work that was happening in other large urban school districts.

But these EWIs were not simply being adopted by local school districts. States had also started creating their own versions of EWIs. In the 2012–2013 school year, Massachusetts began piloting its own Early Warning Indicator System, which flagged students as being at low, medium, or high risk of not graduating or not passing ninth-grade courses. Information on each student's risk label was sent to schools before the beginning of the year and the web portal allowed users to generate their own reports.[20] At around the same time, Wisconsin had also started its Dropout Early Warning System, where machine learning algorithms used historical data, like test scores, disciplinary records, and race, to create student risk categories: low, moderate, and high. These predicted categories were then used by high school counselors to triage support for incoming ninth graders who needed them.[21] The state of Minnesota had also created its own Minnesota Early Indicator and Response System, with local just-in-time early indicator data and a process for school staff to follow in assigning interventions and monitoring progress.[22] But these state-wide systems for dropout prediction have also been criticized for false alarms for Black and Hispanic students, as well as for the individualization of intervention when problems of dropping out in a state are often predicted by the inequitable distribution of resources across schools and districts.[23] Notwithstanding the potential problems with state-wide systems of dropout prediction, different states' "local" adoption of EWIs highlights the knowledge from and adaptation of local examples.

When reading documentation about the initiation of these district and state-level EWIs, webs branch out from places like Chicago and Philadelphia. The knowledge of these EWI systems and their consequences in these large school districts became an important factor for local and state education agencies to adopt them. In addition to interorganizational and inter-district webs, some national organizations also took notice.

## National Web

While many of the changes related to EWIs were driven by local organizations, school districts, or states, national efforts also contributed to these changes. Interestingly, many of these national efforts have been spearheaded by individuals and organizations that initiated EWIs locally in Chicago and Philadelphia. One is a federal government agency that has supported studies on early warning systems in different geographical contexts. The other is a collaborative network of nine partner organizations working to spread EWIs, given the support from a large national philanthropy. In both cases, many actors in these national initiatives were themselves locally involved in EWIs.

When Arne Duncan left his CEO position at the CPS to be the US Secretary of Education in 2009, the work of Freshman OnTrack just-in-time data systems was just beginning in the district. Nonetheless, he saw the potential of the work and spoke about it. When asked about his role in the spread of EWIs, he shared, "I'd like to think I had a little bit to do with that and that I was such a big cheerleader for it. The US Department of Education had a pretty big platform and megaphone and [I talked] about how helpful it was to me." In this sense, local actors taking up national offices became amplifiers for the message of an educational initiative.

Duncan was also joined from Chicago by Easton, who became the director of the Institute of Education Sciences (IES), which handled the Regional Education Laboratories (RELs). The RELs were composed of 10 laboratories that partnered with school districts, state education departments, and other education stakeholders to use evidence to improve learning outcomes for students. Divided into regions like the Northeast (serving Connecticut, Maine, etc.), the Southwest (serving Arkansas, Texas, etc.), and the Midwest (serving Illinois, Iowa, etc.), these RELs created research studies, instructional products, and professional learning across a variety of topics including dropout prevention.[24] Easton spoke about these RELs:

> I'm very familiar with the RELs because when I was director of IES, the RELs were under my leadership. So, when I got there . . . , I wanted the RELs to be working more closely with districts and a lot of them did early warning indicators with networks of school districts.

A number of REL studies focused on indicators and interventions in several districts in Oregon, Washington, and Ohio. In some studies, like the one in Oregon, they did research to understand early warning signals for those who did not graduate on time.[25] Other studies, like one in Washington state, focused on particular subpopulations, like English language learners.[26] Additional studies, like one in Ohio, focused on variations in predictors of dropping out depending on the school district and grade level.[27] One study was a randomized controlled trial across 73 high schools in three Midwestern states. It found that the EWI intervention system had significant effects in reducing chronic absence and course failure but was unrelated to increasing GPA or reducing suspensions.[28] This effort by the federal government to support the spread of EWIs had taken on a local character as many of the efforts were still with particular schools and school districts.

A similar strategy was evident with a national collaborative network, which had worked with local schools. In 2022, diverse school support organizations became part of a collaborative network called the GRAD Partnership, which aimed to work with school districts, schools, communities, and organizations to "create the conditions needed to bring the use of evidence-based Student Success Systems from a new practice to a common practice."[29] Balfanz noted the genesis of the collaboration as:

> The interesting thing that will be a good coda for your story . . . is that we're now going to lead with Chicago, with AIR [American Institutes of Research], with BARR [Center], and a bunch of others a big national effort

> to bring on-track systems to scale. . . . I guess in a way the Gates Foundation brought us together because they're the ones that sort of put the money up. But it started with Bob Hughes [who was the K–12 director] of the Gates Foundation but used to be the head of New Visions in New York and they themselves do early warning work in their schools and they've been big on continuous improvements.

Here, the story of EWIs came full circle as the national work for these indicators had been catalyzed by the NCS in Chicago and TDS in Philadelphia, and supported by the Gates Foundation, whose K–12 education arm was headed by the former president of New Visions, which had pioneered many of the early EWI work in New York City. In addition to these organizations in the three cities, the collaboration also included, among others, the BARR Center with its presence in more than 200 schools; the American Institutes for Research, which led studies with some of the Regional Educational Laboratories; and the Carnegie Foundation for the Advancement of Teaching, which had developed the proposal to expand the adoption of EWIs.

While the GRAD Partnership was a national effort with partners all over the United States, many of the efforts can be more accurately characterized as local efforts to partner with specific schools, school districts, and education departments. While the nine organizations participated in communal events and shared collective resources that had a national perspective, the strategy of engagement was still distinctly local. Patricia Balana, the managing director of the collaborative network, shared:

> We have potential intermediaries come to us to say, "We listened in your launch. We think we're well positioned to support District X. Can you come and build our capacity around this on-track student success work? We will support the five schools in our district because *we are local, we know the context, we know the community, we are a trusted organization*." So, that's kind of happening organically, in a sense. (emphasis added)

Thus, even with the goal of the national spread of these student success systems, the strategy was to partner at the local level. In this sense, nonprofits had taken on the role not just of spreading EWIs but of localizing them and embedding them in school and community contexts. To create a national web, they relied on local changes.

## Spatial Dynamics of Institutional Change

The spread of EWIs from Chicago, Philadelphia, and New York City to different school districts and states in the United States highlighted the spatial dimension of institutional change. EWIs emerged and created shifts within particular local settings and contexts. Even as these EWIs were burgeoning in other places, the changes were still deeply local. However, these local changes were not limited to what happened in a city, a town, a district, or a state. These changes were adopted and adapted in other localities as local organizations were connected to other organizations in other places, as these organizations were contracted in other places, as certain locations became proofs of concept that inspire imitation, and as national agencies created initiatives with local intermediaries. In creating institutional change in a decentralized and disjointed system, the focus was not so much at the national or organizational level, but rather at the local level of interorganizational systems.

This chapter highlights the concept of inter-local changes, where change initially happens in a local system and this change, within the local system, can potentially be transposed in other local systems. I argue that this type of change emerges in contexts that do not have consolidated or centralized powers, and in contexts that value local autonomy and self-determination. In the case of US public education and local school control, change comes not from a large national initiative but from the webs of local initiatives that are connected to each other. Such connections are often brought about by organizations through their presence across local areas and through their ability to network with other organizations across spaces. Thus, our concepts of change in education must account for these spatial dynamics.

Yet educational changes through these inter-local changes are not always optimal. The thing with inter-local changes is that some places change sooner and some later, and some don't change at all. When local areas and their organizations can institute changes at their own time, much of the change is predicted by the civic capacity and political resources within a specific school, district, or city.[30] Such differences in the adoption of changes can lead not only to variation among local settings but also to reproduced or exacerbated inequalities. If one district has EWIs but a nearby district doesn't because of the absence of certain organizational or political resources, inter-local changes may mean that one locality experiences change while another doesn't.

But inter-local changes may also mean that localities that do not need to change are buffered from these changes. Because changes are not wholly applied to all places, individuals and organizations within a specific context have the power to decide whether a policy, program, or proposal makes sense to them. If one district has EWIs and another district doesn't, it might be that EWIs were not necessary in that context. The dynamics of inter-local changes provide this possibility.

This chapter illustrates how educational transformations happen spatially through inter-local changes. In the case of EWIs, organizations focused on local actions and interactions but exhibited consequences that were often inter-local, if not national.

# Conclusion

## Theorizing Change from Outside-In

The problem in education is perhaps not that schools remain the same, but that schools change so frequently and so incoherently that the changes are unhelpful at best and damaging at worst. Scholars have talked about the "spinning wheels" of education reforms that are often stuck at the same spot, or the "Christmas tree effect" of ornamental school changes that are often patchworked together.[1] Many new reforms spread but many also fail. As one sociologist of education would put it, schools are characterized as having so much reform but so little change.[2]

In recent years, organizational scholars have argued that organizational change is less an exceptional case and more the natural state of organizations.[3] But constant organizational change can be incoherent, loosely coupled, and inconsequential. The constant advent of new changes can lead to uncoordinated structures and systems that further the instructional incoherence in schools.[4] In schools' desire to show change, maintain legitimacy, and create confidence in their activities, schools may decouple policy from practice—where the official structure is not what actually happens on the ground.[5] More importantly, even a coherent and tightly coupled system of changes is no assurance of consequential changes in school and student outcomes.[6] But could there be conditions that support the initiation, implementation, and institutionalization of practices that are *coherent*, tightly *coupled*, and actually *consequential*?

The story of early warning indicators (EWIs) provides a case to theorize these conditions. While the initiative was no silver bullet and while the challenges of American schools still remain, evidence suggests important and productive consequences coming from the introduction of data systems and relational processes that support students' transition into high schools. The initiative started neither as a program nor as a policy, but as a research project in Chicago and Philadelphia during a time when longitudinal data systems were only slowly becoming available. The insight, however, that predictors of graduation were discernible as early as the ninth grade provided an organizing and cohering principle for change.

*Subtle Webs*. Jose Eos Trinidad, Oxford University Press. © Oxford University Press (2025).
DOI: 10.1093/9780197786123.003.008

Ninth-grade EWIs became technologies for school accountability, just-in-time identification, tiered intervention, and school improvement. A tighter coupling between policy and practice emerged as organizations outside schools worked with actors inside them. Researchers worked with district data engineers. Philanthropists collaborated with district leadership. School support and ninth-grade instructional coaches organized teams of teachers and school leaders to implement these technologies. Across all these activities, changes were often concentrated at the local level of schools and school districts. For schools and districts that saw steady progress in the number of students on track to graduate, this fed into their belief in EWIs' consequential changes.

Three themes emerged from the story of EWIs regarding the *source*, *scale*, and *space* of educational change. These three themes structure the chapters in this book. The first two chapters highlight the view from inside and outside schools and emphasize that the source of change is not limited to the education bureaucracy. The source of change is at the intersection of "outside" organizations collaborating with individuals "inside" schools and school districts. The next three chapters on the macro-, meso-, and micro-level perspectives on EWIs demonstrate the various scales for change to happen. While they were conceptualized as discrete levels, the interconnections across them were hinted at by the shared stories and concepts. Finally, the last chapter on local systems and national consequences illustrates the underappreciated spatial element of change, as change often happens locally and becomes transposed to other local systems. More than simply about EWIs and educational change, I argue that this conceptualization of change from outside-in and across multiple levels can frame other studies of institutional, organizational, and policy change.

A core argument in the book is how change in a decentralized system must necessarily contend with this characteristic of the system being a constellation of semi-independent and disjointed entities. A large agency may have little direct influence on the core work on the ground because the system was not set up this way. However, if there is a need for changes to spread, how do they happen? While our theories often think of change as either top-down or bottom-up, this book highlights the concept of change from outside-in as "outside" organizations (i.e., elements in the institutional environment) can form an invisible infrastructure and a subtle web to institute these changes. Given a system that is against centralized control, the power of networked outsiders relies on their being local actors with only subtle national connections.

Yet being an outsider is not enough. Organizations work on specific changes across various levels (see Table C.1). At the macro-level, organizations try to influence the ways policies and practices are framed (i.e., their institutional logics) through the technologies being crafted and implemented. The way EWIs became satisfactory for teachers, principals, district leaders, and philanthropists holding varying institutional logics was because of the flexibility and variety in how the technologies can be made sense of. EWIs were not a single technology; they were a set of technologies that adapted to different logics. At the meso-level, organizations created networks of institutional entrepreneurs that leveraged material and social resources. However, instead of thinking of these networks as random, it may be better to think of them as templates spanning an orb web of hubs-and-spoke and a tangled web of closely embedded actors. To get EWIs off the ground, organizations drew on these templates to structure their networks for specific contexts. At the micro-level, the key resources were organizational routines, particularly amid the resistance and skepticism that emerged from grounded actors. Through building relationships and securing routines, these organizations were able to sustain and embed these routines into the web of practices already there in schools. Taken altogether, outsiders had to have one foot in and another foot out of the system.

As change happened across various levels in an institution, one may think that the movement was from the macro-level of institutional logics to the meso-level of entrepreneurial networks to the micro-level of

**Table C.1** Multiple Levels of Institutional Change

| Level | Source of Change | Institutional Theory | Focal actors |
|---|---|---|---|
| Macro-level | Technology and Framing | Institutional Logics | Researchers |
| Meso-level | Networks and Templates | Institutional Entrepreneurship | Networked Leaders |
| Micro-level | Organizational Routines | Inhabited Institutions | On-the-Ground Nonprofit Staff |

organizational routines. However, change often happened across these levels at the same time as people worked on framing, as new technologies were introduced, as organizations were connected, and as new routines were begun. Nonetheless, these changes were often concentrated on the immediate environment, whether it was an organization, a city, or some local context. To more widely spread and sustain these changes, organizations created changes that were adopted and adapted across local systems—transposing ideas, practices, principles, and technologies from one space to another.

## Theoretical Applications

The idea of the subtle web of outside organizations instituting changes across various levels and local contexts provides a perspective to understand other initiatives beyond EWIs. The spread of various reform efforts from the broad political spectrum can be understood with this perspective. Initiatives like charter schools, alternative teacher preparation programs, networked improvement communities, teacher value-added measures, computer science education, and unified enrollment systems have both started and spread because of interventions, interests, and investments by often local philanthropic, nonprofit, research, and advocacy organizations. I illustrate the theoretical richness of this concept by drawing on examples from networked *professional* organizations (e.g., value added models, alternative teacher preparation programs, and charter schools) and networked *parent* organizations (e.g., Moms for Liberty and Moms Demand Action). By documenting examples from both conservative and liberal positions, I show how the subtle web is a larger phenomenon that can be leveraged by various sorts of actors in a decentralized system. While the examples are necessarily short and succinct, they provide new frontiers in investigating the process of change in education.

### Networked Professional Organizations

One initiative that has spread across the United States emerged during the early 2000s with teacher *value-added modeling* (VAM). Coming from the economic literature, these models assumed that the "added value" of a teacher may be measured, given the proximal influence of teachers on students' achievement and given the wide variability in teachers' effectiveness.[7] In addition to measurement, these VAMs have been used for high- and low-stakes accountability, which are particularly consequential for teacher evaluation.[8] At the macro-level, VAMs were intrinsically connected to processes and perspectives that privileged quantification and a "trust in numbers," perspectives that had taken root in public policy in general and education policy in particular.[9] They relied on institutional logics that trusted market forces and state accountability, evident in how the technology was used. At the meso-level, different organizations were interested in getting this taken up. One article documented this as:

> [Economist Eric] Hanushek, now with an appointment at the conservative Hoover Institution, as well as other economists located at think tanks like RAND and the American Institutes for Research sought to legitimize the use of VAM for Department of Education officials by using NCLB funding to research the statistical properties of the method . . . . By the early 2010s VAM reached its public high point . . . . Within a few years, over thirty states had devised ways to incorporate VAM into new evaluation systems, not just to track aggregate performance, but to distinguish among the performance of individual educators.[10]

Despite VAMs exhibiting mixed results, particularly with the misclassification of teachers and concerns regarding their unintended consequences, the technology was taken up through embedded individual and organizational networks—spanning academics, research institutions, for-profit corporations, philanthropies, and government bureaucrats. At the micro-level, teachers and teachers' unions filed lawsuits against VAM-based evaluations, highlighting local resistance to these new technologies and the inability for changes to stick in the absence of direct engagement with people on the ground.[11] The emergence and spread of VAMs has parallels to this multi-level theory of educational change.

*Alternative teacher preparation organizations* like Teach for America (TFA) and The New Teacher Project (TNTP) became common place in US public education. During the writing of this book, TFA was in 52 regions in the United States, including the San Francisco bay area, Dallas-Fort Worth, Kansas City, New Jersey, and Miami-Dade.[12] TNTP had also been in many urban districts like Baltimore, Indianapolis, New Orleans, and Las Vegas.[13]

Other districts also launched their own local version of alternative teacher preparation and certification programs, like the New York City Teaching Fellows[14] and TeachCharleston in South Carolina.[15] The presence of these organizations in predominantly urban and metropolitan areas was often driven by the macro-level meaning-making of these organizations, which some scholar argue constitutes "a mission to rescue and reform schools in America's urban education centers from what was deemed sub-par teaching and teacher training as a result of a national teacher shortage."[16] Similar to EWIs, the spread was not so much across different schools but across urban school districts, often mediated by meso-level interpersonal and interorganizational networks. TFA, for example, created an alumni network of more than 58,000 members, in which alumni in and across their placement areas become embedded actors in influencing public education in different school, district, and state contexts.[17] At the micro-level, these alternative pathways have received criticism about the lack of supports for teachers, the difficulty of retaining them, the modest impacts of their intervention, and the managerial logics employed to reform school systems.[18] However, these organizations continue their presence in school districts as these alternative pathways have become legitimated, taken-for-granted, and annual routines for school districts in need of new teachers.

*Charter schools* in the United States are tuition-free, publicly funded schools that are run by groups, universities, or organizations under a "charter" between the school and an authorizing agency.[19] Originally conceived as a way to spur innovations, some charter schools have functioned as alternatives to district-operated public schools.[20] Across the country, charter schools have expanded to encompass more than 7,000 schools, an indicator of the idea's spread despite many criticism and much resistance.[21] Interestingly, charter school laws are absent in five states in the United States, including Montana, Nebraska, Vermont, North Dakota, and South Dakota.[22] Thus, even if the concept has spread widely, much of it is "locally" determined at specific communities and specific states. Studies of the emergence of charter schools have shown how the local educational organizational environment is core to increasing the number of charter schools in an area.

At the macro-level, these charter schools had to create organizational identities to make them legible and legitimate to various actors, and scholars have shown the dynamics of both mimicry and differentiation in the process of legitimizing this new form.[23] More importantly, recent studies have also shown that charter schools drew on specific organizational identities depending on the racial and socioeconomic composition of the places they inhabit—highlighting the use of varying frames and logics to gain support for them.[24] At the meso-level, charter schools often spread because of the networks of philanthropies, charter management organizations, and research/advocacy groups that had interests and had invested in these changes. In particular, scholars have documented how foundation dollars flow across different states through these charter management and advocacy organizations.[25] At the micro-level, charter schools have created webs of routines embedded in their schools, or what some have referred to as "scripts" that regulate the behavior of both teachers and students.[26] Many of these charter schools did not emerge equally in the United States because they were dependent on the local contexts of particular states and specific school districts.[27] The case of charter schools' emergence can be systematically understood with this theory of subtle webs across various scales and spaces.

## Networked Parent Organizations

The subtle webs of change in education does not happen solely through professional nonprofit organizations. Change can also emerge across seemingly grassroots parent organizations. Two groups, from two separate poles of the political spectrum, provide current examples about how change happens through networked organizations. Moms for Liberty and Moms Demand Action, despite advocating wildly different policies, have used similar strategies that stem from the subtle webs discussed in this book.

Moms for Liberty is a conservative political organization that advocates against school discussions surrounding lesbians, gays, bisexuals, and transgenders (LGBT) and critical race theory (CRT), using "parental rights" as a rallying cry for its members.[28] Its focus on anti-LGBT and anti-CRT ideas is fueled by a macro-level logic of the family and community being against these threats to their values and "how short-sighted and destructive policies directly hurt children and families."[29] These organizations have mushroomed in different counties and states, like Florida, Washington, Oregon, and Montana.[30] Despite the seemingly grassroots orientation, the organization's meso-level interconnections cast doubts on this origin story. Journalist Paige Williams documents:

> Moms for Liberty, which is sometimes referred to as M4L or MFL, is so new that it is hard to parse, from public documents, what its leaders are getting paid. (The founders say that the chairs of local chapters are volunteers.) The group describes itself as a "grassroots" organization, yet its instant absorption by the conservative mediasphere has led some critics to suspect it of being an Astroturf group—an operation secretly funded by moneyed interests . . . .
>
> The leaders had deep G.O.P. connections. One, Marie Rogerson, was a successful Republican political strategist. The other, Bridget Ziegler, a school-board member in Sarasota County, is married to the vice-chair of the Florida G.O.P., Christian Ziegler . . . . A national phalanx of interconnected organizations—including the Manhattan Institute, where [conservative media personality Christopher] Rufo is a fellow, and a group called Moms for America—supported the suite of talking points about C.R.T.[31]

Yet inasmuch as these connections across individuals and organizations were fueling the organization, the main action is happening in micro-level school board meetings where parents demand schools and school districts to remove books, change curricula, and change what they argue are materials exposing their children to "psychological distress."[32] A deeper study of the organization's emergence and spread may clarify how the local and national dynamics played out in their influence on public education.

On the other side of the political spectrum is Moms Demand Action, a grassroots movement that aims to protect people from gun violence. The organization started in the wake of the Sandy Hook, Connecticut, school shooting in late 2012, and describes itself as a "left-of-center activist group that lobbies for the implementation of strict gun control measures."[33] At the macro-level, the organization's members lobby with their state legislators and attend state legislature sessions to speak on gun regulation. Its founder, a public relations practitioner, has used tactics to help frame the debates suitably.[34] At the meso-level, the organization does not act alone as it participates in initiatives by a coalition composed for key left-of-center and far-left organizations, like the National Organization for Women, the Latino Victory Project, the Women's March, the Lawyers Committee for Civil Rights Under Law, and the Center for American Progress.[35] At the micro-level, Moms Demand Action organizes events locally in their different chapters, from membership meetings to memorials for gun violence victims.[36] The organization even has a highly publicized national boycott called "Skip Starbucks

Saturdays" to pressure the coffee chain to not allow guns in their establishments.[37] Many of the changes were driven not by pressure on the national legislation (even as this is part of their strategy), but by local pressures on states and businesses.

The different succinct examples from professional organizations and parent organizations, as well as from right-leaning and left-leaning groups, highlights the potential for understanding change through the work of outside organizations that are locally focused yet nationally connected with each other. Rather than top-down or bottom-up per se, the changes often come through interconnected organizations that operate outside-in.

## Politics of Outside Organizations

If changes in education are driven by subtle webs of outside organizations, this can pose practical problems for schools, districts, and localities that do not have access to such organizations. The variability in organizational and civic capacity can lead not just to differences but to potentially exacerbated inequalities. If the places most in need of EWIs are the places without a research consortium or a school support organization, then the subtle web can actually heighten inequalities. Of course, this is in addition to the concerns already highlighted in the book's introduction about the potential risks of private action on public institutions.

However, in many studies that critique the influence of nonprofit and philanthropic organizations in public education, the focus is on the organizations themselves. But the emergence of nonprofits, philanthropies, and local organizations in education comes as a response to the United States's decentralized system of local schools. In such a system without a strong centralizing force or standardizing institution, other organizations can fill in the void. The ability of organizations to influence, change, and shape American education occurs because the very system itself is suspicious of a central authority, highlighting what some have noted as a fundamental ambiguity in US public opinion: "Americans want government programs but dislike [big] government."[38] Thus, networked organizations provide an opportunity for subtle, nationwide changes to happen, even if such changes are often patchworked.

What I show in this book is not whether we should or shouldn't have this subtle web of organizations, but that this is the reality that public education specifically, and public institutions more generally, are facing. Civic participation and civil associational life are hallmarks of American society, documented as such since Alexis de Tocqueville's visit to the country in 1831. Public schools have often promoted such civic vitality through local school boards and school councils. But this localization of schools has also opened education up to widespread inequalities and a difficulty to institute changes across the country.[39] As I argue, nonprofits and philanthropies have filled this void and become key actors in shaping not just local schools and districts but the larger institution of American education. In this process of crafting networked local changes, organizations show their ability and power to influence national institutions.

## Toward Equitable and Democratic Changes

The story of EWIs provides an illustration of how meaningful change can emerge from local actors who are able to leverage institutional logics to frame policy problems, spin entrepreneurial networks across various levels and organizations, and craft organizational routines to transform work on the ground. The book talks about the power of these outside organizations connected with local schools and districts—who altogether have created a *social learning environment.* As subtle webs try to institute changes in the education system, the book has also shown that these changes are not without risks and unintended consequences. This book ends by highlighting opportunities for organizations and schools to create meaningful and equitable changes that reduce the risks we've explored in this book and improve democratic participation. These are meant as provocations to think of ideas that various stakeholders can accomplish.

*Organizations can create intentional structures for democracy.* One of the core concerns about outside organizations, like research, philanthropic, and nonprofit organizations, is their lack of accountability to the public and their potential to reduce community voice. To address this, outside organizations must consider actions and activities that structure accountability and democracy. How can a private organization ensure that it is accountable to its community and that it represents the voice of those who are often marginalized? One way some organizations have done this is by organizing steering committees to hold the organization and its leaders accountable. The steering committee may be made up of individuals from the community and individuals from diverse socioeconomic, ethnic-racial, gender, and political backgrounds. By creating and cultivating an intentional structure for organizational accountability and democratic voice, local organizations can ensure that no single individual's voice is privileged in the work. This may also help in crafting policies, practices, and routines that are sensitive to local contexts and responsive to cultural assets that already exist. Although the suggestion may pose challenges for speed and focus, it can reap rewards as change can be deeper.

*State education and school district officials can function as sieves of outside initiatives.* Organizations outside the education bureaucracy can sometimes have focused capacity to help institute changes. Given this focus and power, state educational agencies and school districts may be easily buffeted by the influence of these organizations. To guard against this, government officials can act as sieves to clarify the main priorities for which the district needs support, as well as remaining flexible as new needs arise. On the one hand, state and district offices may set out clearly what their priorities are and which of these priorities may be addressed wholly or in part by nonprofits and philanthropies. Rather than depend simply on the presence of financial, material, and social resources, the office may be more deliberate in setting this out beforehand.

On the other hand, there may be particular initiatives and needs that emerge only later, which necessitates a certain flexibility on the part of state education agencies and local school districts. In the context of unforeseen emergencies and crises, like the COVID-19 pandemic, the flexibility to open up to the assistance of nonprofits can create helpful stopgap solutions. However, these temporary solutions must not replace the larger systems-wide changes that are arguably the key space for government intervention. More practically, school boards can develop guidelines for their priorities, relationships, and work alongside nonprofits and philanthropies. But guidelines are not enough as many of these initiatives do not just happen at the state or district offices. They often happen with schools, school leaders, and teachers.

*School leader and teacher preparation programs can focus on adaptations and partnerships.* The most consequential changes in education depend less on the action of outside organizations and more on the action of individuals in the school system. School leaders, teachers, and support staff are the ones who will ultimately implement changes, adapt outside initiatives, and practice daily routines. The example of EWIs showed how schools had different reasons for adopting these data systems and how schools have adapted them, but not without skepticism and resistance. Rather than think of resistance as a deterrent, it can be seen as an opportunity for adaptation and contextualization. Preparation programs for school leaders and teachers can highlight the larger ecosystem of education change—showing how partnerships can lead to mutual learning and contextual adaptation. More practically, these lessons may come through courses on organizational theory with topics like organizational change and interorganizational learning. The interaction with outside organizations can be seen as an opportunity for adaptations to be created and for new safeguards to be introduced. Nonetheless, the ability to adapt and partner in school does not wholly depend on the preparation of schools and principals, but also on the relational trust in these schools as well as between schools and their partners.

*Researchers can complement a problem-pointing perspective with a problem-solving perspective.* Much sociological, organizational, and educational research can focus on pointing out problems with new policies and unintended consequences of new technologies. Although these are important to help alert us to how good intentions can have bad outcomes, an equally important perspective is to highlight organizational "bright spots" that can show important ways forward. Inspired by the work of Monica Prasad on pursuing a problem-solving sociology, I also see this book as contributing to our understanding of potential avenues for meaningful change to happen in education and in our organizations.[40] The book illustrates the potential of EWIs to address dropping out, of nonprofits to spread constructive educational changes, and of outside organizations to give coherence to a decentralized and disjointed system. Future education and organizational research can explore the many opportunities for meaningful change to emerge from the collective learning of actors within schools and their interaction with outside organizations.

*Public policy leaders can leverage the advantages of outside organizations and reduce the potential disadvantages.* Nonprofit, philanthropic, and community-based organizations are a constitutive part of American life. Across various domains from education to health care, these organizations perform different functions. This book has shown the potential advantages of these networked organizations that have the capacity to bring about coherence and standardization across various disparate locations. Place-based research organizations can provide highly specific and contextualized information. Support organizations can build grounded long-term relationships with community members. Local philanthropic and family foundations can support initiatives for innovation and experimentation. And their networks across places can help shape practices in an otherwise decentralized and incoherent system. This book hopes to inspire policy leaders and scholars to notice these subtle webs, and to invite actions that can support their work while attentive to the potential risks the book has already documented.

Dropping out used to be a problem that was thought to be beyond the control of schools, teachers, and policy leaders. However, change started when research, philanthropic, and nonprofit organizations learned *with* schools that dropping out can be predicted and that data can be leveraged to address it. But change was not simply about identifying students at risk but about changing the culture and supporting the context in schools. Some key ingredients for change were technologies that influenced shifts in thinking (i.e., logics), changes in people's ways of relating (i.e., networks), and transformations in everyday practices (i.e., routines). But these changes were highly dependent on the social learning that emerged across networks of schools, bureaucracies, and local organizations. These networks were the subtle webs that transformed data, dropping out, and US school districts.

# Methodological Appendix

## An Integrative Policy Analysis

This chapter highlights concepts for an integrative policy analysis in which scholars study policies holistically and historically from their inception and political tug-of-war to their implementation and adaptation. This analysis privileges *historical*, *multi-level*, and *networked* perspectives in understanding policies to show not just the effect or implementation of a policy but how policies move through their course. This integrative method complements and enriches traditional quantitative studies of policy effects, qualitative studies of policy implementation, and critical studies of policy formation. By understanding a policy from its initiation to its institutionalization and from originators to implementers (and back), researchers may provide a clearer picture about how change transpires, about which aspects of the technology were crucial in the change, about what institutional constraints were preventing change, and about who the key movers and shakers were. I write this methodological appendix first as documentation of the social scientific procedures I used and choices I made to do this research. A second, and perhaps more important, reason for writing this appendix is a pedagogical reason to suggest ideas for doing integrative policy analysis.

The method is not so much one method but a combination of different methods. In this research, I note three important elements of integrative policy analysis. First, it attends to *historical changes* as organizations and policies are neither fixed nor static. Traditionally, researchers analyze policies immediately after they are introduced, whether as a field experiment or as an actual policy on the ground. This is key to understanding if further investments and expansions of the policy are warranted. However, policies are contingent on context. On the one hand, they may be effective in one moment but may no longer be as effective in another (e.g., EWIs might be more effective during a time when large numbers of students drop out but not when many already expect to graduate). On the other hand, the use of policies, programs, and technologies can shift through time, such as the EWIs' increasingly varied uses as schools and organizations learned more about them. One contemporary movement in many sectors, including education, is continuous improvement, which privileges iterative and structured cycles of analysis to solve problems and test solutions for an organization.[1] Given that policies can often still come from districts, states, and the federal government, it will be important to see how schools adopt and change these policies to support their context. Policies are never singular and static; they are multi-faceted and ever changing. Our analysis must then be anchored on these realities.

Second, an integrative policy analysis can happen across multiple scales; that is, both *societal levels* and *local contexts*. In terms of levels, such analysis can focus on the macro-level of the society—constituting general paradigms, principles, processes, and ways of thinking. It can emphasize the meso-level of organizations and communities, which include organizational policies, politics, relationships, cooperation, and competition. It can also highlight the micro-level of individuals, particularly with people's intentions, interests, resistance, and routines. Given the many facets of policies and organizations, the parsing out and distinction between these different levels can provide helpful ways of analyzing the phenomenon at hand. In addition to levels, the local context is an equally important element as the emergence and adaptation of policies depend on the political institutions, cultural norms, and structural barriers within a given context.

Third, an integrative analysis is sensitive to how *networks* of individuals and organizations are key factors in the initiation, implementation, and institutionalization of policies and practices. Change happens less through individual actions and more through dynamic interactions. Proposals become policies as alignment happens across different stakeholders. Policies become resisted or adopted as implementers interact with each other or with more knowledgeable others. Technologies take on new uses as people discover ways around them or ways of harnessing them. To analyze policy emergence and change, it will be helpful to understand what specific ties and interactions bring them about.

These three elements were key aspects I considered in the methodological choices I made regarding the case, data collection strategies, and analytic procedures. I will outline these in the next sections. I will highlight why I used the conceptual case of dropout prediction systems and the empirical cases of Chicago, Philadelphia, and New York City. I will then talk about how I collected data through interviews and documents that were attentive to history, scale, and networks of individuals. Afterward, I will detail how I used the data to map out the historical trajectories of EWIs, to thematically analyze the different levels for these changes, and to create a networked perspective of individual and organizational ties. The final section of this methodological appendix offers some lessons learned in the process of researching—many of which often resulted from trials and errors as well as from happenstance and luck.

## Conceptual Case and Empirical Cases

"What is this a case of?" is a question many sociologists get asked a lot. The study of EWIs, for example, is not simply the study of dropout prediction systems. Its study may be a case of quantification in society, it may be a case of institutional change in a decentralized system, or it may be a case of the influence of civil and private actors on public institutions. Sometimes, a researcher may start with an empirical case, like EWIs in Chicago, but must then think about the larger conceptual case upon which this phenomenon sheds light. Sometimes, a researcher may start with a conceptual case of their desire to study big data in society but must then think about how this broad interest can translate into an empirical study. In both scenarios, the researcher will need to have a *conceptual case* that tries to push theoretical knowledge and an *empirical case* (or *cases*) that provide ground for such insights to emerge.

This book's introduction has provided theoretical reasons for choosing Chicago, Philadelphia, and New York City as cases. Many of these reasons are based on how the three cities are among the first large urban school districts to have scaled EWIs, many of these efforts driven by a constellation of organizations outside schools and many of these initiatives being acknowledged as pioneers in this field. However, these different cities also had significant contextual and demographic differences that made it possible to investigate if specific dynamics were shared despite variations in contexts. These were the theoretical justifications for the choice of these empirical cases.

There were also practical justifications for these empirical choices. I document them here to show how social scientific research is an iterative process with many practical considerations. Such practical considerations become the basis for the project and the theoretical justifications we can leverage. I also highlight here how luck and good fortune can play a role in one's research. The skill is not so much foresight as sensitivity to when fortune comes knocking on the door. I had initially been interested in studying EWIs in New York City, Los Angeles, and Chicago—the three largest urban school districts in the United States. I started interviewing individuals in Chicago because I had become familiar with this work as a graduate student at the University of Chicago. However, one of the first people I interviewed from the To&Through Project mentioned how they also worked in Philadelphia. This became my first stroke of good luck because I didn't realize that I could also study Philadelphia, and that Philadelphia was actually an early pioneer of EWIs. But with good luck came bad luck as well. When I reached out to a research organization in Los Angeles, they respectfully declined my invitation to be part of the research. Thus, I couldn't study the three largest school districts; however, I was able to study the three pioneer cities that had tried to scale EWIs up in the early 2000s.

Once I had decided the city cases, I needed the specific *organizational cases* as well. To do this, I relied on an expansive literature search and on expert informants who connected me to other organizations. In reviewing the literature on EWIs, I found five organizations that had either researched these EWIs or created EWIs in the three cities: the University of Chicago Consortium on School Research, the To&Through Project, researchers at Johns Hopkins University, Research Alliance for New York City Schools, and New Visions for Public Schools. I then reached out to the specific directors of these organizations, asking if they would be willing to participate. As again luck would have it, the organizations opened their doors to my research (something for which I am immensely grateful). As I interviewed individuals in these organizations, they told me about other individuals and organizations in the EWI/data space including philanthropies, school support nonprofits, community-based organizations, and central district officials. Such webs of connections added to the cases I was studying and provided a more holistic picture of the institutional actors in the emergence of EWIs.

## Collecting Data

Data for this research came from 95 informants and more than 2,800 pages of documents about EWIs. Primarily, I relied on semi-structured interviews that I conducted between 2021 and 2023. These interviews, with 73 organizational actors, spanned district officials, nonprofit leaders, philanthropic managers, researchers, data strategists, school improvement coaches, and professors.[2] Many of these individuals were based in Chicago, Philadelphia, and New York City but some of them have since moved to other jobs. To understand what was happening in schools, I supplemented these interviews with data from 22 interviews conducted between 2015 and 2017, during a time when EWIs were being introduced and implemented in Chicago. Such data provided the basis for Chapter 1 of the book. Finally, I assembled company documents, research and annual reports, news articles, websites, journal publications, and other media forms all related to EWIs, spanning 1999 and 2022.

*Access.* The main data sources were expert and elite interviews with people who shared their knowledge about EWIs in their own local contexts and across the United States more generally. These interviews were collectively referred to as expert and elite interviews because they were with individuals who were knowledgeable about EWIs or who were key decision-makers in bringing them about. I learned about these individuals primarily through the literature search on EWIs because they were either authors or leaders in research organizations. Because many of these individuals had public profiles in their organizational websites, I reached out to them through their email addresses. In cases where the individuals did not have email addresses listed, I used their LinkedIn profiles to send a message asking for their email so that I could connect with them more formally. In some cases, individuals I interviewed introduced me via email to another colleague, either in the same organization or a different organization. These different networks of connections helped to bring diverse perspectives on EWIs. However, it must be noted that some individuals declined or did not respond to invitations to be interviewed, even after following up. While admittedly a limitation, these are few in number and, when possible, I would refer to documentary evidence to understand their role on EWIs.

*Interviews.* Before interviews, I read up as much as I could about my informant and about the work they had done. For researchers, in particular, I read the research papers they wrote on EWIs. This knowledge helped me customize the semi-structured interview guide, which was mainly composed of questions about their participation and role on EWI initiatives, challenges and constraints with EWIs, transformations throughout the years, other private actors in education, and the larger ecosystem of school improvement. The interviews happened over Zoom or over the phone, in accordance with health protocols during this time. During the interview, I asked informants if they would be willing to be identified in the research given the difficulty of anonymizing organizations, positions, and individuals, as well as because of their public personality as district leaders, researchers, and nonprofit directors. Only one person declined to be identified. After the interviews, I asked the informants if there were things that they wanted to take off the record. Many did not take anything out; two people asked not to quote a proposal that had not yet been approved during the time of the interview. All these procedures were approved by the Social and Behavioral Sciences Institutional Review Board (IRB) of the University of Chicago. All interviews, which ranged between 30 and 90 minutes, were subsequently transcribed.

*Validity.* I was fully cognizant of the dangers of relying solely on interviews with these elites and experts, who may have had ulterior reasons in painting a positive picture of their efforts. To address this, I had intentionally asked these informants about instances when their efforts were not as productive, or when EWIs did not work, or when they experienced conflicts and resistance. The informants, in turn, were more than frank about their frustrations and mistakes—something that caught me by surprise. I did not need to be critical about them because they themselves were healthily critical about the work they did. They were detailed in their depiction of mistakes and things that did not work, and humble in the risk of relying solely on their improvement work. Moreover, I noted how the responses were in/consistent with the documents I assembled.

*Author Positionality.* While conducting this research, I was a graduate student based at the University of Chicago, and I was familiar with the work of the Consortium and EWIs. As a cisgender, male, international student from a developing country, I was particularly surprised with the US educational system's decentralized character. In the Philippines, where I'm from, changes come from the central/national education department. My status as a doctoral student may have also helped in gaining access to the organizations that

I studied because I was concentrated on doing research and did not have any political or material reasons for studying them.

*Supplementary School Interviews.* To understand what was happening on the ground during the introduction and early implementation of EWIs, I had to rely on sources that had been previously collected. Thus, I gained access to 22 interviews with schoolteachers, counselors, assistant principals, and principals in six schools in Chicago, conducted between 2015 and 2017. No published document had arisen from these interviews, which were commissioned by the University of Chicago Consortium on School Research. (Camille Farrington and Faye Kroshinsky led this qualitative project on Freshman OnTrack.) The goal of the research project was to understand how schools were using Freshman OnTrack, particularly what people were doing and what data had facilitated the work. Through a data sharing agreement with the Consortium, I was added to the IRB application for the original project and was given access to the anonymized interview transcripts. The data were crucial in providing a backdrop to understanding how EWIs were used in schools.

*Supplementary Documents.* Given the potential difficulties of relying solely on narratives and recollections of people's experiences about EWIs, I aimed to triangulate the interview data with documentary data. Thus, I assembled more than 2,800 pages of documentary evidence, including published and unpublished documents, peer-reviewed papers, news articles in local dailies, school district reports, company annual reports, published research, district handbooks, and organizational webpages. These data were arranged chronologically to help assemble the historical trajectory of EWIs. To promote open science, the public documents have been made available at https://doi.org/10.17605/OSF.IO/Z435F.

## Analyzing the Data

The historical, multi-level, and networked perspectives were key in analyzing the interviews and documentary data. Given the various perspectives, I also had to employ different types of data analysis. I detail below the use of historical, thematic, network, and dialogic analysis of the data. Although I divide them into these neat four categories, they did not necessarily proceed one after another, nor was it possible to easily divorce the various elements. The process of analyzing the data was iterative and constructive, with new methods emerging as the data needed to be analyzed in new ways.

First, I assembled a timeline of events, publications, media materials, organizational births and deaths, and interorganizational partnerships connected to EWIs (see Figure A.1 for a stylized version with some key highlights). I used the documents I had collected as well as references in the interviews to show the changes and additions to EWIs from 1999 to 2023. Rather than map out the general changes regarding EWIs, I mapped out these changes in each of the three cities—with particular attention to how the constellation of organizations were changing through time and what new public-interfacing documents were created. In addition to noting the changes in EWIs, I also took note of the other changes in each of the school districts such as changes in district administration (with new CEOs or superintendents), new policies like suspension reduction policies, and changing demographic dynamics like the reduction in the number of students. Attention to these changes formed the foundation for the discussion in Chapters 1 and 2.

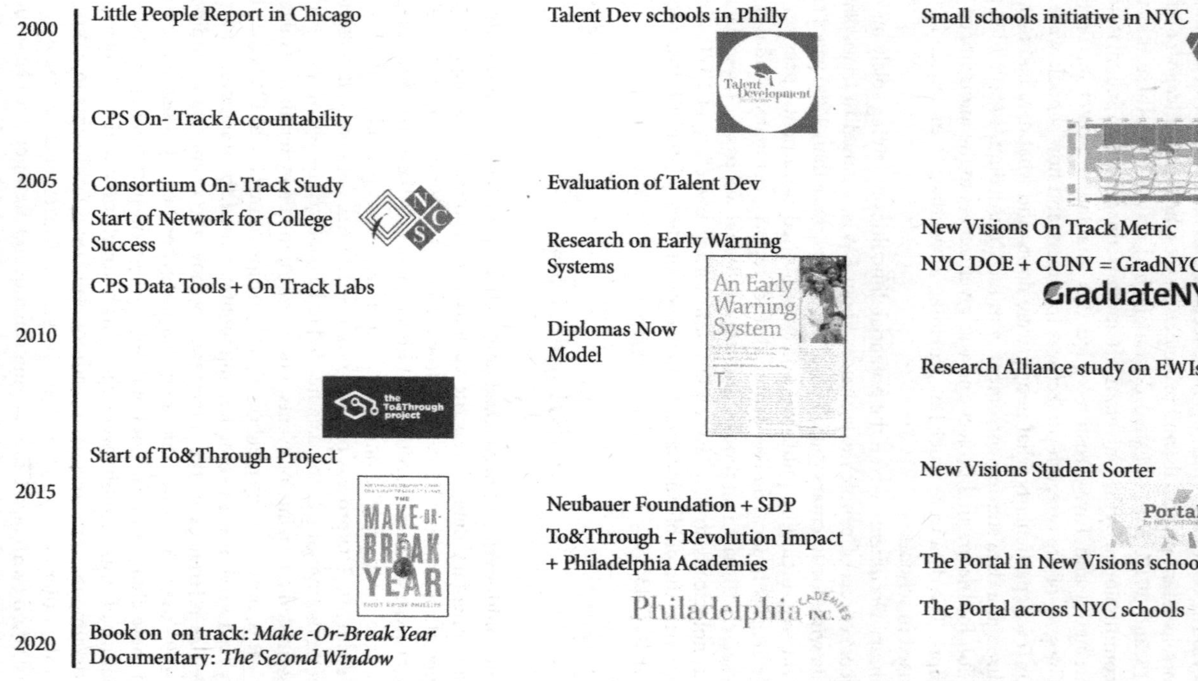


**Figure A.1** Timeline of Early Warning Indicator Development in Chicago, Philadelphia, and New York City

Second, the interview data were analyzed using thematic codes that were sensitive to different institutional dynamics and drawing on institutional theories (e.g., institutional logics, institutional entrepreneurs, interorganizational networks, organizational routines). After reading the transcripts, I created a codebook with large themes regarding changes in EWIs, institutional logics, networks, philanthropy, resistance, and advantages and disadvantages. Under each of these themes were codes regarding their different types, like resistance through ignorance, fear, and double-edged use of data. In creating the codebook, I wrote analytic descriptions and inclusion and exclusion criteria for each code. Once I had these codes set, I trained three undergraduate research assistants to code the data using an online tool called Taguette. Each research assistant had to code a set number of interviews, add codes and descriptions if necessary, check another individual's coding, and bring up any disagreements in meetings. I, too, had coded a number of interviews, and I checked the work of the research assistants. Given the use of an online tool, we could all work on the documents at the same time and we could "call" on a code and to see all the quotes associated with it. I would then use these quotes to weave the narrative and the substantive elements of this research. This systematic method of investigation then led to integrating the story with insight. After seeing the connections of the different themes, I saw the data could be organized according to macro-, meso-, and micro-level perspectives that helped structure the different institutional elements. These coded interviews became the foundation for Chapters 3 to 6.

Third, I used data on interorganizational and interpersonal connections to create exploratory network maps for EWI collaboration. At the interorganizational level, I used data from company websites and documents to show which organizations were connected with which organization. For example, I used website data on funders of the University of Chicago Consortium on School Research, the Network for College Success, and the To&Through Project to show the organizations that funded either or all three organizations (see Figure 4.3, for example). Sometimes, the data on interorganizational connections came from interview informants who mentioned the specific offices to which they were connected, the types of collaborations they had, and the division of labor created. For example, a group working in Philadelphia led by Pranav Kothari mentioned the different offices in the school district they collaborated with and how these organizations related to the nonprofits working outside of it (see Figure 4.4, for example). At the interpersonal level, I created network maps from the interviews, creating a tie whenever an individual mentioned someone they worked with, was supervisor of, or had collaborated with. Although these were not formal network maps in the sense that they were neither extensive nor quantified, they did provide a perspective for seeing the connections across organizations and the templates organizations used in connecting with each other.

Fourth, I used manuscript drafts as a way of starting a dialogue with my informants, inviting them to comment on the quotes attributed to them, to help fact-check the details, and to open conversations about the interpretations. Many individuals to whom I had sent the drafts noted how the draft successfully captured their experience. There were some who requested minor corrections in their quote, either because of the verbatim inclusion of informal words such as "like," "totally," and so on, or because certain quotes sounded more flippant than they intended. Others also corrected certain sections regarding errors of fact, inaccuracy of data, or the potential misinterpretation of readers. For example, one informant mentioned that the words "some officers" may be open to different interpretations and that I should just use "three officers" to be more exact.

I appreciated the opportunity to be corrected. There were cases when the initial document missed something that happened in Philadelphia during the intervening years between the JHU researchers and the Chicago nonprofits. A Philadelphia philanthropic manager pointed this out, and I went back to search for more data on this period. It must be mentioned, however, that none of my informants ever suggested any edits that made a substantive change in the arguments presented in this research. Moreover, I had opportunities to present these data to some of my informants and their organizations, and I have received a warm reception to the ideas I presented. While I had done this aspect of the work to make sure that my research was as accurate and fair as possible, this process also had the latent benefit of fostering trust and goodwill between me and my informants. This is important, particularly in organizational research because one hopes that the relations with these organizations can potentially lead to long-term collaborations.

## Reflections for an Integrative Policy Analysis

This Appendix has provided a sense of how I went about this research and how I suggest going about an integrative policy analysis that can complement and supplement quantitative studies of policy effects, qualitative studies of policy implementation, and critical studies of policy formation. An integrative perspective tries to bring these elements together and highlights the changes that policies can go through. In addition to what I have already written about this set of methods, I also want to write some reflections that might help those who plan similar research studies.

*Caminante, no hay camino, se hace camino al andar.* "Wayfarer, there is no way; the way is made by walking." This is one of my favorite lines from a poem by Antonio Machado. It has taken on a new significance for me as I researched and wrote this book. In some way, I had to create my own path in crafting a study across more than 30 organizations in three cities over a 20-year period. Given that most education research concentrated on actors within the school system, analytic guidance for interviewing K–12 education experts and elites were few and far between. Nonetheless, many generous folks provided ideas like doing comparative studies, creating network graphs, concentrating on the connections across cities, and attending to the spread, instead of the effect, of the policies. To do an integrative policy analysis may likewise entail creating a path for oneself. What I shared here are simply examples and opportunities; researchers could find a path that will lead to more novel ideas and important insights.

*Research is about relationships.* Although most qualitative research anonymizes their informants, this research has gone against the grain by revealing many of the individuals and organizations connected to EWIs. I argue that a researcher should actively decide on whether participants or groups remain anonymous or not. This is particularly salient in organizational research, where anonymity may obscure clarity. In my experience, I have come to appreciate this decision to reveal my participants because I knew I had a "skin in the game." By writing research with people's names in it, I had to go to painstaking lengths to make sure that all details aligned and were consistent. I had to check with multiple people about the facts and the interpretation of those facts. Most importantly, I had to gain trust and goodwill among my informants. I made it a point that my relationship with my informants continued even after our interview. I continued to write them letters updating them on this work and sending them drafts of the research. It was more than just fact-checking; it was a way of keeping a human connection. I've sometimes felt that research can be rather instrumental at times, even extractive. For example, I could just have easily interviewed a group of people, written my paper, and gotten things over with. No follow-ups and no sustained relationship. But, for me, that felt rather exploitative and as if I would be treating my informants only as a means to an end, rather than ends in themselves. And so, I tried my best to keep these relationships that enriched the research, and more importantly, enriched each other's lives.

*An integrative perspective is about clarifying complexity rather than judging a policy.* When I started writing this research, a lot of good and well-meaning individuals asked me if I was trying to discover if EWIs were actually not as good as they are purported to be. After all, so much of the literature on quantification and outside organizations hints at the negative and unintended consequences of efforts to use these technologies. I think it is a disciplinary predisposition in sociology and education to be critical about the policies and practices that claim to support individuals and organizations. However, in the process of research, I saw that the story was not about particular heroes and villains, nor was it about clearly judging whether the programs were effective or not. The story was rather one of different strategies and interactions that experienced success in certain areas, resistance in others, and transformations in many places. To do this type of research is to holistically show the opportunities and tradeoffs that come with new policies. No policy will ever be a silver bullet, but understanding the process of change and its complexity is key to making an honest assessment.

# Bibliography


Aaronson, Daniel, and Bhashkar Mazumder. "The Impact of Rosenwald Schools on Black Achievement." *Journal of Political Economy* 119, no. 5 (October 2011): 821–88. https://doi.org/10.1086/662962.

Abbott, Andrew. *The System of Professions: An Essay on the Division of Expert Labor.* Chicago and London: University of Chicago Press, 1988.

Abrutyn, Seth, and Jonathan H. Turner. "The Old Institutionalism Meets the New Institutionalism." *Sociological Perspectives* 54, no. 3 (September 1, 2011): 283–306. https://doi.org/10.1525/sop.2011.54.3.283.

Adrion, W. Richards, Sarah T. Dunton, Barbara Ericson, Renee Fall, Carol Fletcher, and Mark Guzdial. "U.S. States Must Broaden Participation While Expanding Access to Computer Science Education." *Communications of the ACM* 63, no. 12 (November 17, 2020): 22–25. https://doi.org/10.1145/3430375.

Allensworth, Elaine M. *Graduation and Dropout Trends in Chicago: A Look at Cohorts of Students from 1991 through 2004.* Chicago, IL: Consortium on Chicago School Research, 2005.

Allensworth, Elaine M. "The Use of Ninth-Grade Early Warning Indicators to Improve Chicago Schools." *Journal of Education for Students Placed at Risk (JESPAR)* 18, no. 1 (January 2013): 68–83. https://doi.org/10.1080/10824669.2013.745181.

Allensworth, Elaine M., and John Q. Easton. *The On-Track Indicator as a Predictor of High School Graduation.* Chicago, IL: Consortium on Chicago School Research at the University of Chicago, 2005.

Amin, Ash, and Nigel Thrift. "Neo-Marshallian Nodes in Global Networks." *International Journal of Urban and Regional Research* 16, no. 4 (December 1992): 571–87. https://doi.org/10.1111/j.1468-2427.1992.tb00197.x.

Amin, Reema, and Alex Zimmerman. "NYC's 2021 Graduation Rates Inched up as State Eased Requirements." *Chalkbeat*, February 16, 2022. https://ny.chalkbeat.org/2022/2/16/22937322/bucking-national-trends-nycs-2021-graduation-rates-inched-up-as-state-eased-requirements.

Arthur, James. *Policy Entrepreneurship in Education: Engagement, Influence and Impact.* New York, NY: Routledge, 2017.

Associated Press. "Schools in Chicago Are Called the Worst by Education Chief." *The New York Times*, November 8, 1987, sec. US. https://www.nytimes.com/1987/11/08/us/schools-in-chicago-are-called-the-worst-by-education-chief.html.

Au, Wayne, and Joseph J. Ferrare. *Mapping Corporate Education Reform: Power and Policy Networks in the Neoliberal State.* New York, NY: Routledge, 2015.

Aydarova, Elena. "Shadow Elite of Teacher Education Reforms: Intermediary Organizations' Construction of Accountability Regimes." *Educational Policy* 36, no. 5 (July 1, 2022): 1188–1221. https://doi.org/10.1177/0895904820951121.

Baharav, Hadar, and Laurel Sipes. "Early Warning Indicator Systems in Action: Considerations from Identification to Supports." *Teachers College Record* 122 (2020): 1–24.

Bailey, Drew, Greg J. Duncan, Candice L. Odgers, and Winnie Yu. "Persistence and Fadeout in the Impacts of Child and Adolescent Interventions." *Journal of Research on Educational Effectiveness* 10, no. 1 (2017): 7–39. https://doi.org/10.1080/19345747.2016.1232459.

Baldridge, Bianca J. *Reclaiming Community: Race and the Uncertain Future of Youth Work.* Palo Alto, CA: Stanford University Press, 2019.

Balfanz, Robert, and Vaughan Byrnes. "Early Warning Indicators and Intervention Systems: State of the Field." In *Handbook of Student Engagement Interventions,* 45–55. London, UK: Elsevier, 2019. https://linkinghub.elsevier.com/retrieve/pii/B9780128134139000048.

Balfanz, Robert, and Vaughan Byrnes. "Using Data and the Human Touch: Evaluating the NYC Inter-Agency Campaign to Reduce Chronic Absenteeism." *Journal of Education for Students Placed at Risk* 23, no. 1–2 (April 3, 2018): 107–21. https://doi.org/10.1080/10824669.2018.1435283.

Balfanz, Robert, Liza Herzog, and Douglas J. Mac Iver. "Preventing Student Disengagement and Keeping Students on the Graduation Path in Urban Middle-Grades Schools: Early Identification and Effective Interventions." *Educational Psychologist* 42, no. 4 (November 2, 2007): 223–35. https://doi.org/10.1080/00461520701621079.

Balfanz, Robert, and Nettie Legters. *Locating the Dropout Crisis. Which High Schools Produce the Nation's Dropouts? Where Are They Located? Who Attends Them?* Baltimore, MD: Center for Research on the Education of Students Placed At Risk, Publications Department, 2004. https://eric.ed.gov/?id=ED484525.

Banas, Casey, and Devonda Byers. "Education Chief: City Schools Worst." *Chicago Tribune,* November 8, 1987. https://www.chicagotribune.com/news/ct-xpm-1987-11-08-8703230953-story.html.

Battilana, Julie. "Agency and Institutions: The Enabling Role of Individuals' Social Position." *Organization* 13, no. 5 (September 1, 2006): 653–76. https://doi.org/10.1177/1350508406067008.

Battilana, Julie, Bernard Leca, and Eva Boxenbaum. "How Actors Change Institutions: Towards a Theory of Institutional Entrepreneurship." *Academy of Management Annals* 3, no. 1 (January 2009): 65–107. https://doi.org/10.5465/19416520903053598.

Battin-Pearson, Sara, Michael D. Newcomb, Robert D. Abbott, Karl G. Hill, Richard F. Catalano, and J. David Hawkins. "Predictors of Early High School Dropout: A Test of Five Theories." *Journal of Educational Psychology* 92, no. 3 (2000): 568–82. https://doi.org/10.1037/0022-0663.92.3.568.

Becker, Markus C. "Organizational Routines: A Review of the Literature." *Industrial and Corporate Change* 13, no. 4 (August 1, 2004): 643–78. https://doi.org/10.1093/icc/dth026.

Benjamin, Ruha. *Race After Technology: Abolitionist Tools for the New Jim Code.* Cambridge, UK: Polity Press, 2019.

Berends, Mark. "Sociology and School Choice: What We Know After Two Decades of Charter Schools." *Annual Review of Sociology* 41, no. 1 (2015): 159–80. https://doi.org/10.1146/annurev-soc-073014-112340.

Berman, Elizabeth Popp. *Creating the Market University: How Academic Science Became an Economic Engine.* Princeton, NJ: Princeton University Press, 2012.

Berman, Elizabeth Popp. *Thinking like an Economist: How Efficiency Replaced Equality in U.S. Public Policy.* Princeton, NJ: Princeton University Press, 2022.

Bifulco, Robert, and David J. Schwegman. "Who Benefits from Accountability-Driven School Closure? Evidence from New York City." *Journal of Policy Analysis and Management* 39, no. 1 (2020): 96–130. https://doi.org/10.1002/pam.22140.

Blanchett, Wanda J., Vincent Mumford, and Floyd Beachum. "Urban School Failure and Disproportionality in a Post-Brown Era: Benign Neglect of the Constitutional Rights of Students of Color." *Remedial and Special Education* 26, no. 2 (March 2005): 70–81. https://doi.org/10.1177/07419325050260020201.

Booker, Angela. "Designing for a Productive Politics of Participation in Research Practice Partnerships." *Educational Policy* 37, no. 1 (January 1, 2023): 225–49. https://doi.org/10.1177/08959048221134586.

Brandtner, Christof. "Green American City: Civic Capacity and the Distributed Adoption of Urban Innovations." *American Journal of Sociology* 128, no. 3 (November 2022): 627–79. https://doi.org/10.1086/722965.

Brayne, Sarah. "Big Data Surveillance: The Case of Policing." *American Sociological Review* 82, no. 5 (2017): 977–1008.

Brayne, Sarah. *Predict and Surveil: Data, Discretion, and the Future of Policing.* Oxford, UK: Oxford University Press, 2020.

Brayne, Sarah, and Angèle Christin. "Technologies of Crime Prediction: The Reception of Algorithms in Policing and Criminal Courts." *Social Problems* online first (March 5, 2020): 1–17. https://doi.org/10.1093/socpro/spaa004.

Bridwell-Mitchell, E. N. "Them That's Got? How School Partnerships Can Perpetuate Inequalities." *Phi Delta Kappan* 100, no. 8 (May 1, 2019): 32–36. https://doi.org/10.1177/0031721719846886.

Bridwell-Mitchell, E. N. "Them That's Got: How Tie Formation in Partnership Networks Gives High Schools Differential Access to Social Capital." *American Educational Research Journal* 54, no. 6 (December 1, 2017): 1221–55. https://doi.org/10.3102/0002831217717815.

Bridwell-Mitchell, E. N., James Jack, and Joshua Childs. "The Social Structure of School Resource Disparities: How Social Capital and Interorganizational Relationships Matter for Educational Equity." *Sociology of Education* 96, no. 4 (October 1, 2023): 275–300. https://doi.org/10.1177/00380407231176541.

Brown-Chidsey, Rachel, and Rebekah Bickford. *Practical Handbook of Multi-Tiered Systems of Support: Building Academic and Behavioral Success in Schools.* New York and London: The Guilford Press, 2015.

Bruce, Mary, John M. Bridgeland, Joanna Hornig Fox, and Robert Balfanz. *On Track for Success: The Use of Early Warning Indicator and Intervention Systems to Build a Grad Nation.* Washington, DC: Civic Enterprises, 2011.

Bryk, Anthony S. "2014 AERA Distinguished Lecture: Accelerating How We Learn to Improve." *Educational Researcher* 44, no. 9 (December 1, 2015): 467–77. https://doi.org/10.3102/0013189X15621543.

Bryk, Anthony S. "Organizing Schools for Improvement." *Phi Delta Kappan* 91, no. 7 (April 1, 2010): 23–30. https://doi.org/10.1177/003172171009100705.

Bryk, Anthony S., Louis M. Gomez, and Alicia Grunow. "Getting Ideas into Action: Building Networked Improvement Communities in Education." In *Frontiers in Sociology of Education*, edited by Maureen T. Hallinan, 127–62. Dordrecht: Springer Netherlands, 2011. https://doi.org/10.1007/978-94-007-1576-9_7.

Bryk, Anthony S., Sharon Greenberg, Albert Bertani, Penny Sebring, Steven E. Tozer, and Timothy Knowles. *How a City Learned to Improve Its Schools.* Cambridge, MA: Harvard Education Press, 2023.

Bryk, Anthony S., and Barbara Schneider. *Trust in Schools: A Core Resource for Improvement.* New York, NY: Russell Sage Foundation, 2002.

Bryk, Anthony S., Penny Bender Sebring, David Kerbow, Sharon Rollow, and John Q. Easton. *Charting Chicago School Reform: Democratic Localism as a Lever for Change.* New York, NY: Routledge, 2018.

Bulkley, Katrina E., and Patricia Burch. "The Changing Nature of Private Engagement in Public Education: For-Profit and Nonprofit Organizations and Educational Reform." *Peabody Journal of Education* 86, no. 3 (July 1, 2011): 236–51. https://doi.org/10.1080/0161956X.2011.578963.

Burch, Patricia. *Hidden Markets: The New Education Privatization.* New York, NY: Routledge, 2009.

Burdick-Will, Julia, Jeffrey A. Grigg, Kiara Millay Nerenberg, and Faith Connolly. "Socially-Structured Mobility Networks and School Segregation Dynamics: The Role of Emergent Consideration Sets." *American Sociological Review* 85, no. 4 (August 1, 2020): 675–708. https://doi.org/10.1177/0003122420934739.

Burke, Arthur. *Early Identification of High School Graduation Outcomes in Oregon Leadership Network Schools. REL 2015-079.* Portland, OR: Regional Educational Laboratory at Education Northwest, 2015. https://eric.ed.gov/?id=ED556119.

Bush-Mecenas, Susan. "'The Business of Teaching and Learning': Institutionalizing Equity in Educational Organizations Through Continuous Improvement." *American Educational Research Journal* 59, no. 3 (June 1, 2022): 461–99. https://doi.org/10.3102/00028312221074404.

Campbell, Donald T. "Assessing the Impact of Planned Social Change." *Evaluation and Program Planning* 2, no. 1 (January 1, 1979): 67–90. https://doi.org/10.1016/0149-7189(79)90048-X.

Canales, Rodrigo. "From Ideals to Institutions: Institutional Entrepreneurship and the Growth of Mexican Small Business Finance." *Organization Science* 27, no. 6 (December 2016): 1548–73. https://doi.org/10.1287/orsc.2016.1093.

Canbolat, Yusuf. "Early Warning for Whom? Regression Discontinuity Evidence from the Effect of Early Warning System on Student Absence." *Educational Evaluation and Policy Analysis* online first (February 5, 2024): 1–26. https://doi.org/10.3102/01623737231221503.

Carl, Bradley, Jed T. Richardson, Emily Cheng, HeeJin Kim, and Robert H. Meyer. "Theory and Application of Early Warning Systems for High School and Beyond." *Journal of Education for Students Placed at Risk (JESPAR)* 18, no. 1 (January 2013): 29–49. https://doi.org/10.1080/10824669.2013.745374.

Carnoy, Martin. "Educational Policies in the Face of Globalization." In *The Handbook of Global Education Policy*, edited by Karen Mundy, Andy Green, Bob Lingard, and Antoni Verger, 27–42. John Wiley & Sons, Ltd, 2016. https://doi.org/10.1002/9781118468005.ch1.

Carruthers, Bruce G., and Wendy Nelson Espeland. "Accounting for Rationality: Double-Entry Bookkeeping and the Rhetoric of Economic Rationality." *American Journal of Sociology* 97, no. 1 (July 1991): 31–69. https://doi.org/10.1086/229739.

Caven, Meg. "Quantification, Inequality, and the Contestation of School Closures in Philadelphia." *Sociology of Education* 92, no. 1 (January 1, 2019): 21–40. https://doi.org/10.1177/0038040718815167.

Chicago Public Schools Department of School Quality Measurement and Research. *School Quality Rating Policy (SQRP) Handbook: Guide to the Policy, Indicators, and Ratings*. Chicago, IL: Author, 2019. https://www.cps.edu/globalassets/cps-pages/about-cps/district-data/metrics/school-quality-rating-policy-sqrp/sqrp-handbook.pdf.

Coburn, Cynthia E., Willow S. Mata, and Linda Choi. "The Embeddedness of Teachers' Social Networks: Evidence from a Study of Mathematics Reform." *Sociology of Education* 86, no. 4 (October 1, 2013): 311–42. https://doi.org/10.1177/0038040713501147.

Coburn, Cynthia E., and William R. Penuel. "Research–Practice Partnerships in Education: Outcomes, Dynamics, and Open Questions." *Educational Researcher* 45, no. 1 (January 1, 2016): 48–54. https://doi.org/10.3102/0013189X16631750.

Coburn, Cynthia E., William R. Penuel, and Caitlin C. Farrell. "Fostering Educational Improvement with Research–Practice Partnerships." *Phi Delta Kappan* 102, no. 7 (April 1, 2021): 14–19. https://doi.org/10.1177/00317217211007332.

Coburn, Cynthia E., and Jennifer Lin Russell. "District Policy and Teachers' Social Networks." *Educational Evaluation and Policy Analysis* 30, no. 3 (September 1, 2008): 203–35. https://doi.org/10.3102/0162373708321829.

Cohen, David K., and Jal D. Mehta. "Why Reform Sometimes Succeeds: Understanding the Conditions That Produce Reforms That Last." *American Educational Research Journal* 54, no. 4 (August 1, 2017): 644–90. https://doi.org/10.3102/0002831217700078.

Cohen, David K., and Susan L. Moffitt. *The Ordeal of Equality: Did Federal Regulation Fix the Schools?* Cambridge, MA: Harvard University Press, 2010.

Collins, Briana. "Hundreds of Chicago Public Schools Seniors Begin Their Higher Education Journey at City Colleges of Chicago During 2024 Enrollment Days." *City Colleges of Chicago* (blog), May 17, 2024. https://colleges.ccc.edu/2024/05/

17/hundreds-of-chicago-public-schools-seniors-begin-their-higher-education-journey-at-city-colleges-of-chicago-during-2024-enrollment-days/.

Craig, Tim. "Moms for Liberty Has Turned 'Parental Rights' into a Rallying Cry for Conservative Parents." *Washington Post*, October 15, 2021. https://www.washingtonpost.com/national/moms-for-liberty-parents-rights/2021/10/14/bf3d9ccc-286a-11ec-8831-a31e7b3de188_story.html.

Cullen, Julie Berry, Brian A. Jacob, and Steven D. Levitt. "The Impact of School Choice on Student Outcomes: An Analysis of the Chicago Public Schools." *Journal of Public Economics* 89, no. 5 (June 1, 2005): 729–60. https://doi.org/10.1016/j.jpubeco.2004.05.001.

Daly, Alan J., ed. *Social Network Theory and Educational Change*. Cambridge, MA: Harvard Education Press, 2010.

Davis, Marcia H., Martha Abele Mac Iver, Robert W. Balfanz, Marc L. Stein, and Joanna Hornig Fox. "Implementation of an Early Warning Indicator and Intervention System." *Preventing School Failure: Alternative Education for Children and Youth* 63, no. 1 (January 2, 2019): 77–88. https://doi.org/10.1080/1045988X.2018.1506977.

Davis, Marcia, Liza Herzog, and Nettie Legters. "Organizing Schools to Address Early Warning Indicators (EWIs): Common Practices and Challenges." *Journal of Education for Students Placed at Risk (JESPAR)* 18, no. 1 (January 1, 2013): 84–100. https://doi.org/10.1080/10824669.2013.745210.

DeBray, Elizabeth, Johanna Hanley, Janelle Scott, and Christopher Lubienski. "Money and Influence: Philanthropies, Intermediary Organisations, and Atlanta's 2017 School Board Election." *Journal of Educational Administration and History* 52, no. 1 (January 2, 2020): 63–79. https://doi.org/10.1080/00220620.2019.1689103.

Dee, Thomas S., and Brian Jacob. "The Impact of No Child Left Behind on Student Achievement." *Journal of Policy Analysis and Management* 30, no. 3 (2011): 418–46. https://doi.org/10.1002/pam.20586.

#DegreesNYC. "About #DegreesNYC." #DegreesNYC, 2022. https://www.degreesnyc.org/about.

DeSanto, Barbara. "Moms Demand Action: Using Public Relations to Combat Gun Violence." In *Public Relations Cases*, Danny Moss, Barbara DeSanto, 16–23. New York City: Routledge, 2022.

Deussen, Theresa, Havala Hanson, and Biraj Bisht. *Are Two Commonly Used Early Warning Indicators Accurate Predictors of Dropout for English Learner Students? Evidence from Six Districts in Washington State. REL 2017-261*. Washington, DC: Regional Educational Laboratory Northwest, 2017. https://eric.ed.gov/?id=ED573197.

Diamond, John B. "Accountability Policy, School Organization, and Classroom Practice: Partial Recoupling and Educational Opportunity." *Education and Urban Society* 44, no. 2 (March 1, 2012): 151–82. https://doi.org/10.1177/0013124511431569.

Diamond, John B., and James P. Spillane. "High-Stakes Accountability in Urban Elementary Schools: Challenging or Reproducing Inequality." *Teachers College Record*, 2004, 1145–76.

DiMaggio, Paul J. "Interest and Agency in Institutional Theory." In *Institutional Patterns and Organization*, edited by L. Zuker, 3–22. Cambridge, MA: Ballinger, 1988.

DiMaggio, Paul J., and Walter W. Powell. "The Iron Cage Revisited: Institutional Isomorphism and Collective Rationality in Organizational Fields." *American Sociological Review* 48, no. 2 (1983): 147–60. https://doi.org/10.2307/2095101.

Dunn, Mary B., and Candace Jones. "Institutional Logics and Institutional Pluralism: The Contestation of Care and Science Logics in Medical Education, 1967–2005." *Administrative Science Quarterly* 55, no. 1 (March 1, 2010): 114–49. https://doi.org/10.2189/asqu.2010.55.1.114.

Eddy, Carrie, and Julia Ballenger. "The Effectiveness of an Online Credit Recovery Program on Improving the Graduation Rates of Students at Risk of School Failure." *School Leadership Review* 11, no. 1 (2016): 34–46.

Eddy-Spicer, David, Paula Arce-Trigatti, and Michelle D. Young. "Field Building through Strategic Bricolage: System Leadership and the Institutionalizing Role of Intermediary Organizations." *Journal of Professional Capital and Community* 6, no. 1 (January 1, 2020): 29–43. https://doi.org/10.1108/JPCC-11-2019-0032.

Erichsen, Kristen, and John Reynolds. "Public School Accountability, Workplace Culture, and Teacher Morale." *Social Science Research* 85 (January 1, 2020). https://doi.org/10.1016/j.ssresearch.2019.102347.

Espeland, Wendy Nelson, and Mitchell L. Stevens. "A Sociology of Quantification." *European Journal of Sociology* 49, no. 3 (2008): 401–36.

Everson, Kimberlee C. "Value-Added Modeling and Educational Accountability: Are We Answering the Real Questions?" *Review of Educational Research* 87, no. 1 (February 1, 2017): 35–70. https://doi.org/10.3102/0034654316637199.

Ewing, Eve L. *Ghosts in the Schoolyard: Racism and School Closings on Chicago's South Side*. Chicago and London: University of Chicago Press, 2020.

Fairchild, Susan, Gerard Carrino, Brad Gunton, Chris Soderquist, Andrew Hsiao, Beverly Donohue, and Timothy Farrell. *Student Progress to Graduation in New York City High Schools. Part II. Student Achievement as Stock and Flow: Reimagining Early Warning Systems for At-Risk Students*. New York, NY: New Visions for Public Schools, 2012.

Fairchild, Susan, Brad Gunton, Beverly Donohue, Carolyn Berry, Ruth Genn, and Jessica Knevals. *Student Progress to Graduation in New York City High Schools: A Metric Designed by New Visions for Public Schools*. New York, NY: New Visions for Public Schools, 2011.

Faria, Ann-Marie, Nicholas Sorensen, Jessica Heppen, Jill Bowdon, Suzanne Taylor, Ryan Eisner, and Shandu Foster. *Getting Students on Track for Graduation: Impacts of the Early Warning Intervention and Monitoring System after One Year*. Washington, DC: US Department of Education, Institute of Education Sciences, National Center for Education Evaluation and Regional Assistance, Regional Educational Laboratory Midwest, 2017.

Farrell, Caitlin C., William R. Penuel, Cynthia E. Coburn, Julia Daniel, and Louisa Steup. *Research–Practice Partnerships in Education: The State of the Field*. New York, NY: William T. Grant Foundation, 2021.

Feathers, Todd. "How Wisconsin Uses Race and Income to Label Students 'High Risk.'" *Chalkbeat*, April 27, 2023. https://www.chalkbeat.org/2023/4/27/23699361/dropout-early-warning-system-dews-student-dropouts-race-income-data.

Feathers, Todd. "This Dropout Warning System Flags 'High-Risk' Students. The False Alarms Might Hurt Them Instead." *Chalkbeat*, April 27, 2023. https://www.chalkbeat.org/2023/4/27/23699361/dropout-early-warning-system-dews-student-dropouts-race-income-data.

Feldman, Martha S., Luciana D'Adderio, Katharina Dittrich, and Paula Jarzabkowski. "Introduction: Routine Dynamics in Action." In *Routine Dynamics in Action: Replication and Transformation*, edited by Martha S. Feldman, Luciana D'Aderio, Katharina Dittrich, and Paula Jarzabkowski, 61:1–10. Leeds, UK: Emerald Publishing Limited, 2019. https://doi.org/10.1108/S0733-558X20190000061001.

Feldman, Martha S., and Brian T. Pentland. "Reconceptualizing Organizational Routines as a Source of Flexibility and Change." *Administrative Science Quarterly* 48, no. 1 (March 1, 2003): 94–118. https://doi.org/10.2307/3556620.

Ferrare, Joseph J., and R. Renee Setari. "Converging on Choice: The Interstate Flow of Foundation Dollars to Charter School Organizations." *Educational Researcher* 47, no. 1 (January 1, 2018): 34–45. https://doi.org/10.3102/0013189X17736524.

Fien, Hank, David J. Chard, and Scott K. Baker. "Can the Evidence Revolution and Multi-Tiered Systems of Support Improve Education Equity and Reading Achievement?" *Reading Research Quarterly* 56, no. S1 (2021): S105–18. https://doi.org/10.1002/rrq.391.

Figlio, David N., and Susanna Loeb. "Chapter 8: School Accountability." In *Handbook of the Economics of Education*, edited by Eric A. Hanushek, Stephen Machin, and Ludger Woessmann, 3:383–421. Elsevier, 2011.

Fligstein, Neil. "Social Skill and the Theory of Fields." *Sociological Theory* 19, no. 2 (July 1, 2001): 105–25. https://doi.org/10.1111/0735-2751.00132.

Frank, Kenneth A., Yong Zhao, and Kathryn Borman. "Social Capital and the Diffusion of Innovations Within Organizations: The Case of Computer Technology in Schools." *Sociology of Education* 77, no. 2 (April 1, 2004): 148–71. https://doi.org/10.1177/003804070407700203.

Frazelle, Sarah, and Aisling Nagel. *A Practitioner's Guide to Implementing Early Warning Systems*. Washington, DC: US Department of Education, Institute of Education Sciences, National Center for Education Evaluation and Regional Assistance, Regional Educational Laboratory Northwest, 2015.

Frey, William H. *2020 Census: Big Cities Grew and Became More Diverse, Especially among Their Youth*. Washington, DC: Brookings Institution, 2021. https://www.brookings.edu/research/2020-census-big-cities-grew-and-became-more-diverse-especially-among-their-youth/.

Friedland, Roger, and Robert R. Alford. "Bringing Society Back In: Symbols, Practices, and Institutional Contradictions." In *The New Institutionalism in Organizational Analysis*, edited by Walter W. Powell and Paul J. DiMaggio, 232–63. Chicago and London: University of Chicago Press, 1991. https://cir.nii.ac.jp/crid/1573105975595180032.

Fruchter, Norm. "New York City's Affinity District (Part 1): What Is It?" New York University, June 16, 2020. https://steinhardt.nyu.edu/news/new-york-citys-affinity-district-part-1-what-it.

Fuller, Bruce. *When Schools Work: Pluralist Politics and Institutional Reform in Los Angeles.* Baltimore, MD: Johns Hopkins University Press, 2022.

Fusarelli, Lance D. "Tightly Coupled Policy in Loosely Coupled Systems: Institutional Capacity and Organizational Change." *Journal of Educational Administration* 40, no. 6 (January 1, 2002): 561–75. https://doi.org/10.1108/09578230210446045.

Gates, Bill. "On the Right Track in Chicago." gatesnotes.com, 2019. https://www.gatesnotes.com/Education/On-the-right-track-in-Chicago.

Gill, Brian, Ron Zimmer, Jolley Christman, and Suzanne Blanc. "State Takeover, School Restructuring, Private Management, and Student Achievement in Philadelphia." Santa Monica, CA: RAND Corporation, January 22, 2007. https://www.rand.org/pubs/monographs/MG533.html.

Gillborn, David, Paul Warmington, and Sean Demack. "QuantCrit: Education, Policy, 'Big Data' and Principles for a Critical Race Theory of Statistics." *Race Ethnicity and Education* 21, no. 2 (March 4, 2018): 158–79. https://doi.org/10.1080/13613324.2017.1377417.

Glazer, Joshua, and Donald J. Peurach. "School Improvement Networks as a Strategy for Large-Scale Education Reform: The Role of Educational Environments." *Educational Policy* 27 (July 1, 2013): 676–710. https://doi.org/10.1177/0895904811429283.

Glazerman, Steven, Daniel Mayer, and Paul Decker. "Alternative Routes to Teaching: The Impacts of Teach for America on Student Achievement and Other Outcomes." *Journal of Policy Analysis and Management* 25, no. 1 (2006): 75–96. https://doi.org/10.1002/pam.20157.

Golann, Joanne W. *Scripting the Moves: Culture and Control in a "No-Excuses" Charter School.* Princeton, NJ: Princeton University Press, 2021.

Goren, Paul. "Data, Data, and More Data—What's an Educator to Do?" *American Journal of Education* 118, no. 2 (February 2012): 233–37. https://doi.org/10.1086/663273.

Graham, Kristen A. "1 in 3 Philly Students Doesn't Graduate on Time. To Fix That, High Schools Focus on Freshmen." *The Philadelphia Inquirer*, May 18, 2018. https://www.inquirer.com/philly/education/1-in-3-philly-students-doesnt-graduate-on-time-to-fix-that-high-schools-focus-on-freshmen-20180521.html.

Grayson, Jessica L., and Heather K. Alvarez. "School Climate Factors Relating to Teacher Burnout: A Mediator Model." *Teaching and Teacher Education* 24, no. 5 (July 1, 2008): 1349–63. https://doi.org/10.1016/j.tate.2007.06.005.

Griffen, Zachary, and Aaron Panofsky. "Ambivalent Economizations: The Case of Value Added Modeling in Teacher Evaluation." *Theory and Society* 50, no. 3 (April 1, 2021): 515–39. https://doi.org/10.1007/s11186-020-09417-x.

Gwynne, Julia, Joy Lesnick, Holly M. Hart, and Elaine M. Allensworth. *What Matters for Staying On-Track and Graduating in Chicago Public Schools: A Focus on Students with Disabilities. Research Report.* Chicago, IL: Consortium on Chicago School Research, 2009. https://eric.ed.gov/?id=ED507419.

Gwynne, Julia, Amber Stitziel Pareja, Stacy B. Ehrlich, and Elaine M. Allensworth. *What Matters for Staying On-Track and Graduating in Chicago Public Schools: A Focus on English Language Learners. Research Report.* Chicago, IL: Consortium on Chicago School Research, 2012. https://eric.ed.gov/?id=ED532513.

Haber, Jaren R. "Sorting Schools: A Computational Analysis of Charter School Identities and Stratification." *Sociology of Education* 94, no. 1 (January 1, 2021): 43–64. https://doi.org/10.1177/0038040720953218.

Hallett, Tim. "The Myth Incarnate: Recoupling Processes, Turmoil, and Inhabited Institutions in an Urban Elementary School." *American Sociological Review* 75, no. 1 (February 1, 2010): 52–74. https://doi.org/10.1177/0003122409357044.

Hallett, Tim, and Amelia Hawbaker. "The Case for an Inhabited Institutionalism in Organizational Research: Interaction, Coupling, and Change Reconsidered." *Theory and Society* 50, no. 1 (January 2021): 1–32. https://doi.org/10.1007/s11186-020-09412-2.

Hallett, Tim, and Marc J. Ventresca. "Inhabited Institutions: Social Interactions and Organizational Forms in Gouldner's Patterns of Industrial Bureaucracy." *Theory and Society* 35, no. 2 (April 2006): 213–36. https://doi.org/10.1007/s11186-006-9003-z.

Handsman, Emily, Caitlin Farrell, and Cynthia Coburn. "Solving for X: Constructing Algebra and Algebra Policy During a Time of Change." *Sociology of Education online first* (2022): 1–17.

Hannan, Michael T., and John Freeman. "Structural Inertia and Organizational Change." *American Sociological Review* 49, no. 2 (1984): 149–64. https://doi.org/10.2307/2095567.

Hansen, John. *Information as Intervention: Effects of an Early Warning System.* Cambridge, MA: Center for Education Policy Research at Harvard University, 2018.

Hanushek, Eric A. "Testing, Accountability, and the American Economy." *The ANNALS of the American Academy of Political and Social Science* 683, no. 1 (May 1, 2019): 110–28. https://doi.org/10.1177/0002716219841299.

Harris, Donna M. "Postscript: Urban Schools, Accountability, and Equity: Insights Regarding NCLB and Reform." *Education and Urban Society* 44, no. 2 (March 1, 2012): 203–10. https://doi.org/10.1177/0013124511431571.

Harris, Douglas N. *Charter School City: What the End of Traditional Public Schools in New Orleans Means for American Education.* Chicago and London: University of Chicago Press, 2020.

Harris, Douglas N., Lihan Liu, Nathan Barrett, and Ruoxi Li. "Is the Rise in High School Graduation Rates Real? High-Stakes School Accountability and Strategic Behavior." *Labour Economics* 82 (June 1, 2023): 1–16. https://doi.org/10.1016/j.labeco.2023.102355.

Haveman, Heather A. *The Power of Organizations: A New Approach to Organizational Theory.* Princeton, NJ: Princeton University Press, 2022.

Haveman, Heather A., and Gillian Gualtieri. "Institutional Logics." In *Oxford Research Encyclopedia of Business and Management.* Oxford University Press, 2017. http://business.oxfordre.com/view/10.1093/acrefore/9780190224851.001.0001/acrefore-9780190224851-e-137.

Henry, Kimberly L., Kelly E. Knight, and Terence P. Thornberry. "School Disengagement as a Predictor of Dropout, Delinquency, and Problem Substance Use During Adolescence and Early Adulthood." *Journal of Youth and Adolescence* 41, no. 2 (February 2012): 156–66. https://doi.org/10.1007/s10964-011-9665-3.

Heppen, Jessica B., and Susan Bowles Therriault. *Developing Early Warning Systems to Identify Potential High School Dropouts. Issue Brief.* Washington, DC: National High School Center, American Institutes of Research, 2008. https://eric.ed.gov/?id=ED521558.

Herlihy, Corinne M., and James J. Kemple. *The Talent Development Middle School Model: Context, Components, and Initial Impacts on Students' Performance and Attendance.* New York, NY: MDRC, 2004.

Hess, Frederick M. *Spinning Wheels: The Politics of Urban School Reform.* Washington, DC: Brookings Institution Press, 2011.

Hess, Frederick M., and Jeffrey R. Henig. *The New Education Philanthropy: Politics, Policy, and Reform. Educational Innovations Series.* Harvard Education Press, 2015.

Hess, Frederick M., and Michael B. Horn. *Private Enterprise and Public Education.* New York, NY: Teachers College Press, 2015.

Hibel, Jacob, and Daphne M. Penn. "Bad Apples or Bad Orchards? An Organizational Analysis of Educator Cheating on Standardized Accountability Tests." *Sociology of Education* 93, no. 4 (October 1, 2020): 331–52. https://doi.org/10.1177/0038040720927234.

Honig, Meredith I. "The New Middle Management: Intermediary Organizations in Education Policy Implementation." *Educational Evaluation and Policy Analysis* 26, no. 1 (March 1, 2004): 65–87. https://doi.org/10.3102/01623737026001065.

Horsford, Sonya Douglass, Janelle T. Scott, and Gary L. Anderson. *The Politics of Education Policy in an Era of Inequality: Possibilities for Democratic Schooling.* New York, NY: Routledge, 2018.

Howell, William G., ed. *Besieged: School Boards and the Future of Education Politics.* Washington, DC: Brookings Institution Press, 2005.

Hursh, David. "Assessing No Child Left Behind and the Rise of Neoliberal Education Policies." *American Educational Research Journal* 44, no. 3 (September 1, 2007): 493–518. https://doi.org/10.3102/0002831207306764.

Hursh, David. "The Growth of High-Stakes Testing in the USA: Accountability, Markets and the Decline in Educational Equality." *British Educational Research Journal* 31, no. 5 (2005): 605–22. https://doi.org/10.1080/01411920500240767.

InfluenceWatch. "Moms Demand Action for Gun Sense." *InfluenceWatch*, 2023. https://www.influencewatch.org/organization/moms-demand-action-for-gun-sense/.

Ingersoll, Richard M., and Gregory J. Collins. "Accountability and Control in American Schools." *Journal of Curriculum Studies* 49, no. 1 (February 2017): 75–95. https://doi.org/10.1080/00220272.2016.1205142.

Jabbar, Huriya, Marisa Cannata, Emily Germain, and Andrene Castro. "It's Who You Know: The Role of Social Networks in a Changing Labor Market." *American Educational Research Journal* 57, no. 4 (August 1, 2020): 1485–1524. https://doi.org/10.3102/0002831219879092.

Jacob, Brian A. "Accountability, Incentives and Behavior: The Impact of High-Stakes Testing in the Chicago Public Schools." *Journal of Public Economics* 89, no. 5 (June 1, 2005): 761–96. https://doi.org/10.1016/j.jpubeco.2004.08.004.

Jacob, Brian A., and Steven D. Levitt. "Rotten Apples: An Investigation of the Prevalence and Predictors of Teacher Cheating." *Quarterly Journal of Economics* 118, no. 3 (August 1, 2003): 843–77. https://doi.org/10.1162/00335530360698441.

Jacobs, Richard M. "U.S. Catholic Schools and the Religious Who Served in Them: Contributions in the 18th and 19th Centuries." *Journal of Catholic Education* 1, no. 4 (June 1, 1998): 364–83. https://doi.org/10.15365/joce.0104022013.

Jahnukainen, Markku, and Tiina Itkonen. "Tiered Intervention: History and Trends in Finland and the United States." *European Journal of Special Needs Education* 31, no. 1 (January 2, 2016): 140–50. https://doi.org/10.1080/08856257.2015.1108042.

Jennings, Jennifer L. "Below the Bubble: 'Educational Triage' and the Texas Accountability System." *American Educational Research Journal* 42, no. 2 (January 1, 2005): 231–68. https://doi.org/10.3102/00028312042002231.

Jennings, Jennifer L., and Jonathan Marc Bearak. "'Teaching to the Test' in the NCLB Era: How Test Predictability Affects Our Understanding of Student Performance." *Educational Researcher* 43, no. 8 (November 1, 2014): 381–89. https://doi.org/10.3102/0013189X14554449.

Keels, Micere, Julia Burdick-Will, and Sara Keene. "The Effects of Gentrification on Neighborhood Public Schools." *City & Community* 12, no. 3 (September 1, 2013): 238–59. https://doi.org/10.1111/cico.12027.

Keltner, Brent R. *Funding Comprehensive School Reform*. Santa Barbara, CA: RAND Corporation, 1998. https://www.rand.org/pubs/issue_papers/IP175.html.

Kemple, James J., Corinne M. Herlihy, and Thomas J. Smith. *Making Progress Toward Graduation: Evidence from the Talent Development High School Model*. New York, NY: MDRC, 2005.

Kemple, James J., Micha D. Segeritz, and Nickisha Stephenson. "Building On-Track Indicators for High School Graduation and College Readiness: Evidence from New York City." *Journal of Education for Students Placed at Risk (JESPAR)* 18, no. 1 (January 2013): 7–28. https://doi.org/10.1080/10824669.2013.747945.

Kim, Robert. "Under the Law: 'Anti-Critical Race Theory' Laws and the Assault on Pedagogy." *Phi Delta Kappan* 103, no. 1 (September 1, 2021): 64–65. https://doi.org/10.1177/00317217211043637.

King, Brayden G., Elisabeth S. Clemens, and Melissa Fry. "Identity Realization and Organizational Forms: Differentiation and Consolidation of Identities Among Arizona's Charter Schools." *Organization Science* 22, no. 3 (June 1, 2011): 554–72. https://doi.org/10.1287/orsc.1100.0548.

Kingkade, Tyler, Brandy Zadrozny, and Ben Collins. "Critical Race Theory Battle Invades School Boards—with Help from Conservative Groups." *NBC News*, June 15, 2021. https://www.nbcnews.com/news/us-news/critical-race-theory-invades-school-boards-help-conservative-groups-n1270794.

Knudson, Joel, and Mark Garibaldi. *None of Us Are as Good as All of Us: Early Lessons From the CORE Districts*. Washington, DC: American Institutes for Research, 2015.

Koedel, Cory, Kata Mihaly, and Jonah E. Rockoff. "Value-Added Modeling: A Review." *Economics of Education Review* 47 (August 1, 2015): 180–95. https://doi.org/10.1016/j.econedurev.2015.01.006.

Kretchmar, Kerry, Beth Sondel, and Joseph J. Ferrare. "Mapping the Terrain: Teach For America, Charter School Reform, and Corporate Sponsorship." *Journal of Education Policy* 29, no. 6 (November 2, 2014): 742–59. https://doi.org/10.1080/02680939.2014.880812.

Kretchmar, Kerry, Beth Sondel, and Joseph J. Ferrare. "The Power of the Network: Teach For America's Impact on the Deregulation of Teacher Education." *Educational Policy* 32, no. 3 (May 1, 2018): 423–53. https://doi.org/10.1177/0895904816637687.

Kroezen, Jochem J., and Pursey P. M. A. R. Heugens. "What Is Dead May Never Die: Institutional Regeneration through Logic Reemergence in Dutch Beer Brewing." *Administrative Science Quarterly* 64, no. 4 (December 1, 2019): 976–1019. https://doi.org/10.1177/0001839218817520.

La Londe, Priya G., T. Jameson Brewer, and Christopher A. Lubienski. "Teach For America and Teach for All: Creating an Intermediary Organization Network for Global Education Reform." *Education Policy Analysis Archives* 23, no. 47 (April 20, 2015). https://eric.ed.gov/?id=EJ1070361.

Labaree, David. "Teach For America and Teacher Ed: Heads They Win, Tails We Lose." *Journal of Teacher Education* 61, no. 1–2 (January 1, 2010): 48–55. https://doi.org/10.1177/0022487109347317.

Lankford, Hamilton, Susanna Loeb, and James Wyckoff. "Teacher Sorting and the Plight of Urban Schools: A Descriptive Analysis." *Educational Evaluation and Policy Analysis* 24, no. 1 (March 1, 2002): 37–62. https://doi.org/10.3102/01623737024001037.

Lee, Valerie E., and David T. Burkam. "Dropping Out of High School: The Role of School Organization and Structure." *American Educational Research Journal* 40, no. 2 (January 1, 2003): 353–93. https://doi.org/10.3102/00028312040002353.

Lessard, Anne, Lynn Butler-Kisber, Laurier Fortin, Diane Marcotte, Pierre Potvin, and Égide Royer. "Shades of Disengagement: High School Dropouts Speak Out." *Social Psychology of Education* 11, no. 1 (February 1, 2008): 25–42. https://doi.org/10.1007/s11218-007-9033-z.

Lortie, Dan C. *Schoolteacher: A Sociological Study*. Chicago, IL: University of Chicago Press, 1975.

Loughran, Kevin. "The Philadelphia Negro and the Canon of Classical Urban Theory." *Du Bois Review: Social Science Research on Race* 12, no. 2 (2015): 249–67. https://doi.org/10.1017/S1742058X15000132.

Lounsbury, Michael, Christopher W. J. Steele, Milo Shaoqing Wang, and Madeline Toubiana. "New Directions in the Study of Institutional Logics: From Tools to Phenomena." *Annual Review of Sociology* 47, no. 1 (2021): 261–80. https://doi.org/10.1146/annurev-soc-090320-111734.

Lubienski, Christopher, Miri Yemini, and Claire Maxwell, eds. *The Rise of External Actors in Education: Shifting Boundaries Globally and Locally*. Bristol: Bristol University Press, 2022.

Luo, Jiao, Jia Chen, and Dongjie Chen. "Coming Back and Giving Back: Transposition, Institutional Actors, and the Paradox of Peripheral Influence." *Administrative Science Quarterly* 66, no. 1 (March 1, 2021): 133–76. https://doi.org/10.1177/0001839220929736.

Lusardo, Lonnie. "Moms for Liberty Spreads Its Anti-LGBTQ+ Hatred to the Northwest." *The Seattle Times*, June 13, 2023. https://www.seattletimes.com/opinion/moms-for-liberty-spreads-its-anti-lgbtq-hatred-to-the-northwest/.

Mac Iver, Martha Abele. "Early Warning Indicators of High School Outcomes." *Journal of Education for Students Placed at Risk (JESPAR)* 18, no. 1 (January 2013): 1–6. https://doi.org/10.1080/10824669.2013.745375.

Mac Iver, Martha Abele, and Matthew Messel. "The ABCs of Keeping On Track to Graduation: Research Findings from Baltimore." *Journal of Education for Students Placed at Risk (JESPAR)* 18, no. 1 (January 2013): 50–67. https://doi.org/10.1080/10824669.2013.745207.

Mac Iver, Martha Abele, Marc L. Stein, Marcia H. Davis, Robert W. Balfanz, and Joanna Hornig Fox. "An Efficacy Study of a Ninth-Grade Early Warning Indicator Intervention." *Journal of Research on Educational Effectiveness* 12, no. 3 (July 3, 2019): 363–90. https://doi.org/10.1080/19345747.2019.1615156.

Maguire, Steve, Cynthia Hardy, and Thomas B. Lawrence. "Institutional Entrepreneurship in Emerging Fields: HIV/AIDS Treatment Advocacy in Canada." *Academy of Management Journal* 47, no. 5 (2004): 657–79. https://doi.org/10.2307/20159610.

Malinen, Olli-Pekka, and Hannu Savolainen. "The Effect of Perceived School Climate and Teacher Efficacy in Behavior Management on Job Satisfaction and Burnout: A Longitudinal Study." *Teaching and Teacher Education* 60 (November 1, 2016): 144–52. https://doi.org/10.1016/j.tate.2016.08.012.

Marsh, Julie A., Taylor N. Allbright, Danica R. Brown, Katrina E. Bulkley, Katharine O. Strunk, and Douglas N. Harris. "The Process and Politics of Educational Governance Change in New Orleans, Los Angeles, and Denver." *American Educational Research Journal* 58, no. 1 (February 1, 2021): 107–59. https://doi.org/10.3102/0002831220921475.

Martin, John Levi. "What Is Field Theory?" *American Journal of Sociology* 109, no. 1 (July 2003): 1–49. https://doi.org/10.1086/375201.

McKenzie, Kathryn Bell, and James Joseph Scheurich. "Teacher Resistance to Improvement of Schools with Diverse Students." *International Journal of Leadership in Education* 11, no. 2 (April 1, 2008): 117–33. https://doi.org/10.1080/13603120801950122.

McMahon, Brian M., and Sabrina F. Sembiante. "Re-Envisioning the Purpose of Early Warning Systems: Shifting the Mindset from Student Identification to Meaningful Prediction and Intervention." *Review of Education* 8, no. 1 (2020): 266–301. https://doi.org/10.1002/rev3.3183.

Mehta, Jal. "How Paradigms Create Politics: The Transformation of American Educational Policy, 1980–2001." *American Educational Research Journal* 50, no. 2 (April 1, 2013): 285–324. https://doi.org/10.3102/0002831212471417.

Mennicken, Andrea, and Wendy Nelson Espeland. "What's New with Numbers? Sociological Approaches to the Study of Quantification." *Annual Review of Sociology* 45, no. 1 (2019): 223–45. https://doi.org/10.1146/annurev-soc-073117-041343.

Meyer, John W. "The Effects of Education as an Institution." *American Journal of Sociology* 83, no. 1 (July 1977): 55–77. https://doi.org/10.1086/226506.

Meyer, John W., and Brian Rowan. "Institutionalized Organizations: Formal Structure as Myth and Ceremony." *American Journal of Sociology* 83, no. 2 (1977): 340–63. https://doi.org/10.1086/226550.

Miller, Shazia Rafiullah, and Elaine M. Allensworth. "Progress and Problems: Student Performance in CPS High Schools, 1993 to 2000." In *Reforming Chicago's High Schools: Research Perspectives on School and System Level Change*, edited by Valerie E. Lee, 51–84. Chicago, IL: Consortium on Chicago School Research, 2002.

Miller, Shazia Rafiullah, Stuart Luppescu, Robert M. Gladden, and John Q. Easton. *How Do Barton Graduates Perform in CPS High Schools?* Chicago: Consortium on Chicago School Research, 1999.

Mintrom, Michael. "Policy Entrepreneurs and the Diffusion of Innovation." *American Journal of Political Science* 41, no. 3 (1997): 738–70. https://doi.org/10.2307/2111674.

Miskel, Cecil, and Mengli Song. "Passing Reading First: Prominence and Processes in an Elite Policy Network." *Educational Evaluation and Policy Analysis* 26, no. 2 (June 1, 2004): 89–109. https://doi.org/10.3102/01623737026002089.

Moeller, Eliza, and Alex Seeskin. "Practice-Driven Data: Lessons from Chicago's Approach to Research, Data, and Practice in Education." *Teachers College Record* 122, no. 14 (2020): 1–30.

Moeller, Eliza, Alex Seeskin, and Jenny Nagaoka. *Practice-Driven Data: Lessons from Chicago's Approach to Research, Data, and Practice in Education*. Chicago, IL: UChicago Consortium on School Research, 2018.

Monarrez, Tomás, Brian Kisida, and Matthew Chingos. "The Effect of Charter Schools on School Segregation." *American Economic Journal: Economic Policy* 14, no. 1 (February 1, 2022): 301–40. https://doi.org/10.1257/pol.20190682.

Morel, Richard Paquin, and Cynthia Coburn. "Access, Activation, and Influence: How Brokers Mediate Social Capital Among Professional Development Providers." *American Educational Research Journal* 56, no. 2 (April 2019): 247–88. https://doi.org/10.3102/0002831218788528.

Munir, Kamal A., and Nelson Phillips. "The Birth of the 'Kodak Moment': Institutional Entrepreneurship and the Adoption of New Technologies." *Organization Studies* 26, no. 11 (November 1, 2005): 1665–87. https://doi.org/10.1177/0170840605056395.

Murray, Brittany, Thurston Domina, Linda Renzulli, and Rebecca Boylan. "Civil Society Goes to School: Parent–Teacher Associations and the Equality of Educational Opportunity." *The Russell Sage Foundation Journal of the Social Sciences* 5, no. 3 (2019): 41. https://doi.org/10.7758/rsf.2019.5.3.03.

Nagaoka, Jenny, Alex Seeskin, and Vanessa M Coca. *The Educational Attainment of Chicago Public Schools Students: 2016*. Chicago, IL: University of Chicago Consortium on School Research, 2016.

National Center for Education Statistics. "Digest of Education Statistics, 2020." National Center for Education Statistics, 2020. https://nces.ed.gov/programs/digest/d20/tables/dt20_215.30.asp.

National Center for Education Statistics. "Public Charter School Enrollment." In *Condition of Education*. Washington, DC: US Department of Education, Institute of Education Sciences, 2023. https://nces.ed.gov/programs/coe/indicator/cgb.

Neal, Derek A., and Diane Whitmore Schanzenbach. "Left Behind by Design: Proficiency Counts and Test-Based Accountability." *Review of Economics and Statistics* 92, no. 2 (February 17, 2010): 263–83. https://doi.org/10.1162/rest.2010.12318.

Neild, Ruth Curran, and Robert Balfanz. *Unfulfilled Promise: The Dimensions and Characteristics of Philadelphia's Dropout Crisis, 2000–2005*. Philadelphia, PA: Philadelphia Youth Network, 2006.

Neild, Ruth Curran, Robert Balfanz, and Liza Herzog. "An Early Warning System." *Educational Leadership* 1 (2007), 28–33.

Neild, Ruth Curran, Scott Stoner-Eby, and Frank Furstenberg. "Connecting Entrance and Departure: The Transition to Ninth Grade and High School Dropout." *Education and Urban Society* 40, no. 5 (July 1, 2008): 543–69. https://doi.org/10.1177/0013124508316438.

Neill, Monty. "The Testing Resistance and Reform Movement." *Monthly Review* 67, no. 10 (March 2, 2016): 8–28. https://doi.org/10.14452/MR-067-10-2016-03_2.

Nelson, Ashlyn Aiko, and Beth Gazley. "The Rise of School-Supporting Nonprofits." *Education Finance and Policy* 9, no. 4 (2014): 541–66.

Nelson, Richard R., and Sidney G. Winter. *An Evolutionary Theory of Economic Change*. Cambridge, MA: Harvard University Press, 1982.

New Visions for Public Schools. "The Portal by New Visions." New Visions for Public Schools, 2022. https://portal.newvisions.org/.

Newman, Maria. "Graduation Rate Declines to Lowest in Eight Years." *The New York Times*, December 30, 1994, sec. New York. https://www.nytimes.com/1994/12/30/nyregion/graduation-rate-declines-to-lowest-in-eight-years.html.

Noguera, Pedro. *City Schools and the American Dream: Reclaiming the Promise of Public Education*. New York and London: Teachers College Press, 2003.

Oberfield, Zachary W. *Are Charters Different?: Public Education, Teachers, and the Charter School Debate*. Cambridge, MA: Harvard Education Press, 2017.

O'Neil, Cathy. *Weapons of Math Destruction: How Big Data Increases Inequality and Threatens Democracy*. New York, NY: Crown, 2016.

Orton, J. Douglas, and Karl E. Weick. "Loosely Coupled Systems: A Reconceptualization." *Academy of Management Review* 15, no. 2 (1990): 203–23. https://doi.org/10.2307/258154.

Patterson, Orlando. "Making Sense of Culture." *Annual Review of Sociology* 40, no. 1 (July 30, 2014): 1–30. https://doi.org/10.1146/annurev-soc-071913-043123.

Payne, Charles M. "Claim No Easy Victories: Some Notes toward a Fearless Sociology of Education." In *Education in a New Society: Renewing the Sociology of Education*, edited by Jal Mehta and Scott Davies, 387–406. Chicago and London: University of Chicago Press, 2018.

Payne, Charles M. *So Much Reform, So Little Change: The Persistence of Failure in Urban Schools.* Cambridge, MA: Harvard Education Press, 2008.

Penuel, William, Robbin Riedy, Michael Barber, Donald Peurach, Whitney LeBouef, and Tiffany Clark. "Principles of Collaborative Education Research with Stakeholders: Toward Requirements for a New Research and Development Infrastructure." *Review of Educational Research* 90 (July 3, 2020): 1–48. https://doi.org/10.3102/0034654320938126.

Perdomo, Juan C., Tolani Britton, Moritz Hardt, and Rediet Abebe. "Difficult Lessons on Social Prediction from Wisconsin Public Schools." *arXiv*, April 12, 2023. https://doi.org/10.48550/arXiv.2304.06205.

Peurach, Donald J. "Innovating at the Nexus of Impact and Improvement: Leading Educational Improvement Networks." *Educational Researcher* 45, no. 7 (October 1, 2016): 421–29. https://doi.org/10.3102/0013189X16670898.

Peurach, Donald J. *Seeing Complexity in Public Education: Problems, Possibilities, and Success for All.* New York, NY: Oxford University Press, 2011.

Peurach, Donald J., and Joshua L. Glazer. "Reconsidering Replication: New Perspectives on Large-Scale School Improvement." *Journal of Educational Change* 13, no. 2 (May 2012): 155–90. https://doi.org/10.1007/s10833-011-9177-7.

Phillips, Emily Krone. *The Make-or-Break Year: Solving the Dropout Crisis One Ninth Grader at a Time.* New York, NY: The New Press, 2019.

Phillips, Meredith, Kyo Yamashiro, Adina Farrukh, Cynthia Lim, Katherine Hayes, Nicole Wagner, Jeffrey White, and Hansheng Chen. "Using Research to Improve College Readiness: A Research Partnership Between the Los Angeles Unified School District and the Los Angeles Education Research Institute." *Journal of Education for Students Placed at Risk* 20, no. 1–2 (2015): 141–68. https://doi.org/10.1080/10824669.2014.990562.

Pierson, Paul. *Politics in Time: History, Institutions, and Social Analysis.* Princeton, NJ: Princeton University Press, 2004. https://www.degruyter.com/document/doi/10.1515/9781400841080/html.

Pileggi, Molly, Lindsey Liu, and Alyn Turner. *Back On Track: How Off-Track Ninth Graders Progressed in Later Years of High School, Class of 2017 and 2018.* Philadelphia, PA: Philadelphia Education Research Consortium, 2020.

Pinkus, Lyndsay. *Using Early-Warning Data to Improve Graduation Rates: Closing Cracks in the Education System.* Washington, DC: Alliance for Excellent Education, 2008.

Porter, Theodore M. *Trust in Numbers: The Pursuit of Objectivity in Science and Public Life.* Princeton, NJ: Princeton University Press, 1996.

Powell, Walter W. "Neither Market nor Hierarchy: Network Forms of Organization." *Research in Organizational Behavior* 12 (1990): 295–336.

Powell, Walter W., and Elisabeth S. Clemens. *Private Action and the Public Good.* New Haven, CT: Yale University Press, 1998.

Prasad, Monica. "Problem-Solving Sociology." *Contemporary Sociology: A Journal of Reviews* 47, no. 4 (July 2018): 393–98. https://doi.org/10.1177/0094306118779810.

Putnam, Robert D. *Bowling Alone: The Collapse and Revival of American Community.* New York, NY: Simon and Schuster, 2000.

Pylvainen, Helena. *2020–21 High School Graduation Rates in Philadelphia*. Philadelphia, PA: School District of Philadelphia Office of Research and Evaluation, 2022.

Quinn, Rand, Megan Tompkins-Stange, and Debra Meyerson. "Beyond Grantmaking: Philanthropic Foundations as Agents of Change and Institutional Entrepreneurs." *Nonprofit and Voluntary Sector Quarterly* 43, no. 6 (December 1, 2014): 950–68. https://doi.org/10.1177/0899764013488836.

Rao, Hayagreeva. *Market Rebels: How Activists Make or Break Radical Innovations*. Princeton, NJ: Princeton University Press, 2008.

Rao, Hayagreeva, Philippe Monin, and Rodolphe Durand. "Institutional Change in Toque Ville: Nouvelle Cuisine as an Identity Movement in French Gastronomy." *American Journal of Sociology* 108 (January 1, 2003): 795–843. https://doi.org/10.1086/367917.

Ravitch, Diane. *The Death and Life of the Great American School System: How Testing and Choice Are Undermining Education*. New York, NY: Basic Books, 2016.

Ravitch, Diane. *Reign of Error: The Hoax of the Privatization Movement and the Danger to America's Public Schools*. New York, NY: Vintage Books, 2014.

Raymond, Margaret E., and Eric A. Hanushek. "High-Stakes Research: The Campaign against Accountability Has Brought Forth a Tide of Negative Anecdotes and Deeply Flawed Research. Solid Analysis Reveals a Brighter Picture." *Education Next* 3, no. 3 (June 22, 2003): 48–56.

Reay, Trish, and C.R. Hinings. "Managing the Rivalry of Competing Institutional Logics." *Organization Studies* 30, no. 6 (June 1, 2009): 629–52. https://doi.org/10.1177/0170840609104803.

Reckhow, Sarah. *Follow the Money: How Foundation Dollars Change Public School Politics*. Oxford, UK: Oxford University Press, 2013.

Reckhow, Sarah, and Jeffrey W. Snyder. "The Expanding Role of Philanthropy in Education Politics." *Educational Researcher* 43, no. 4 (May 1, 2014): 186–95. https://doi.org/10.3102/0013189X14536607.

Reich, Rob. *Just Giving: Why Philanthropy Is Failing Democracy and How It Can Do Better*. Princeton, NJ: Princeton University Press, 2018.

Reikosky, Nora. "Pipeline Philanthropy: Understanding Philanthropic Corporate Action in Education During the COVID-19 Era and Beyond." *Educational Policy* online first (April 18, 2023): 1–31. https://doi.org/10.1177/08959048231163802.

Renzulli, Linda A. "Organizational Environments and the Emergence of Charter Schools in the United States." *Sociology of Education* 78, no. 1 (January 1, 2005): 1–26. https://doi.org/10.1177/003804070507800101.

Rerup, Claus, and Martha S. Feldman. "Routines as a Source of Change in Organizational Schemata: The Role of Trial-and-Error Learning." *Academy of Management Journal* 54, no. 3 (June 2011): 577–610. https://doi.org/10.5465/amj.2011.61968107.

Research Alliance for New York City Schools. "How Have NYC's High School Graduation and College Enrollment Rates Changed Over Time?," 2018. https://steinhardt.nyu.edu/research-alliance/research/spotlight-nyc-schools/how-have-nycs-high-school-graduation-and-college.

Research Alliance for New York City Schools. "Projects | Supporting the #DegreesNYC Data Co-Op and Learning Network | NYU Steinhardt." NYU Steinhardt, 2021. https://steinhardt.nyu.edu/research-alliance/research/projects/supporting-degreesnyc-data-co-op-and-learning-network.

Roderick, Melissa, and Eric Camburn. "Risk and Recovery from Course Failure in the Early Years of High School." *American Educational Research Journal* 36, no. 2 (January 1, 1999): 303–43. https://doi.org/10.3102/00028312036002303.

Roderick, Melissa, Vanessa Coca, and Jenny Nagaoka. "Potholes on the Road to College: High School Effects in Shaping Urban Students' Participation in College Application, Four-Year College Enrollment, and College Match." *Sociology of Education* 84, no. 3 (July 1, 2011): 178–211. https://doi.org/10.1177/0038040711411280.

Roderick, Melissa, and John Q. Easton. *Developing New Roles for Research in New Policy Environments: The Consortium on Chicago School Research.* Chicago, IL: University of Chicago, 2007.

Roderick, Melissa, John Q. Easton, and Penny Bender Sebring. *The Consortium on Chicago School Research: A New Model for the Role of Research in Supporting Urban School Reform.* Chicago, IL: Consortium on Chicago School Research, 2009. https://eric.ed.gov/?id=ED505883.

Roderick, Melissa, Thomas Kelley-Kemple, David W. Johnson, and Nicole O. Beechum. *Preventable Failure: Improvements in Long-Term Outcomes When High Schools Focused on the Ninth Grade Year. Research Summary.* Chicago, IL: University of Chicago Consortium on Chicago School Research, 2014. https://eric.ed.gov/?id=ED553174.

Roderick, Melissa, Jenny Nagaoka, and Vanessa Coca. "College Readiness for All: The Challenge for Urban High Schools." *The Future of Children* 19, no. 1 (2009): 185–210.

Rouse, Cecilia Elena, Jane Hannaway, Dan Goldhaber, and David N. Figlio. "Feeling the Florida Heat? How Low-Performing Schools Respond to Voucher and Accountability Pressure." *American Economic Journal: Economic Policy* 5, no. 2 (May 2013): 251–81. https://doi.org/10.1257/pol.5.2.251.

Rowan, Brian. "Does the School Improvement 'Industry' (Organizations Providing Schools and Governing Agencies with Information, Training, Materials, and Programmatic Resources Relevant to Instructional Improvement Problems) Help or Prevent Deep and Sound Change?" *Journal of Educational Change* 9, no. 2 (June 2008): 197–202. https://doi.org/10.1007/s10833-007-9062-6.

Rowan, Brian. "The Ecology of School Improvement: Notes on the School Improvement Industry in the United States." *Journal of Educational Change* 3 (2002): 283–314.

Russakoff, Dale. *The Prize: Who's in Charge of America's Schools?* New York, NY: Houghton Mifflin Harcourt, 2015.

Safransky, Sara. "Geographies of Algorithmic Violence: Redlining the Smart City." *International Journal of Urban and Regional Research* 44, no. 2 (March 2020): 200–18. https://doi.org/10.1111/1468-2427.12833.

Saltman, Kenneth J. *The Gift of Education: Public Education and Venture Philanthropy.* New York, NY: Palgrave MacMillan, 2010.

Sarafidou, Jasmin-Olga, and Georgios Chatziioannidis. "Teacher Participation in Decision Making and Its Impact on School and Teachers." *International Journal of Educational Management* 27, no. 2 (January 1, 2013): 170–83. https://doi.org/10.1108/09513541311297586.

Schildkamp, Kim, Cindy L. Poortman, and Pasi Sahlberg. "Data-Based Decision Making in Developing Countries: Balancing Accountability Measures and Improvement Efforts." *Journal of Professional Capital and Community* 4, no. 3 (January 1, 2019): 166–71. https://doi.org/10.1108/JPCC-07-2019-037.

Schildkamp, Kim, Cindy Poortman, Hans Luyten, and Johanna Ebbeler. "Factors Promoting and Hindering Data-Based Decision Making in Schools." *School Effectiveness and School Improvement* 28, no. 2 (April 3, 2017): 242–58. https://doi.org/10.1080/09243453.2016.1256901.

Schneiberg, Marc, and Elisabeth S. Clemens. "The Typical Tools for the Job: Research Strategies in Institutional Analysis*." *Sociological Theory* 24, no. 3 (2006): 195–227. https://doi.org/10.1111/j.1467-9558.2006.00288.x.

Schoen, LaTefy, and Lance D. Fusarelli. "Innovation, NCLB, and the Fear Factor: The Challenge of Leading 21st-Century Schools in an Era of Accountability." *Educational Policy* 22, no. 1 (January 1, 2008): 181–203. https://doi.org/10.1177/0895904807311291.

Schoff, Frederic. "The National Congress of Mothers and Parent–Teacher Associations." *The ANNALS of the American Academy of Political and Social Science* 67, no. 1 (September 1, 1916): 139–47. https://doi.org/10.1177/000271621606700119.

School District of Philadelphia. "Fast Facts—The School District of Philadelphia," 2024. https://www.philasd.org/fast-facts/.

Scott, Janelle. "The Politics of Venture Philanthropy in Charter School Policy and Advocacy." *Educational Policy* 23, no. 1 (January 1, 2009): 106–36. https://doi.org/10.1177/0895904808328531.

Scott, Janelle, Elizabeth DeBray, Christopher Lubienski, Priya Goel La Londe, Elise Castillo, and Stephen Owens. "Urban Regimes, Intermediary Organization Networks, and Research Use: Patterns Across Three School Districts." *Peabody Journal of Education* 92, no. 1 (January 2017): 16–28. https://doi.org/10.1080/0161956X.2016.1264800.

Scott, Janelle, and Huriya Jabbar. "The Hub and the Spokes: Foundations, Intermediary Organizations, Incentivist Reforms, and the Politics of Research Evidence." *Educational Policy* 28, no. 2 (March 1, 2014): 233–57. https://doi.org/10.1177/0895904813515327.

Scott, Janelle, Christopher Lubienski, and Elizabeth DeBray-Pelot. "The Politics of Advocacy in Education." *Educational Policy* 23, no. 1 (January 1, 2009): 3–14. https://doi.org/10.1177/0895904808328530.

Scott, W. Richard, Martin Ruef, Peter J. Mendel, and Carol A. Caronna. *Institutional Change and Healthcare Organizations: From Professional Dominance to Managed Care*. Chicago and London: University of Chicago Press, 2000.

Shapiro, Aaron. "Predictive Policing for Reform? Indeterminacy and Intervention in Big Data Policing." *Surveillance & Society* 17, no. 3/4 (September 7, 2019): 456–72. https://doi.org/10.24908/ss.v17i3/4.10410.

Shen, Jianping, Xingyuan Gao, and Jiangang Xia. "School as a Loosely Coupled Organization? An Empirical Examination Using National SASS 2003–04 Data." *Educational Management Administration & Leadership* 45, no. 4 (July 1, 2017): 657–81. https://doi.org/10.1177/1741143216628533.

Shen-Berro, Julian. "NYC Graduation Rates Remained Essentially Flat in 2023." *Chalkbeat*, March 21, 2024. https://www.chalkbeat.org/newyork/2024/03/21/nyc-graduation-rates-dipped-slightly-last-year/.

Sherer, Jennifer Zoltners, and James P. Spillane. "Constancy and Change in Work Practice in Schools: The Role of Organizational Routines." *Teachers College Record* 113, no. 3 (March 1, 2011): 611–57. https://doi.org/10.1177/016146811111300302.

Silver, David, Marisa Saunders, and Estela Zarate. *What Factors Predict High School Graduation in the Los Angeles Unified School District: California Dropout Research Project Report.* Santa Barbara, CA: University of California Santa Barbara, 2008.

Slaughter, Austin, Ruth Curran Neild, and Molly Crofton. *Ready From the Start: Identifying and Supporting At-Risk Ninth Graders from Their Earliest Days in High School.* Philadelphia, PA: Philadelphia Education Research Consortium, 2018. https://www.aera.net/Publications/Online-Paper-Repository/AERA-Online-Paper-Repository-Viewer/ID/1439900.

Smith, Neil. "New Globalism, New Urbanism: Gentrification as Global Urban Strategy." *Antipode* 34, no. 3 (June 2002): 427–50. https://doi.org/10.1111/1467-8330.00249.

Song, Mengli, and Cecil G. Miskel. "Who Are the Influentials? A Cross-State Social Network Analysis of the Reading Policy Domain." *Educational Administration Quarterly* 41, no. 1 (February 1, 2005): 7–48. https://doi.org/10.1177/0013161X04269515.

Sparks, Sarah D. "Most Schools Have Early-Warning Systems. Some Kids Are Still Getting Lost." Education Week, February 27, 2024, sec. Leadership, School & District Management. https://www.edweek.org/leadership/most-schools-have-early-warning-systems-how-well-do-they-work/2024/02.

Spillane, James P., Naomi L. Blaushild, Christine M. Neumerski, Jennifer L. Seelig, and Donald J. Peurach. "Striving for Coherence, Struggling with Incoherence: A Comparative Study of Six Educational Systems Organizing for Instruction." *Educational Evaluation and Policy Analysis* 44, no. 4 (December 1, 2022): 567–92. https://doi.org/10.3102/01623737221093382.

Spillane, James P., Leigh Mesler Parise, and Jennifer Zoltners Sherer. "Organizational Routines as Coupling Mechanisms: Policy, School Administration, and the Technical Core." *American Educational Research Journal* 48, no. 3 (June 1, 2011): 586–619. https://doi.org/10.3102/0002831210385102.

Spitzmueller, Matthew C. "Remaking 'Community' Mental Health: Contested Institutional Logics and Organizational Change." *Human Service Organizations: Management, Leadership & Governance* 42, no. 2 (March 15, 2018): 123–45. https://doi.org/10.1080/23303131.2017.1422071.

Steffes, Tracy L. *School, Society, and State: A New Education to Govern Modern America, 1890–1940.* Chicago and London: University of Chicago Press, 2011.

Stid, Daniel, Kate O'Neill, and Susan Colby. "Portland Public Schools: From Data and Decisions to Implementation and Results on Dropout Prevention." Boston, MA: Bridgespan Group, January 2009. https://eric.ed.gov/?id=ED535867.

Stuit, David, Mindee O'Cummings, Heather Norbury, Jessica Heppen, Sonica Dhillon, Jim Lindsay, and Bo Zhu. *Identifying Early Warning Indicators in Three Ohio School Districts. REL 2016-118.* Washington, DC: Regional Educational Laboratory Midwest, 2016. https://eric.ed.gov/?id=ED566958.

Swartz, Tracy. "CPS Touts Record-High Graduation Rate, Record-Low Dropout Rate." *Chicago Tribune*, October 21, 2021. https://www.chicagotribune.com/news/breaking/ct-chicago-schools-graduation-dropout-rates-20211021-2u3liqwlzre4pchcbh6tvpni64-story.html.

Terhart, Ewald. "Teacher Resistance against School Reform: Reflecting an Inconvenient Truth." *School Leadership & Management* 33, no. 5 (November 1, 2013): 486–500. https://doi.org/10.1080/13632434.2013.793494.

The GRAD Partnership. "Organizing Partners, The GRAD Partnership." *The GRAD Partnership* (blog), 2023. https://www.gradpartnership.org/partners/.

The GRAD Partnership. "Student Success Systems." *The GRAD Partnership* (blog), 2023. https://www.gradpartnership.org/student-success-systems/.

Thiner, Andrea Jean. "Minnesota Early Indicator and Response System Impact on Graduation Rates: An Analysis of an Early Warning Intervention and Monitoring Systems in an Alternative Learning Center." Thesis, North Dakota State University, 2021. https://library.ndsu.edu/ir/handle/10365/31987.

Thornton, Patricia H. *Markets from Culture: Institutional Logics and Organizational Decisions in Higher Education Publishing.* Palo Alto, CA: Stanford University Press, 2004.

Thornton, Patricia H., William Ocasio, and Michael Lounsbury. *The Institutional Logics Perspective: A New Approach to Culture, Structure and Process.* Oxford, UK: Oxford University Press, 2012. https://oxford.universitypressscholarship.com/10.1093/acprof:oso/9780199601936.001.0001/acprof-9780199601936.

Tocqueville, Alexis de. *Democracy in America.* New York, NY: G. Dearborn & Co., 1838. https://www.gutenberg.org/ebooks/815.

Tompkins-Stange, Megan E. *Policy Patrons: Philanthropy, Education Reform, and the Politics of Influence.* Cambridge, MA: Harvard Education Press, 2016.

Tong, Tong, Shelby Leigh Smith, Michael Fienberg, and Adam Kho. "Charter Schools: An Alternative Option in American Schooling." *Encyclopedia* 3, no. 1 (March 2023): 362–70. https://doi.org/10.3390/encyclopedia3010022.

Tracey, Paul, Nelson Phillips, and Owen Jarvis. "Bridging Institutional Entrepreneurship and the Creation of New Organizational Forms: A Multilevel Model." *Organization Science* 22, no. 1 (February 2011): 60–80. https://doi.org/10.1287/orsc.1090.0522.

Trinidad, Jose Eos. "Material Resources, School Climate, and Achievement Variations in the Philippines: Insights from PISA 2018." *International Journal of Educational Development* 75 (May 1, 2020): 1–9. https://doi.org/10.1016/j.ijedudev.2020.102174.

Trinidad, Jose Eos. "Meaning-Making, Negotiation, and Change in School Accountability, Or What Sociology Can Offer Policy Studies." *Sociological Inquiry* online first (2022): 1–26. https://doi.org/10.1111/soin.12485.

Trinidad, Jose Eos. "Rethinking School Improvement Organizations: Understanding Their Variety, Benefits, Risks, and Future Directions." *Educational Researcher* online first (June 12, 2023): 1–8. https://doi.org/10.3102/0013189X231179116.

Trinidad, Jose Eos. "Teacher Response Process to Bureaucratic Control: Individual and Group Dynamics Influencing Teacher Responses." *Leadership and Policy in Schools* 18, no. 4 (October 2, 2019): 533–43. https://doi.org/10.1080/15700763.2018.1475573.

Trujillo, Tina. "The Modern Cult of Efficiency: Intermediary Organizations and the New Scientific Management." *Educational Policy* 28, no. 2 (March 1, 2014): 207–32. https://doi.org/10.1177/0895904813513148.

Trujillo, Tina, Janelle Scott, and Marialena Rivera. "Follow the Yellow Brick Road: Teach For America and the Making of Educational Leaders." *American Journal of Education* 123, no. 3 (May 2017): 353–91. https://doi.org/10.1086/691232.

Tsoukas, Haridimos, and Robert Chia. "On Organizational Becoming: Rethinking Organizational Change." *Organization Science* 13, no. 5 (October 2002): 567–82. https://doi.org/10.1287/orsc.13.5.567.7810.

Turnbull, Barbara. "Teacher Participation and Buy-in: Implications for School Reform Initiatives." *Learning Environments Research* 5, no. 3 (October 1, 2002): 235–52. https://doi.org/10.1023/A:1021981622041.

United Way of Greater Philadelphia and Southern New Jersey. "United Way and Philadelphia Education Fund Boost Academic Success for Philadelphia Students." Cision, October 29, 2014. https://www.prnewswire.com/news-releases/united-way-and-philadelphia-education-fund-boost-academic-success-for-philadelphia-students-280771892.html.

US Department of Education. *Issue Brief: Early Warning Systems.* Washington, DC: US Department of Education, Office of Planning, Evaluation, and Policy Development (Policy and Program Studies Service), 2016.

Useem, Elizabeth, Ruth Curran Neild, and William Morrison. *Philadelphia's Talent Development High Schools: Second-Year Results, 2000–01.* Philadelphia, PA: Philadelphia Education Fund, 2001.

Weick, Karl E. "Educational Organizations as Loosely Coupled Systems." *Administrative Science Quarterly* 21, no. 1 (1976): 1–19. https://doi.org/10.2307/2391875.

Wentworth, Laura, and Jenny Nagaoka. "Early Warning Indicators in Education: Innovations, Uses, and Optimal Conditions for Effectiveness." *Teachers College Record* 122, no. 14 (2020): 1–22.

Whitford, Denise K., Dake Zhang, and Antonis Katsiyannis. "Traditional vs. Alternative Teacher Preparation Programs: A Meta-Analysis." *Journal of Child and Family Studies* 27, no. 3 (March 1, 2018): 671–85. https://doi.org/10.1007/s10826-017-0932-0.

Williams, Paige. "The Right-Wing Mothers Fuelling the School-Board Wars." *Annals of Education* 1 (2022): 1–17.

Wolf, Verena, and Daniel Beverungen. "Conceptualizing the Impact of Workarounds—An Organizational Routines' Perspective." In *Proceedings of the 27th European Conference on Information Systems (ECIS)*. Stockholm-Uppsala, Sweden, 2019. https://ris.uni-paderborn.de/record/9676.

Woulfin, Sarah L., and Jessica G. Rigby. "Coaching for Coherence: How Instructional Coaches Lead Change in the Evaluation Era." *Educational Researcher* 46, no. 6 (August 1, 2017): 323–28. https://doi.org/10.3102/0013189X17725525.

Woulfin, Sarah L., Isobel Stevenson, and Kerry Lord. *Making Coaching Matter: Leading Continuous Improvement in Schools.* New York, NY: Teachers College Press, 2023.

Woyshner, Christine. "Black Parent–Teacher Associations and the Origins of the National Congress of Colored Parents and Teachers, 1896–1926," April 2000. https://eric.ed.gov/?id=ED442722.

Yi, Sangyoon, Thorbjørn Knudsen, and Markus C. Becker. "Inertia in Routines: A Hidden Source of Organizational Variation." *Organization Science* 27, no. 3 (June 2016): 782–800. https://doi.org/10.1287/orsc.2016.1059.

Young, Viki M. "Teachers' Use of Data: Loose Coupling, Agenda Setting, and Team Norms." *American Journal of Education* 112, no. 4 (August 2006): 521–48. https://doi.org/10.1086/505058.

Zald, Mayer N., and Michael Lounsbury. "The Wizards of Oz: Towards an Institutional Approach to Elites, Expertise and Command Posts." *Organization Studies* 31, no. 7 (July 1, 2010): 963–96. https://doi.org/10.1177/0170840610373201.

Zhao, Yong, and Kenneth A. Frank. "Factors Affecting Technology Uses in Schools: An Ecological Perspective." *American Educational Research Journal* 40, no. 4 (January 1, 2003): 807–40. https://doi.org/10.3102/00028312040004807.

Zimmerman, Alex. "DOE Backs Off Plan to Overhaul How 164 Schools Are Supervised." *The City*, July 22, 2020. https://www.thecity.nyc/2020/7/21/21333583/doe-backing-off-plan-to-overhaul-how-affinity-schools-are-supervised.

# Notes

## Inroduction

1. Robert Balfanz and Nettie Legters, *Locating the Dropout Crisis. Which High Schools Produce the Nation's Dropouts? Where Are They Located? Who Attends Them?* (Baltimore, MD: Center for Research on the Education of Students Placed At Risk, Publications Department, 2004), https://eric.ed.gov/?id=ED484525.
2. Douglas N. Harris et al., "Is the Rise in High School Graduation Rates Real? High-Stakes School Accountability and Strategic Behavior," *Labour Economics* 82 (June 1, 2023): 1–16, https://doi.org/10.1016/j.labeco.2023.102355.
3. Elaine M. Allensworth, *Graduation and Dropout Trends in Chicago: A Look at Cohorts of Students from 1991 through 2004* (Chicago, IL: Consortium on Chicago School Research, 2005); Briana Collins, "Hundreds of Chicago Public Schools Seniors Begin Their Higher Education Journey at City Colleges of Chicago During 2024 Enrollment Days," *City Colleges of Chicago* (blog), May 17, 2024, https://colleges.ccc.edu/2024/05/17/hundreds-of-chicago-public-schools-seniors-begin-their-higher-education-journey-at-city-colleges-of-chicago-during-2024-enrollment-days/; Tracy Swartz, "CPS Touts Record-High Graduation Rate, Record-Low Dropout Rate," *Chicago Tribune*, October 21, 2021, https://www.chicagotribune.com/news/breaking/ct-chicago-schools-graduation-dropout-rates-20211021-2u3liqwlzre4pchcbh6tvpni64-story.html.
4. Ruth Curran Neild and Robert Balfanz, *Unfulfilled Promise: The Dimensions and Characteristics of Philadelphia's Dropout Crisis, 2000–2005* (Philadelphia, PA: Philadelphia Youth Network, 2006); Helena Pylvainen, *2020–21 High School Graduation Rates in Philadelphia* (Philadelphia, PA: School District of Philadelphia Office of Research and Evaluation, 2022); School District of Philadelphia, "Fast Facts—The School District of Philadelphia," 2024, https://www.philasd.org/fast-facts/.
5. Research Alliance for New York City Schools, "How Have NYC's High School Graduation and College Enrollment Rates Changed Over Time?," 2018, https://steinhardt.nyu.edu/research-alliance/research/spotlight-nyc-schools/how-have-nycs-high-school-graduation-and-college; Reema Amin and Alex Zimmerman, "NYC's 2021 Graduation Rates Inched up as State Eased Requirements," Chalkbeat New York, February 16, 2022, https://ny.chalkbeat.org/2022/2/16/22937322/bucking-national-trends-nycs-2021-graduation-rates-inched-up-as-state-eased-requirements; Julian Shen-Berro, "NYC Graduation Rates Remained Essentially Flat in 2023," *Chalkbeat*, March 21, 2024, https://www.chalkbeat.org/newyork/2024/03/21/nyc-graduation-rates-dipped-slightly-last-year/.
6. Wanda J. Blanchett, Vincent Mumford, and Floyd Beachum, "Urban School Failure and Disproportionality in a Post-Brown Era: Benign Neglect of the Constitutional Rights of Students of Color," *Remedial and Special Education* 26, no. 2 (March 2005): 70–81, https://doi.org/10.1177/07419325050260020201; Frederick M. Hess, *Spinning Wheels: The Politics of Urban School Reform* (Washington, DC: Brookings Institution Press, 2011).
7. Carrie Eddy and Julia Ballenger, "The Effectiveness of an Online Credit Recovery Program on Improving the Graduation Rates of Students at Risk of School Failure," *School Leadership Review* 11, no. 1 (2016): 34–46.
8. Jennifer L. Jennings, "Below the Bubble: 'Educational Triage' and the Texas Accountability System," *American Educational Research Journal* 42, no. 2 (January 1, 2005): 231–68, https://doi.org/10.3102/00028312042002231.
9. Harris et al., "Is the Rise in High School Graduation Rates Real?" 15.
10. Charles M. Payne, "Claim No Easy Victories: Some Notes toward a Fearless Sociology of Education," in *Education in a New Society: Renewing the Sociology of Education*, ed. Jal Mehta and Scott Davies (Chicago and London: University of Chicago Press, 2018), 398–99.

11. Shazia Rafiullah Miller and Elaine M. Allensworth, "Progress and Problems: Student Performance in CPS High Schools, 1993 to 2000," in *Reforming Chicago's High Schools: Research Perspectives on School and System Level Change*, ed. Valerie E. Lee (Chicago, IL: Consortium on Chicago School Research, 2002); Ruth Curran Neild, Robert Balfanz, and Liza Herzog, "An Early Warning System," *Educational Leadership*, 2007, 28–33.
12. Martha Abele Mac Iver and Matthew Messel, "The ABCs of Keeping On Track to Graduation: Research Findings from Baltimore," *Journal of Education for Students Placed at Risk (JESPAR)* 18, no. 1 (January 2013): 50–67, https://doi.org/10.1080/10824669.2013.745207; Laura Wentworth and Jenny Nagaoka, "Early Warning Indicators in Education: Innovations, Uses, and Optimal Conditions for Effectiveness," *Teachers College Record* 122, no. 14 (2020): 1–22.
13. Elaine M. Allensworth, "The Use of Ninth-Grade Early Warning Indicators to Improve Chicago Schools," *Journal of Education for Students Placed at Risk (JESPAR)* 18, no. 1 (January 2013): 68–83, https://doi.org/10.1080/10824669.2013.745181; Robert Balfanz and Vaughan Byrnes, "Early Warning Indicators and Intervention Systems: State of the Field," in *Handbook of Student Engagement Interventions* (London, UK: Elsevier, 2019), 45–55, https://linkinghub.elsevier.com/retrieve/pii/B9780128134139000048.
14. Martin Carnoy, "Educational Policies in the Face of Globalization," in *The Handbook of Global Education Policy* (John Wiley & Sons, Ltd, 2016), 27–42, https://doi.org/10.1002/9781118468005.ch1; John B. Diamond, "Accountability Policy, School Organization, and Classroom Practice: Partial Recoupling and Educational Opportunity," *Education and Urban Society* 44, no. 2 (March 1, 2012): 151–82, https://doi.org/10.1177/0013124511431569; David N. Figlio and Susanna Loeb, "Chapter 8—School Accountability," in *Handbook of the Economics of Education*, ed. Eric A. Hanushek, Stephen Machin, and Ludger Woessmann, vol. 3 (Elsevier, 2011), 383–421; John B. Diamond and James P. Spillane, "High-Stakes Accountability in Urban Elementary Schools: Challenging or Reproducing Inequality," *The Teachers College Record*, 2004, 1145–76.
15. Martha Abele Mac Iver et al., "An Efficacy Study of a Ninth-Grade Early Warning Indicator Intervention," *Journal of Research on Educational Effectiveness* 12, no. 3 (July 3, 2019): 363–90, https://doi.org/10.1080/19345747.2019.1615156; John Hansen, "Information as Intervention: Effects of an Early Warning System" (Cambridge, MA: Center for Education Policy Research at Harvard University, 2018); Juan C. Perdomo et al., "Difficult Lessons on Social Prediction from Wisconsin Public Schools" (arXiv, April 12, 2023), https://doi.org/10.48550/arXiv.2304.06205.
16. Marcia Davis, Liza Herzog, and Nettie Legters, "Organizing Schools to Address Early Warning Indicators (EWIs): Common Practices and Challenges," *Journal of Education for Students Placed at Risk (JESPAR)* 18, no. 1 (January 1, 2013): 84–100, https://doi.org/10.1080/10824669.2013.745210; Emily Krone Phillips, *The Make-or-Break Year: Solving the Dropout Crisis One Ninth Grader at a Time* (New York, NY: The New Press, 2019).
17. Janelle Scott, "The Politics of Venture Philanthropy in Charter School Policy and Advocacy," *Educational Policy* 23, no. 1 (January 1, 2009): 106–36, https://doi.org/10.1177/0895904808328531; Janelle Scott and Huriya Jabbar, "The Hub and the Spokes: Foundations, Intermediary Organizations, Incentivist Reforms, and the Politics of Research Evidence," *Educational Policy* 28, no. 2 (March 1, 2014): 233–57, https://doi.org/10.1177/0895904813515327; Christopher Lubienski, Miri Yemini, and Claire Maxwell, eds., *The Rise of External Actors in Education: Shifting Boundaries Globally and Locally* (Bristol: Bristol University Press, 2022); Elizabeth DeBray et al., "Money and Influence: Philanthropies, Intermediary Organisations, and Atlanta's 2017 School Board Election," *Journal of Educational Administration and History* 52, no. 1 (January 2, 2020): 63–79, https://doi.org/10.1080/00220620.2019.1689103; Sarah Reckhow, *Follow the Money: How Foundation Dollars Change Public School Politics* (Oxford, UK: Oxford University Press, 2013).
18. David K. Cohen and Jal D. Mehta, "Why Reform Sometimes Succeeds: Understanding the Conditions That Produce Reforms That Last," *American Educational Research Journal* 54, no. 4 (August 1, 2017): 644–90, https://doi.org/10.3102/0002831217700078.
19. Charles M. Payne, *So Much Reform, So Little Change: The Persistence of Failure in Urban Schools* (Cambridge, MA: Harvard Education Press, 2008).
20. David K. Cohen and Susan L. Moffitt, *The Ordeal of Equality: Did Federal Regulation Fix the Schools?* (Cambridge, MA: Harvard University Press, 2010); Cohen and Mehta, "Why Reform Sometimes Succeeds."

21. LaTefy Schoen and Lance D. Fusarelli, "Innovation, NCLB, and the Fear Factor: The Challenge of Leading 21st-Century Schools in an Era of Accountability," *Educational Policy* 22, no. 1 (January 1, 2008): 181–203, https://doi.org/10.1177/0895904807311291.
22. Jal Mehta, "How Paradigms Create Politics: The Transformation of American Educational Policy, 1980–2001," *American Educational Research Journal* 50, no. 2 (April 1, 2013): 285–324, https://doi.org/10.3102/0002831212471417.
23. Eric A. Hanushek, "Testing, Accountability, and the American Economy," *The ANNALS of the American Academy of Political and Social Science* 683, no. 1 (May 1, 2019): 110–28, https://doi.org/10.1177/0002716219841299; Margaret E. Raymond and Eric A. Hanushek, "High-Stakes Research: The Campaign against Accountability Has Brought Forth a Tide of Negative Anecdotes and Deeply Flawed Research. Solid Analysis Reveals a Brighter Picture," *Education Next* 3, no. 3 (June 22, 2003): 48–56.
24. Diane Ravitch, *The Death and Life of the Great American School System: How Testing and Choice Are Undermining Education* (New York, NY: Basic Books, 2016).
25. Robert Bifulco and David J. Schwegman, "Who Benefits from Accountability-Driven School Closure? Evidence from New York City," *Journal of Policy Analysis and Management* 39, no. 1 (2020): 96–130, https://doi.org/10.1002/pam.22140; Jacob Hibel and Daphne M. Penn, "Bad Apples or Bad Orchards? An Organizational Analysis of Educator Cheating on Standardized Accountability Tests," *Sociology of Education* 93, no. 4 (October 1, 2020): 331–52, https://doi.org/10.1177/0038040720927234; Brian A. Jacob and Steven D. Levitt, "Rotten Apples: An Investigation of the Prevalence and Predictors of Teacher Cheating," *The Quarterly Journal of Economics* 118, no. 3 (August 1, 2003): 843–77, https://doi.org/10.1162/00335530360698441; Jennings, "Below the Bubble."
26. Cohen and Moffitt, *The Ordeal of Equality*.
27. Yong Zhao and Kenneth A. Frank, "Factors Affecting Technology Uses in Schools: An Ecological Perspective," *American Educational Research Journal* 40, no. 4 (January 1, 2003): 807–40, https://doi.org/10.3102/00028312040004807; Kenneth A. Frank, Yong Zhao, and Kathryn Borman, "Social Capital and the Diffusion of Innovations Within Organizations: The Case of Computer Technology in Schools," *Sociology of Education* 77, no. 2 (April 1, 2004): 148–71, https://doi.org/10.1177/003804070407700203.
28. Cynthia E. Coburn and Jennifer Lin Russell, "District Policy and Teachers' Social Networks," *Educational Evaluation and Policy Analysis* 30, no. 3 (September 1, 2008): 203–35, https://doi.org/10.3102/0162373708321829.
29. Dan C. Lortie, *Schoolteacher: A Sociological Study* (Chicago, IL: University of Chicago Press, 1975).
30. US Department of Education, *Issue Brief: Early Warning Systems* (Washington, DC: US Department of Education, Office of Planning, Evaluation, and Policy Development (Policy and Program Studies Service), 2016); Balfanz and Byrnes, "Early Warning Indicators and Intervention Systems."
31. Tong Tong et al., "Charter Schools: An Alternative Option in American Schooling," *Encyclopedia* 3, no. 1 (March 2023): 362–70, https://doi.org/10.3390/encyclopedia3010022; Tomás Monarrez, Brian Kisida, and Matthew Chingos, "The Effect of Charter Schools on School Segregation," *American Economic Journal: Economic Policy* 14, no. 1 (February 1, 2022): 301–40, https://doi.org/10.1257/pol.20190682.
32. W. Richards Adrion et al., "U.S. States Must Broaden Participation While Expanding Access to Computer Science Education," *Communications of the ACM* 63, no. 12 (November 17, 2020): 22–25, https://doi.org/10.1145/3430375.
33. Denise K. Whitford, Dake Zhang, and Antonis Katsiyannis, "Traditional vs. Alternative Teacher Preparation Programs: A Meta-Analysis," *Journal of Child and Family Studies* 27, no. 3 (March 1, 2018): 671–85, https://doi.org/10.1007/s10826-017-0932-0.
34. Robert Kim, "Under the Law: 'Anti-Critical Race Theory' Laws and the Assault on Pedagogy," *Phi Delta Kappan* 103, no. 1 (September 1, 2021): 64–65, https://doi.org/10.1177/00317217211043637; Tyler Kingkade, Brandy Zadrozny, and Ben Collins, "Critical Race Theory Battle Invades School Boards—with Help from Conservative Groups," *NBC News*, June 15, 2021, https://www.nbcnews.com/news/us-news/critical-race-theory-invades-school-boards-help-conservative-groups-n1270794.
35. Reckhow, *Follow the Money*; Bruce Fuller, *When Schools Work: Pluralist Politics and Institutional Reform in Los Angeles* (Baltimore, MD: Johns Hopkins University Press, 2022); Anthony

S. Bryk et al., *How a City Learned to Improve Its Schools* (Cambridge, MA: Harvard Education Press, 2023); Julie A. Marsh et al., "The Process and Politics of Educational Governance Change in New Orleans, Los Angeles, and Denver," *American Educational Research Journal* 58, no. 1 (February 1, 2021): 107–59, https://doi.org/10.3102/0002831220921475; DeBray et al., "Money and Influence."

36. Frederic Schoff, "The National Congress of Mothers and Parent–Teacher Associations," *The ANNALS of the American Academy of Political and Social Science* 67, no. 1 (September 1, 1916): 139, https://doi.org/10.1177/000271621606700119.
37. Christine Woyshner, *Black Parent–Teacher Associations and the Origins of the National Congress of Colored Parents and Teachers, 1896–1926*, April 2000, https://eric.ed.gov/?id=ED442722.
38. Daniel Aaronson and Bhashkar Mazumder, "The Impact of Rosenwald Schools on Black Achievement," *Journal of Political Economy* 119, no. 5 (October 2011): 821–88, https://doi.org/10.1086/662962.
39. Richard M Jacobs, "U.S. Catholic Schools and the Religious Who Served in Them: Contributions in the 18th and 19th Centuries," *Journal of Catholic Education* 1, no. 4 (June 1, 1998): 364–83, https://doi.org/10.15365/joce.0104022013.
40. Ashlyn Aiko Nelson and Beth Gazley, "The Rise of School-Supporting Nonprofits," *Education Finance and Policy* 9, no. 4 (2014): 541–66.
41. Ibid.
42. Megan E. Tompkins-Stange, *Policy Patrons: Philanthropy, Education Reform, and the Politics of Influence* (Cambridge, MA: Harvard Education Press, 2016).
43. David Eddy-Spicer, Paula Arce-Trigatti, and Michelle D. Young, "Field Building through Strategic Bricolage: System Leadership and the Institutionalizing Role of Intermediary Organizations," *Journal of Professional Capital and Community* 6, no. 1 (January 1, 2020): 29–43, https://doi.org/10.1108/JPCC-11-2019-0032; Caitlin C Farrell et al., *Research-Practice Partnerships in Education: The State of the Field* (New York, NY: William T. Grant Foundation, 2021).
44. Donald J. Peurach, *Seeing Complexity in Public Education: Problems, Possibilities, and Success for All* (New York, NY: Oxford University Press, 2011); Meredith I. Honig, "The New Middle Management: Intermediary Organizations in Education Policy Implementation," *Educational Evaluation and Policy Analysis* 26, no. 1 (March 1, 2004): 65–87, https://doi.org/10.3102/01623737026001065.
45. Steven Glazerman, Daniel Mayer, and Paul Decker, "Alternative Routes to Teaching: The Impacts of Teach for America on Student Achievement and Other Outcomes," *Journal of Policy Analysis and Management* 25, no. 1 (2006): 75–96, https://doi.org/10.1002/pam.20157; Priya G. La Londe, T. Jameson Brewer, and Christopher A. Lubienski, "Teach for America and Teach for All: Creating an Intermediary Organization Network for Global Education Reform," *Education Policy Analysis Archives* 23, no. 47 (April 20, 2015), https://eric.ed.gov/?id=EJ1070361.
46. Jose Eos Trinidad, "Rethinking School Improvement Organizations: Understanding Their Variety, Benefits, Risks, and Future Directions," *Educational Researcher* online first (June 12, 2023): 1–8, https://doi.org/10.3102/0013189X231179116; Honig, "The New Middle Management"; Lubienski, Yemini, and Maxwell, *The Rise of External Actors in Education*.
47. Walter W. Powell and Elisabeth S. Clemens, *Private Action and the Public Good* (New Haven, CT: Yale University Press, 1998).
48. Brian Rowan, "The Ecology of School Improvement: Notes on the School Improvement Industry in the United States," *Journal of Educational Change* 3 (2002): 283–314.
49. Honig, "The New Middle Management."
50. Patricia Burch, *Hidden Markets: The New Education Privatization* (New York: Routledge, 2009); Katrina E. Bulkley and Patricia Burch, "The Changing Nature of Private Engagement in Public Education: For-Profit and Nonprofit Organizations and Educational Reform," *Peabody Journal of Education* 86, no. 3 (July 1, 2011): 236–51, https://doi.org/10.1080/0161956X.2011.578963.
51. Lubienski, Yemini, and Maxwell, *The Rise of External Actors in Education*.
52. Alexis de Tocqueville, *Democracy in America* (New York, NY: G. Dearborn & Co., 1838), https://www.gutenberg.org/ebooks/815.

53. Robert D. Putnam, *Bowling Alone: The Collapse and Revival of American Community* (New York, NY: Simon and Schuster, 2000).
54. Bryk et al., *How a City Learned to Improve Its Schools.*
55. DeBray et al., "Money and Influence."
56. Dale Russakoff, *The Prize: Who's in Charge of America's Schools?* (New York, NY: Houghton Mifflin Harcourt, 2015).
57. Rob Reich, *Just Giving: Why Philanthropy Is Failing Democracy and How It Can Do Better* (Princeton, NJ: Princeton University Press, 2018); Diane Ravitch, *Reign of Error: The Hoax of the Privatization Movement and the Danger to America's Public Schools* (New York, NY: Vintage Books, 2014).
58. Donald J. Peurach and Joshua L. Glazer, "Reconsidering Replication: New Perspectives on Large-Scale School Improvement," *Journal of Educational Change* 13, no. 2 (May 2012): 155–90, https://doi.org/10.1007/s10833-011-9177-7; Cynthia E. Coburn, William R. Penuel, and Caitlin C. Farrell, "Fostering Educational Improvement with Research-Practice Partnerships," *Phi Delta Kappan* 102, no. 7 (April 1, 2021): 14–19, https://doi.org/10.1177/0031721721 1007332; Sarah L. Woulfin, Isobel Stevenson, and Kerry Lord, *Making Coaching Matter: Leading Continuous Improvement in Schools* (New York, NY: Teachers College Press, 2023).
59. Brittany Murray et al., "Civil Society Goes to School: Parent–Teacher Associations and the Equality of Educational Opportunity," *RSF: The Russell Sage Foundation Journal of the Social Sciences* 5, no. 3 (2019): 41, https://doi.org/10.7758/rsf.2019.5.3.03.
60. Nelson and Gazley, "The Rise of School-Supporting Nonprofits."
61. E. N. Bridwell-Mitchell, "Them That's Got: How Tie Formation in Partnership Networks Gives High Schools Differential Access to Social Capital," *American Educational Research Journal* 54, no. 6 (2017): 1221–55.
62. Murray et al., "Civil Society Goes to School."
63. Reich, *Just Giving.*
64. This is an idea that many of my research informants have talked about. For example, philanthropies can support initiatives even as there are new leaders in the district. Also, research organizations can act as a repository for institutional memory as district staff and leaders can come and go.
65. Sarah Reckhow and Jeffrey W. Snyder, "The Expanding Role of Philanthropy in Education Politics," *Educational Researcher* 43, no. 4 (May 1, 2014): 186–95, https://doi.org/10.3102/0013189X14536607.
66. Ibid.
67. Bryk et al., *How a City Learned to Improve Its Schools.*
68. Fuller, *When Schools Work.*
69. Douglas N. Harris, *Charter School City: What the End of Traditional Public Schools in New Orleans Means for American Education* (Chicago and London: University of Chicago Press, 2020).
70. Marc Schneiberg and Elisabeth S. Clemens, "The Typical Tools for the Job: Research Strategies in Institutional Analysis*," *Sociological Theory* 24, no. 3 (2006): 195–227, https://doi.org/10.1111/j.1467-9558.2006.00288.x.
71. John W. Meyer and Brian Rowan, "Institutionalized Organizations: Formal Structure as Myth and Ceremony," *American Journal of Sociology* 83, no. 2 (1977): 340–63.
72. Paul J. DiMaggio and Walter W. Powell, "The Iron Cage Revisited: Institutional Isomorphism and Collective Rationality in Organizational Fields," *American Sociological Review* 48, no. 2 (1983): 147–60, https://doi.org/10.2307/2095101.
73. John Levi Martin, "What Is Field Theory?," *American Journal of Sociology* 109, no. 1 (July 2003): 1–49, https://doi.org/10.1086/375201.
74. Michael Lounsbury et al., "New Directions in the Study of Institutional Logics: From Tools to Phenomena," *Annual Review of Sociology* 47, no. 1 (2021): 261–80, https://doi.org/10.1146/annurev-soc-090320-111734; Heather A. Haveman, *The Power of Organizations: A New Approach to Organizational Theory* (Princeton, NJ: Princeton University Press, 2022).
75. Julie Battilana, "Agency and Institutions: The Enabling Role of Individuals' Social Position," *Organization* 13, no. 5 (September 1, 2006): 653–76, https://doi.org/10.1177/1350508406067008.

76. Tim Hallett and Amelia Hawbaker, "The Case for an Inhabited Institutionalism in Organizational Research: Interaction, Coupling, and Change Reconsidered," *Theory and Society* 50, no. 1 (January 2021): 1–32, https://doi.org/10.1007/s11186-020-09412-2.
77. Mehta, "How Paradigms Create Politics."
78. Rand Quinn, Megan Tompkins-Stange, and Debra Meyerson, "Beyond Grantmaking: Philanthropic Foundations as Agents of Change and Institutional Entrepreneurs," *Nonprofit and Voluntary Sector Quarterly* 43, no. 6 (December 1, 2014): 950–68, https://doi.org/10.1177/0899764013488836.
79. Tim Hallett, "The Myth Incarnate: Recoupling Processes, Turmoil, and Inhabited Institutions in an Urban Elementary School," *American Sociological Review* 75, no. 1 (February 1, 2010): 52–74, https://doi.org/10.1177/0003122409357044.
80. Roger Friedland and Robert R. Alford, "Bringing Society Back In: Symbols, Practices, and Institutional Contradictions," in *The New Institutionalism in Organizational Analysis* (Chicago and London: University of Chicago Press, 1991), 248, https://cir.nii.ac.jp/crid/1573105975595180032.
81. Seth Abrutyn and Jonathan H. Turner, "The Old Institutionalism Meets the New Institutionalism," *Sociological Perspectives* 54, no. 3 (September 1, 2011): 283–306, https://doi.org/10.1525/sop.2011.54.3.283; Patricia H. Thornton, William Ocasio, and Michael Lounsbury, *The Institutional Logics Perspective: A New Approach to Culture, Structure and Process* (Oxford, UK: Oxford University Press, 2012), https://oxford.universitypressscholarship.com/10.1093/acprof:oso/9780199601936.001.0001/acprof-9780199601936.
82. Ibid.
83. Mary B. Dunn and Candace Jones, "Institutional Logics and Institutional Pluralism: The Contestation of Care and Science Logics in Medical Education, 1967–2005," *Administrative Science Quarterly* 55, no. 1 (March 1, 2010): 114–49, https://doi.org/10.2189/asqu.2010.55.1.114; Trish Reay and C. R. Hinings, "Managing the Rivalry of Competing Institutional Logics," *Organization Studies* 30, no. 6 (June 1, 2009): 629–52, https://doi.org/10.1177/0170840609104803.
84. Heather A. Haveman and Gillian Gualtieri, "Institutional Logics," in *Oxford Research Encyclopedia of Business and Management*, by Heather A. Haveman and Gillian Gualtieri (Oxford University Press, 2017), http://business.oxfordre.com/view/10.1093/acrefore/9780190224851.001.0001/acrefore-9780190224851-e-137.
85. Matthew C. Spitzmueller, "Remaking 'Community' Mental Health: Contested Institutional Logics and Organizational Change," *Human Service Organizations: Management, Leadership & Governance* 42, no. 2 (March 15, 2018): 123–45, https://doi.org/10.1080/23303131.2017.1422071.
86. Paul J. DiMaggio, "Interest and Agency in Institutional Theory," in *Institutional Patterns and Organization*, ed. L Zuker (Cambridge, MA: Ballinger, 1988), 3–22.
87. Julie Battilana, Bernard Leca, and Eva Boxenbaum, "How Actors Change Institutions: Towards a Theory of Institutional Entrepreneurship," *Academy of Management Annals* 3, no. 1 (January 2009): 65–107, https://doi.org/10.5465/19416520903053598; Hayagreeva Rao, *Market Rebels: How Activists Make or Break Radical Innovations* (Princeton, NJ: Princeton University Press, 2008); Neil Fligstein, "Social Skill and the Theory of Fields," *Sociological Theory* 19, no. 2 (July 1, 2001): 105–25, https://doi.org/10.1111/0735-2751.00132.
88. Kamal A. Munir and Nelson Phillips, "The Birth of the 'Kodak Moment': Institutional Entrepreneurship and the Adoption of New Technologies," *Organization Studies* 26, no. 11 (November 1, 2005): 1665–87, https://doi.org/10.1177/0170840605056395; Hayagreeva Rao, Philippe Monin, and Rodolphe Durand, "Institutional Change in Toque Ville: Nouvelle Cuisine as an Identity Movement in French Gastronomy," *American Journal of Sociology* 108 (January 1, 2003): 795–843, https://doi.org/10.1086/367917; Steve Maguire, Cynthia Hardy, and Thomas B. Lawrence, "Institutional Entrepreneurship in Emerging Fields: HIV/AIDS Treatment Advocacy in Canada," *The Academy of Management Journal* 47, no. 5 (2004): 657–79, https://doi.org/10.2307/20159610; Rodrigo Canales, "From Ideals to Institutions: Institutional Entrepreneurship and the Growth of Mexican Small Business Finance," *Organization Science* 27, no. 6 (December 2016): 1548–73, https://doi.org/10.1287/orsc.2016.1093.

89. Paul Tracey, Nelson Phillips, and Owen Jarvis, "Bridging Institutional Entrepreneurship and the Creation of New Organizational Forms: A Multilevel Model," *Organization Science* 22, no. 1 (February 2011): 60–80, https://doi.org/10.1287/orsc.1090.0522.
90. Payne, *So Much Reform, So Little Change.*
91. Martha S. Feldman and Brian T. Pentland, "Reconceptualizing Organizational Routines as a Source of Flexibility and Change," *Administrative Science Quarterly* 48, no. 1 (March 1, 2003): 94–118, https://doi.org/10.2307/3556620.
92. Martha S. Feldman et al., "Introduction: Routine Dynamics in Action," in *Routine Dynamics in Action: Replication and Transformation*, ed. Martha S. Feldman et al., vol. 61, Research in the Sociology of Organizations (Emerald Publishing Limited, 2019), 1–10, https://doi.org/10.1108/S0733-558X20190000061001.
93. Markus C. Becker, "Organizational Routines: A Review of the Literature," *Industrial and Corporate Change* 13, no. 4 (August 1, 2004): 643–78, https://doi.org/10.1093/icc/dth026.
94. Jennifer Zoltners Sherer and James P. Spillane, "Constancy and Change in Work Practice in Schools: The Role of Organizational Routines," *Teachers College Record* 113, no. 3 (March 1, 2011): 611–57, https://doi.org/10.1177/016146811111300302.
95. Elaine M Allensworth and John Q Easton, *The On-Track Indicator as a Predictor of High School Graduation* (Chicago, IL: Consortium on Chicago School Research at the University of Chicago, 2005).
96. Ibid.
97. Robert Balfanz, Liza Herzog, and Douglas J. Mac Iver, "Preventing Student Disengagement and Keeping Students on the Graduation Path in Urban Middle-Grades Schools: Early Identification and Effective Interventions," *Educational Psychologist* 42, no. 4 (November 2, 2007): 223–35, https://doi.org/10.1080/00461520701621079.
98. Neild, Balfanz, and Herzog, "An Early Warning System."
99. James J. Kemple, Micha D. Segeritz, and Nickisha Stephenson, "Building On-Track Indicators for High School Graduation and College Readiness: Evidence from New York City," *Journal of Education for Students Placed at Risk (JESPAR)* 18, no. 1 (January 2013): 7–28, https://doi.org/10.1080/10824669.2013.747945; Lyndsay Pinkus, *Using Early-Warning Data to Improve Graduation Rates: Closing Cracks in the Education System* (Washington, DC: Alliance for Excellent Education, 2008); Meredith Phillips et al., "Using Research to Improve College Readiness: A Research Partnership Between the Los Angeles Unified School District and the Los Angeles Education Research Institute," *Journal of Education for Students Placed at Risk* 20, no. 1–2 (2015): 141–68, https://doi.org/10.1080/10824669.2014.990562; Bradley Carl et al., "Theory and Application of Early Warning Systems for High School and Beyond," *Journal of Education for Students Placed at Risk (JESPAR)* 18, no. 1 (January 2013): 29–49, https://doi.org/10.1080/10824669.2013.745374; Daniel Stid, Kate O'Neill, and Susan Colby, "Portland Public Schools: From Data and Decisions to Implementation and Results on Dropout Prevention" (Boston, MA: Bridgespan Group, January 2009), https://eric.ed.gov/?id=ED535867; Mac Iver and Messel, "The ABCs of Keeping On Track to Graduation"; Sarah Frazelle and Aisling Nagel, *A Practitioner's Guide to Implementing Early Warning Systems* (Washington, DC: US Department of Education, Institute of Education Sciences, National Center for Education Evaluation and Regional Assistance, Regional Educational Laboratory Northwest, 2015).
100. US Department of Education, *Issue Brief: Early Warning Systems.*
101. Balfanz and Byrnes, "Early Warning Indicators and Intervention Systems."
102. Sarah D. Sparks, "Most Schools Have Early-Warning Systems. Some Kids Are Still Getting Lost," *Education Week*, February 27, 2024, sec. Leadership, School & District Management, https://www.edweek.org/leadership/most-schools-have-early-warning-systems-how-well-do-they-work/2024/02.
103. Mac Iver and Messel, "The ABCs of Keeping On Track to Graduation."
104. Julia Gwynne, Joy Lesnick, et al., *What Matters for Staying On-Track and Graduating in Chicago Public Schools: A Focus on Students with Disabilities. Research Report* (Chicago, IL: Consortium on Chicago School Research, 2009), https://eric.ed.gov/?id=ED507419; Julia Gwynne, Amber Stitziel Pareja, et al., *What Matters for Staying On-Track and Graduating in Chicago Public Schools: A Focus on English Language Learners. Research Report* (Chicago, IL: Consortium on Chicago School Research, 2012), https://eric.ed.gov/?id=ED532513.
105. Kemple, Segeritz, and Stephenson, "Building On-Track Indicators for High School Graduation and College Readiness."

106. Perdomo et al., "Difficult Lessons on Social Prediction from Wisconsin Public Schools."
107. Mary Bruce et al., *On Track for Success: The Use of Early Warning Indicator and Intervention Systems to Build a Grad Nation* (Washington, DC: Civic Enterprises, 2011).
108. Jessica B. Heppen and Susan Bowles Therriault, *Developing Early Warning Systems to Identify Potential High School Dropouts. Issue Brief* (Washington, DC: National High School Center, American Institutes of Research, 2008), https://eric.ed.gov/?id=ED521558; Melissa Roderick et al., *Preventable Failure: Improvements in Long-Term Outcomes When High Schools Focused on the Ninth Grade Year. Research Summary* (Chicago, IL: University of Chicago Consortium on Chicago School Research, 2014), https://eric.ed.gov/?id=ED553174; Drew Bailey et al., "Persistence and Fadeout in the Impacts of Child and Adolescent Interventions," *Journal of Research on Educational Effectiveness* 10, no. 1 (2017): 7–39, https://doi.org/10.1080/19345747.2016.1232459.
109. Ann-Marie Faria et al., *Getting Students on Track for Graduation: Impacts of the Early Warning Intervention and Monitoring System after One Year* (Washington, DC: US Department of Education, Institute of Education Sciences, National Center for Education Evaluation and Regional Assistance, Regional Educational Laboratory Midwest, 2017).
110. Robert Balfanz and Vaughan Byrnes, "Using Data and the Human Touch: Evaluating the NYC Inter-Agency Campaign to Reduce Chronic Absenteeism," *Journal of Education for Students Placed at Risk* 23, no. 1–2 (April 3, 2018): 107–21, https://doi.org/10.1080/10824669.2018.1435283.
111. Marcia H. Davis, Martha Abele Mac Iver, et al., "Implementation of an Early Warning Indicator and Intervention System," *Preventing School Failure: Alternative Education for Children and Youth* 63, no. 1 (January 2, 2019): 77–88, https://doi.org/10.1080/1045988X.2018.1506977.
112. Yusuf Canbolat, "Early Warning for Whom? Regression Discontinuity Evidence from the Effect of Early Warning System on Student Absence," *Educational Evaluation and Policy Analysis* online first (February 5, 2024): 1–26, https://doi.org/10.3102/01623737231221503.
113. Hansen, "Information as Intervention: Effects of an Early Warning System."
114. Eliza Moeller, Alex Seeskin, and Jenny Nagaoka, *Practice-Driven Data: Lessons from Chicago's Approach to Research, Data, and Practice in Education* (Chicago, IL: UChicago Consortium on School Research, 2018).
115. Wentworth and Nagaoka, "Early Warning Indicators in Education: Innovations, Uses, and Optimal Conditions for Effectiveness."
116. Perdomo et al., "Difficult Lessons on Social Prediction from Wisconsin Public Schools."
117. Allensworth, "The Use of Ninth-Grade Early Warning Indicators to Improve Chicago Schools."
118. Hadar Baharav and Laurel Sipes, "Early Warning Indicator Systems in Action: Considerations from Identification to Supports," *Teachers College Record* 122 (2020): 1–24.
119. Todd Feathers, "How Wisconsin Uses Race and Income to Label Students 'High Risk,'" Chalkbeat, April 27, 2023, https://www.chalkbeat.org/2023/4/27/23699361/dropout-early-warning-system-dews-student-dropouts-race-income-data.
120. Davis, Herzog, and Legters, "Organizing Schools to Address Early Warning Indicators (EWIs)."
121. Phillips, *The Make-or-Break Year.*
122. Blanchett, Mumford, and Beachum, "Urban School Failure and Disproportionality in a Post-Brown Era."
123. Hamilton Lankford, Susanna Loeb, and James Wyckoff, "Teacher Sorting and the Plight of Urban Schools: A Descriptive Analysis," *Educational Evaluation and Policy Analysis* 24, no. 1 (March 1, 2002): 37–62, https://doi.org/10.3102/01623737024001037.
124. Payne, *So Much Reform, So Little Change.*
125. Pedro Noguera, *City Schools and the American Dream: Reclaiming the Promise of Public Education* (New York, NY: Teachers College Press, 2003).
126. National Center for Education Statistics, "Digest of Education Statistics, 2020," National Center for Education Statistics, 2020, https://nces.ed.gov/programs/digest/d20/tables/dt20_215.30.asp.
127. Poverty thresholds are based on the size of the family and number of children. The US Census Bureau has a matrix for the poverty threshold every year available at census.gov/data/tables/time-series/demo/income-poverty/historical-poverty-thresholds.html

128. William H. Frey, *2020 Census: Big Cities Grew and Became More Diverse, Especially among Their Youth* (Washington, DC: Brookings Institution, 2021), https://www.brookings.edu/research/2020-census-big-cities-grew-and-became-more-diverse-especially-among-their-youth/.
129. While part of the reason for relying on historical interviews was the theoretical reason given, another part of the reason was because of the lack of access to Chicago Public Schools teachers during the COVID-19 pandemics when the district research office provided limited permission for new research.

## Chapter 1

1. Balfanz and Legters, *Locating the Dropout Crisis.*
2. Ibid.
3. Valerie E. Lee and David T. Burkam, "Dropping Out of High School: The Role of School Organization and Structure," American Educational Research Journal 40, no. 2 (January 2003): 353–93, https://doi.org/10.3102/00028312040002353; Sara Battin-Pearson et al., "Predictors of Early High School Dropout: A Test of Five Theories," Journal of Educational Psychology 92, no. 3 (2000): 568–82, https://doi.org/10.1037/0022-0663.92.3.568.
4. Anne Lessard et al., "Shades of Disengagement: High School Dropouts Speak Out," Social Psychology of Education 11, no. 1 (February 1, 2008): 25–42, https://doi.org/10.1007/s11218-007-9033-z.
5. Allensworth and Easton, The On-Track Indicator as a Predictor of High School Graduation; Balfanz and Byrnes, "Early Warning Indicators and Intervention Systems"; Frazelle and Nagel, A Practitioner's Guide to Implementing Early Warning Systems.
6. Heppen and Therriault, Developing Early Warning Systems; Roderick et al., Preventable Failure; Phillips, The Make-or-Break Year.
7. Allensworth, "The Use of Ninth-Grade Early Warning Indicators to Improve Chicago Schools," 68.
8. Wendy Nelson Espeland and Mitchell L. Stevens, "A Sociology of Quantification," European Journal of Sociology 49, no. 3 (2008): 401–36; Andrea Mennicken and Wendy Nelson Espeland, "What's New with Numbers? Sociological Approaches to the Study of Quantification," Annual Review of Sociology 45, no. 1 (2019): 223–45, https://doi.org/10.1146/annurev-soc-073117-041343.
9. David Figlio and Susanna Loeb, "School Accountability," in Handbook of the Economics of Education, vol. 3 (Elsevier, 2011), 383–421, https://doi.org/10.1016/B978-0-444-53429-3.00008-9; Jose Eos Trinidad, "Meaning-Making, Negotiation, and Change in School Accountability, Or What Sociology Can Offer Policy Studies," Sociological Inquiry online first (2022): 1–26, https://doi.org/10.1111/soin.12485; Diamond, "Accountability Policy, School Organization, and Classroom Practice."
10. Figlio and Loeb, "School Accountability"; Cecilia Elena Rouse et al., "Feeling the Florida Heat? How Low-Performing Schools Respond to Voucher and Accountability Pressure," American Economic Journal: Economic Policy 5, no. 2 (May 2013): 251–81, https://doi.org/10.1257/pol.5.2.251; Thomas S. Dee and Brian Jacob, "The Impact of No Child Left Behind on Student Achievement," Journal of Policy Analysis and Management 30, no. 3 (2011): 418–46, https://doi.org/10.1002/pam.20586.
11. Hibel and Penn, "Bad Apples or Bad Orchards?"; Jennifer L. Jennings and Jonathan Marc Bearak, "'Teaching to the Test' in the NCLB Era: How Test Predictability Affects Our Understanding of Student Performance," Educational Researcher 43, no. 8 (November 1, 2014): 381–89, https://doi.org/10.3102/0013189X14554449; Jennings, "Below the Bubble"; Derek A. Neal and Diane Whitmore Schanzenbach, "Left Behind by Design: Proficiency Counts and Test-Based Accountability," The Review of Economics and Statistics 92, no. 2 (February 17, 2010): 263–83, https://doi.org/10.1162/rest.2010.12318; Jacob and Levitt, "Rotten Apples."
12. These school interviews were done by the University of Chicago Consortium on School Research between 2016 and 2018 with 22 teachers, counselors, support staff, assistant principals, and principals. I received permission from the original staff who did the interviews to use and analyze these transcripts to understand how EWIs were being implemented. The information from these transcripts has not been published before and this publication is an attempt to use these data. I am grateful for Jenny Nagaoka and Faye Kroshinsky for their help.

13. In 2022, other performance indicators in the school accountability metric include SAT (Scholastic Aptitude Test) annual growth, average daily attendance rate, percentage of students meeting college readiness benchmarks, 1-year dropout rate, 4-year cohort graduation rate, 5 Essential survey results, etc. Chicago Public Schools Department of School Quality Measurement and Research, School Quality Rating Policy (SQRP) Handbook: Guide to the Policy, Indicators, and Ratings (Chicago, IL: Department of School Quality Measurement and Research, 2019), https://www.cps.edu/globalassets/cps-pages/about-cps/district-data/metrics/school-quality-rating-policy-sqrp/sqrp-handbook.pdf.
14. Allensworth and Easton, The On-Track Indicator as a Predictor of High School Graduation; Chicago Public Schools Department of School Quality Measurement and Research, School Quality Rating Policy (SQRP) Handbook.
15. Chicago Public Schools Department of School Quality Measurement and Research, School Quality Rating Policy (SQRP) Handbook.
16. All the names of the schools are pseudonyms provided by the original interviewers from the University of Chicago Consortium on School Research.
17. Ravitch, The Death and Life of the Great American School System.
18. Donald T. Campbell, "Assessing the Impact of Planned Social Change," Evaluation and Program Planning 2, no. 1 (January 1, 1979): 85, https://doi.org/10.1016/0149-7189(79)90048-X.
19. Allensworth, "The Use of Ninth-Grade Early Warning Indicators to Improve Chicago Schools."
20. Roderick et al., Preventable Failure; Moeller, Seeskin, and Nagaoka, Practice-Driven Data: Lessons from Chicago's Approach to Research, Data, and Practice in Education; Eliza Moeller and Alex Seeskin, "Practice-Driven Data: Lessons From Chicago's Approach to Research, Data, and Practice in Education," Teachers College Record 122, no. 14 (2020): 1–30; Bill Gates, "On the Right Track in Chicago," gatesnotes.com, 2019, https://www.gatesnotes.com/Education/On-the-right-track-in-Chicago.
21. Davis, Herzog, and Legters, "Organizing Schools to Address Early Warning Indicators (EWIs)"; Davis, Iver, et al., "Implementation of an Early Warning Indicator and Intervention System"; Balfanz and Byrnes, "Using Data and the Human Touch."
22. Meyer and Rowan, "Institutionalized Organizations: Formal Structure as Myth and Ceremony."
23. Drew Bailey et al., "Persistence and Fadeout in the Impacts of Child and Adolescent Interventions," Journal of Research on Educational Effectiveness 10, no. 1 (January 2, 2017): 7–39, https://doi.org/10.1080/19345747.2016.1232459.
24. Davis, Iver, et al., "Implementation of an Early Warning Indicator and Intervention System"; Mac Iver et al., "An Efficacy Study of a Ninth-Grade Early Warning Indicator Intervention."
25. Baharav and Sipes, "Early Warning Indicator Systems in Action."
26. Kimberly L. Henry, Kelly E. Knight, and Terence P. Thornberry, "School Disengagement as a Predictor of Dropout, Delinquency, and Problem Substance Use During Adolescence and Early Adulthood," Journal of Youth and Adolescence 41, no. 2 (February 2012): 156–66, https://doi.org/10.1007/s10964-011-9665-3.
27. Rachel Brown-Chidsey and Rebekah Bickford, Practical Handbook of Multi-Tiered Systems of Support: Building Academic and Behavioral Success in Schools (New York and London: The Guilford Press, 2015).
28. This idea of changes being concentrated on the system rather than schools was also evident in conversations with individuals from the Network for College Success as they highlighted the role of out-of-the-classroom interventions (e.g., tutoring, credit recovery, calling chronic absentees) rather than in-classroom instructional changes. These will be detailed in later chapters.
29. Mac Iver et al., "An Efficacy Study of a Ninth-Grade Early Warning Indicator Intervention"; Wentworth and Nagaoka, "Early Warning Indicators in Education"; Perdomo et al., "Difficult Lessons on Social Prediction from Wisconsin Public Schools"; Davis, Iver, et al., "Implementation of an Early Warning Indicator and Intervention System"; Balfanz and Byrnes, "Using Data and the Human Touch."
30. Paul Pierson, Politics in Time: History, Institutions, and Social Analysis (Princeton, NJ: Princeton University Press, 2004), 79, https://www.degruyter.com/document/doi/10.1515/9781400841080/html.
31. Mac Iver et al., "An Efficacy Study of a Ninth-Grade Early Warning Indicator Intervention," 383–84.

## Chapter 2


1. Associated Press, "Schools in Chicago Are Called the Worst by Education Chief," *The New York Times*, November 8, 1987, sec. US, https://www.nytimes.com/1987/11/08/us/schools-in-chicago-are-called-the-worst-by-education-chief.html.
2. Casey Banas and Devonda Byers, "Education Chief: City Schools Worst," *Chicago Tribune*, November 8, 1987, https://www.chicagotribune.com/news/ct-xpm-1987-11-08-8703230953-story.html.
3. Julie Berry Cullen, Brian A. Jacob, and Steven D. Levitt, "The Impact of School Choice on Student Outcomes: An Analysis of the Chicago Public Schools," *Journal of Public Economics* 89, no. 5 (June 1, 2005): 729–60, https://doi.org/10.1016/j.jpubeco.2004.05.001; Anthony S. Bryk et al., *Charting Chicago School Reform: Democratic Localism as a Lever for Change* (New York, NY: Routledge, 2018); Banas and Byers, "Education Chief: City Schools Worst."
4. Neild and Balfanz, *Unfulfilled Promise*; Brian Gill et al., "State Takeover, School Restructuring, Private Management, and Student Achievement in Philadelphia" (Santa Monica, CA: RAND Corporation, January 22, 2007), https://www.rand.org/pubs/monographs/MG533.html; Maria Newman, "Graduation Rate Declines To Lowest in Eight Years," *The New York Times*, December 30, 1994, sec. New York, https://www.nytimes.com/1994/12/30/nyregion/graduation-rate-declines-to-lowest-in-eight-years.html; David Silver, Marisa Saunders, and Estela Zarate, "What Factors Predict High School Graduation in the Los Angeles Unified School District: California Dropout Research Project Report" (Santa Barbara, CA: University of California Santa Barbara, 2008).
5. Trinidad, "Rethinking School Improvement Organizations"; Brian Rowan, "Does the School Improvement 'Industry' (Organizations Providing Schools and Governing Agencies with Information, Training, Materials, and Programmatic Resources Relevant to Instructional Improvement Problems) Help or Prevent Deep and Sound Change?," *Journal of Educational Change* 9, no. 2 (June 2008): 197–202, https://doi.org/10.1007/s10833-007-9062-6; Rowan, "The Ecology of School Improvement."
6. Honig, "The New Middle Management"; Burch, *Hidden Markets*; Lubienski, Yemini, and Maxwell, *The Rise of External Actors in Education.*
7. Melissa Roderick and John Q. Easton, *Developing New Roles for Research in New Policy Environments: The Consortium on Chicago School Research* (Chicago, IL: University of Chicago, 2007); Cynthia E. Coburn and William R. Penuel, "Research–Practice Partnerships in Education: Outcomes, Dynamics, and Open Questions," *Educational Researcher* 45, no. 1 (January 1, 2016): 48–54, https://doi.org/10.3102/0013189X16631750.
8. The School of Social Service Administration at the University of Chicago has been subsequently renamed the Crown Family School of Social Work, Policy, and Practice. The University of Chicago Consortium on School Research (Consortium) was originally named the Consortium on Chicago School Research. Elaine Allensworth has stayed at the Consortium, and she is its executive director. Shazia Miller has moved to different research organizations, like the American Institutes of Research, National Opinion Research Center (NORC), and Mathematica.
9. Melissa Roderick and Eric Camburn, "Risk and Recovery from Course Failure in the Early Years of High School," *American Educational Research Journal* 36, no. 2 (January 1, 1999): 303–43, https://doi.org/10.3102/00028312036002303.
10. Ibid., 336.
11. Miller and Allensworth, "Progress and Problems."
12. Ibid., 70.
13. James J. Kemple, Corinne M. Herlihy, and Thomas J. Smith, *Making Progress Toward Graduation: Evidence from the Talent Development High School Model* (New York, NY: MDRC, 2005).
14. Elizabeth Useem, Ruth Curran Neild, and William Morrison, *Philadelphia's Talent Development High Schools: Second-Year Results, 2000–01* (Philadelphia, PA: Philadelphia Education Fund, 2001).
15. Ibid.
16. Balfanz, Herzog, and Mac Iver, "Preventing Student Disengagement," 223.
17. Neild, Balfanz, and Herzog, "An Early Warning System."

18. Ruth Curran Neild, Scott Stoner-Eby, and Frank Furstenberg, "Connecting Entrance and Departure: The Transition to Ninth Grade and High School Dropout," *Education and Urban Society* 40, no. 5 (July 1, 2008): 543–69, https://doi.org/10.1177/0013124508316438.
19. United Way of Greater Philadelphia and Southern New Jersey, "United Way and Philadelphia Education Fund Boost Academic Success for Philadelphia Students," October 29, 2014, https://www.prnewswire.com/news-releases/united-way-and-philadelphia-education-fund-boost-academic-success-for-philadelphia-students-280771892.html.
20. Molly Pileggi, Lindsey Liu, and Alyn Turner, *Back On Track: How Off-Track Ninth Graders Progressed in Later Years of High School, Class of 2017 and 2018* (Philadelphia, PA: Philadelphia Education Research Consortium, 2020); Austin Slaughter, Ruth Curran Neild, and Molly Crofton, *Ready From the Start: Identifying and Supporting At-Risk Ninth Graders From Their Earliest Days in High School* (Philadelphia, PA: Philadelphia Education Research Consortium, 2018), https://www.aera.net/Publications/Online-Paper-Repository/AERA-Online-Paper-Repository-Viewer/ID/1439900.
21. Kristen A. Graham, "1 in 3 Philly Students Doesn't Graduate on Time. To Fix That, High Schools Focus on Freshmen," *The Philadelphia Inquirer*, May 18, 2018, https://www.inquirer.com/philly/education/1-in-3-philly-students-doesnt-graduate-on-time-to-fix-that-high-schools-focus-on-freshmen-20180521.html.
22. Kemple, Segeritz, and Stephenson, "Building On-Track Indicators for High School Graduation and College Readiness," 8.
23. Ibid., 26. In New York state, to earn a diploma, students must pass their courses and also pass five Regents exams in English, math, science, social studies, and an additional exam.
24. Pinkus, *Using Early-Warning Data to Improve Graduation Rates*, 6.
25. Susan Fairchild et al., *Student Progress to Graduation in New York City High Schools. Part II. Student Achievement as Stock and Flow: Reimagining Early Warning Systems for At-Risk Students* (New York, NY: New Visions for Public Schools, 2012).
26. Susan Fairchild et al., *Student Progress to Graduation in New York City High Schools: A Metric Designed by New Visions for Public Schools* (New York City, NY: New Visions for Public Schools, 2011).
27. Reich, *Just Giving*; Frederick M. Hess and Jeffrey R. Henig, *The New Education Philanthropy: Politics, Policy, and Reform. Educational Innovations Series* (Cambridge, MA: Harvard Education Press, 2015); Frederick M. Hess and Michael B. Horn, *Private Enterprise and Public Education* (New York, NY: Teachers College Press, 2015); Reckhow, *Follow the Money*; Joshua Glazer and Donald J. Peurach, "School Improvement Networks as a Strategy for Large-Scale Education Reform: The Role of Educational Environments," *Educational Policy* 27 (July 1, 2013): 676–710, https://doi.org/10.1177/0895904811429283; Anthony S. Bryk, Louis M. Gomez, and Alicia Grunow, "Getting Ideas into Action: Building Networked Improvement Communities in Education," in *Frontiers in Sociology of Education*, ed. Maureen T. Hallinan (Dordrecht: Springer Netherlands, 2011), 127–62, https://doi.org/10.1007/978-94-007-1576-9_7.
28. Sonya Douglass Horsford, Janelle T. Scott, and Gary L. Anderson, *The Politics of Education Policy in an Era of Inequality: Possibilities for Democratic Schooling* (New York, NY: Routledge, 2018).
29. Hess, *Spinning Wheels*.
30. Powell and Clemens, *Private Action and the Public Good*.
31. Ibid., xvi.
32. Wayne Au and Joseph J. Ferrare, *Mapping Corporate Education Reform: Power and Policy Networks in the Neoliberal State* (New York, NY: Routledge, 2015); Kenneth J. Saltman, *The Gift of Education: Public Education and Venture Philanthropy* (New York, NY: Palgrave MacMillan, 2010); Scott and Jabbar, "The Hub and the Spokes"; Horsford, Scott, and Anderson, *The Politics of Education Policy in an Era of Inequality*; Janelle Scott, Christopher Lubienski, and Elizabeth DeBray-Pelot, "The Politics of Advocacy in Education," *Educational Policy* 23, no. 1 (January 1, 2009): 3–14, https://doi.org/10.1177/0895904808328530.
33. William G. Howell, ed., *Besieged: School Boards and the Future of Education Politics* (Washington, DC: Brookings Institution Press, 2005); Janelle Scott et al., "Urban Regimes, Intermediary Organization Networks, and Research Use: Patterns Across Three School Districts," *Peabody Journal of Education* 92, no. 1 (January 2017): 16–28, https://doi.org/10.1080/0161956X.2016.1264800; DeBray et al., "Money and Influence"; Au and Ferrare, *Mapping Corporate*

*Education Reform*; Bianca J. Baldridge, *Reclaiming Community: Race and the Uncertain Future of Youth Work* (Palo Alto, CA: Stanford University Press, 2019); Donald J. Peurach, "Innovating at the Nexus of Impact and Improvement: Leading Educational Improvement Networks," *Educational Researcher* 45, no. 7 (October 1, 2016): 421–29, https://doi.org/10.3102/0013189X16670898; E. N. Bridwell-Mitchell, "Them That's Got? How School Partnerships Can Perpetuate Inequalities," *Phi Delta Kappan* 100, no. 8 (May 1, 2019): 32–36, https://doi.org/10.1177/0031721719846886; E. N. Bridwell-Mitchell, James Jack, and Joshua Childs, "The Social Structure of School Resource Disparities: How Social Capital and Interorganizational Relationships Matter for Educational Equity," *Sociology of Education* 96, no. 4 (October 1, 2023): 275–300, https://doi.org/10.1177/00380407231176541.

34. Frank, Zhao, and Borman, "Social Capital and the Diffusion of Innovations Within Organizations"; Coburn and Russell, "District Policy and Teachers' Social Networks"; Cecil Miskel and Mengli Song, "Passing Reading First: Prominence and Processes in an Elite Policy Network," *Educational Evaluation and Policy Analysis* 26, no. 2 (June 1, 2004): 89–109, https://doi.org/10.3102/01623737026002089; Mengli Song and Cecil G. Miskel, "Who Are the Influentials? A Cross-State Social Network Analysis of the Reading Policy Domain," *Educational Administration Quarterly* 41, no. 1 (February 1, 2005): 7–48, https://doi.org/10.1177/0013161X04269515.
35. Russakoff, *The Prize*; Tompkins-Stange, *Policy Patrons*; Eve L. Ewing, *Ghosts in the Schoolyard: Racism and School Closings on Chicago's South Side* (Chicago and London: University of Chicago Press, 2020); Nora Reikosky, "Pipeline Philanthropy: Understanding Philanthropic Corporate Action in Education During the COVID-19 Era and Beyond," *Educational Policy* online first (April 18, 2023): 1–31, https://doi.org/10.1177/08959048231163802.

## Chapter 3

1. Haveman and Gualtieri, "Institutional Logics."
2. Haveman, *The Power of Organizations.*
3. Patricia H. Thornton, *Markets from Culture: Institutional Logics and Organizational Decisions in Higher Education Publishing* (Palo Alto, CA: Stanford University Press, 2004).
4. Elizabeth Popp Berman, *Creating the Market University: How Academic Science Became an Economic Engine* (Princeton, NJ: Princeton University Press, 2012).
5. Lounsbury et al., "New Directions in the Study of Institutional Logics."
6. Spitzmueller, "Remaking 'Community' Mental Health."
7. W. Richard Scott et al., *Institutional Change and Healthcare Organizations: From Professional Dominance to Managed Care* (Chicago and London: University of Chicago Press, 2000).
8. Mayer N. Zald and Michael Lounsbury, "The Wizards of Oz: Towards an Institutional Approach to Elites, Expertise and Command Posts," *Organization Studies* 31, no. 7 (July 1, 2010): 963–96, https://doi.org/10.1177/0170840610373201; Andrew Abbott, *The System of Professions: An Essay on the Division of Expert Labor* (Chicago and London: University of Chicago Press, 1988); Jochem J. Kroezen and Pursey P. M. A. R. Heugens, "What Is Dead May Never Die: Institutional Regeneration through Logic Reemergence in Dutch Beer Brewing," *Administrative Science Quarterly* 64, no. 4 (December 1, 2019): 976–1019, https://doi.org/10.1177/0001839218817520.
9. Shazia Rafiullah Miller et al., *How Do Barton Graduates Perform in CPS High Schools?* (Chicago: Consortium on Chicago School Research, 1999).
10. Allensworth and Easton, *The On-Track Indicator as a Predictor of High School Graduation.*
11. Ibid., 7.
12. David Hursh, "Assessing No Child Left Behind and the Rise of Neoliberal Education Policies," *American Educational Research Journal* 44, no. 3 (September 1, 2007): 493–518, https://doi.org/10.3102/0002831207306764; Donna M. Harris, "Postscript: Urban Schools, Accountability, and Equity: Insights Regarding NCLB and Reform," *Education and Urban Society* 44, no. 2 (March 1, 2012): 203–10, https://doi.org/10.1177/0013124511431571.
13. Brian A. Jacob, "Accountability, Incentives and Behavior: The Impact of High-Stakes Testing in the Chicago Public Schools," *Journal of Public Economics* 89, no. 5 (June 1, 2005): 761–96, https://doi.org/10.1016/j.jpubeco.2004.08.004; Jacob and Levitt, "Rotten Apples."
14. Allensworth and Easton, *The On-Track Indicator as a Predictor of High School Graduation*, 7.

15. Bruce G. Carruthers and Wendy Nelson Espeland, "Accounting for Rationality: Double-Entry Bookkeeping and the Rhetoric of Economic Rationality," *American Journal of Sociology* 97, no. 1 (July 1991): 31–69, https://doi.org/10.1086/229739.
16. Richard M. Ingersoll and Gregory J. Collins, "Accountability and Control in American Schools," *Journal of Curriculum Studies* 49, no. 1 (February 2017): 75–95, https://doi.org/10.1080/00220272.2016.1205142.
17. Chicago Public Schools Department of School Quality Measurement and Research, *School Quality Rating Policy (SQRP) Handbook.*
18. Paul Goren, "Data, Data, and More Data—What's an Educator to Do?," *American Journal of Education* 118, no. 2 (February 2012): 233–37, https://doi.org/10.1086/663273; Kim Schildkamp, Cindy L. Poortman, and Pasi Sahlberg, "Data-Based Decision Making in Developing Countries: Balancing Accountability Measures and Improvement Efforts," *Journal of Professional Capital and Community* 4, no. 3 (January 1, 2019): 166–71, https://doi.org/10.1108/JPCC-07-2019-037; Kim Schildkamp et al., "Factors Promoting and Hindering Data-Based Decision Making in Schools," *School Effectiveness and School Improvement* 28, no. 2 (April 3, 2017): 242–58, https://doi.org/10.1080/09243453.2016.1256901.
19. New Visions for Public Schools, "The Portal by New Visions," New Visions for Public Schools, 2022, https://portal.newvisions.org/.
20. Abbott, *The System of Professions*, 2.
21. The GRAD Partnership, "Organizing Partners, The GRAD Partnership," *The GRAD Partnership* (blog), 2023, https://www.gradpartnership.org/partners/.
22. Ibid.
23. The GRAD Partnership, "Student Success Systems," *The GRAD Partnership* (blog), 2023, https://www.gradpartnership.org/student-success-systems/.
24. Anthony S. Bryk and Barbara Schneider, *Trust in Schools: A Core Resource for Improvement* (New York, NY: Russell Sage Foundation, 2002).
25. Martha Abele Mac Iver, "Early Warning Indicators of High School Outcomes," *Journal of Education for Students Placed at Risk (JESPAR)* 18, no. 1 (January 2013): 1–6, https://doi.org/10.1080/10824669.2013.745375; Balfanz and Byrnes, "Using Data and the Human Touch"; Mac Iver et al., "An Efficacy Study of a Ninth-Grade Early Warning Indicator Intervention"; Faria et al., *Getting Students On Track for Graduation.*
26. Scott, Lubienski, and DeBray-Pelot, "The Politics of Advocacy in Education."
27. Reikosky, "Pipeline Philanthropy"; Sarah L. Woulfin and Jessica G. Rigby, "Coaching for Coherence: How Instructional Coaches Lead Change in the Evaluation Era," *Educational Researcher* 46, no. 6 (August 1, 2017): 323–28, https://doi.org/10.3102/0013189X17725525; Melissa Roderick, John Q. Easton, and Penny Bender Sebring, *The Consortium on Chicago School Research: A New Model for the Role of Research in Supporting Urban School Reform* (Chicago, IL: Consortium on Chicago School Research, 2009), https://eric.ed.gov/?id=ED505883; Bryk, Gomez, and Grunow, "Getting Ideas into Action."

## Chapter 4

1. Battilana, "Agency and Institutions," 654.
2. Battin-Pearson et al., "Predictors of Early High School Dropout"; Lessard et al., "Shades of Disengagement"; Allensworth, "The Use of Ninth-Grade Early Warning Indicators to Improve Chicago Schools."
3. Brian M. McMahon and Sabrina F. Sembiante, "Re-Envisioning the Purpose of Early Warning Systems: Shifting the Mindset from Student Identification to Meaningful Prediction and Intervention," *Review of Education* 8, no. 1 (2020): 266–301, https://doi.org/10.1002/rev3.3183.
4. Battilana, Leca, and Boxenbaum, "2 How Actors Change Institutions."
5. Michael Mintrom, "Policy Entrepreneurs and the Diffusion of Innovation," *American Journal of Political Science* 41, no. 3 (1997): 738–70, https://doi.org/10.2307/2111674; James Arthur, *Policy Entrepreneurship in Education: Engagement, Influence and Impact* (New York, NY: Routledge, 2017).
6. Battilana, "Agency and Institutions"; Maguire, Hardy, and Lawrence, "Institutional Entrepreneurship in Emerging Fields."
7. Fligstein, "Social Skill and the Theory of Fields."

8. Emily Handsman, Caitlin Farrell, and Cynthia Coburn, "Solving for X: Constructing Algebra and Algebra Policy During a Time of Change," *Sociology of Education* online first (2022): 1–17; Quinn, Tompkins-Stange, and Meyerson, "Beyond Grantmaking"; Rao, *Market Rebels*.
9. Jiao Luo, Jia Chen, and Dongjie Chen, "Coming Back and Giving Back: Transposition, Institutional Actors, and the Paradox of Peripheral Influence," *Administrative Science Quarterly* 66, no. 1 (March 1, 2021): 133–76, https://doi.org/10.1177/0001839220929736; Bulkley and Burch, "The Changing Nature of Private Engagement in Public Education."
10. Jose Eos Trinidad, "Teacher Response Process to Bureaucratic Control: Individual and Group Dynamics Influencing Teacher Responses," *Leadership and Policy in Schools* 18, no. 4 (October 2, 2019): 533–43, https://doi.org/10.1080/15700763.2018.1475573; Burch, *Hidden Markets*; David Hursh, "The Growth of High-Stakes Testing in the USA: Accountability, Markets and the Decline in Educational Equality," *British Educational Research Journal* 31, no. 5 (2005): 605–22, https://doi.org/10.1080/01411920500240767.
11. Walter W. Powell, "Neither Market nor Hierarchy: Network Forms of Organization," *Research in Organizational Behavior* 12 (1990): 295–336.
12. Tina Trujillo, "The Modern Cult of Efficiency: Intermediary Organizations and the New Scientific Management," *Educational Policy* 28, no. 2 (March 1, 2014): 207–32, https://doi.org/10.1177/0895904813513148.
13. Honig, "The New Middle Management."
14. Scott et al., "Urban Regimes, Intermediary Organization Networks, and Research Use"; Elena Aydarova, "Shadow Elite of Teacher Education Reforms: Intermediary Organizations' Construction of Accountability Regimes," *Educational Policy* 36, no. 5 (July 1, 2022): 1188–1221, https://doi.org/10.1177/0895904820951121.
15. Norm Fruchter, "New York City's Affinity District (Part 1): What Is It?," New York University, June 16, 2020, https://steinhardt.nyu.edu/news/new-york-citys-affinity-district-part-1-what-it.
16. Alex Zimmerman, "DOE Backs Off Plan to Overhaul How 164 Schools Are Supervised," *The City*, July 22, 2020, https://www.thecity.nyc/2020/7/21/21333583/doe-backing-off-plan-to-overhaul-how-affinity-schools-are-supervised.
17. Pinkus, *Using Early-Warning Data to Improve Graduation Rates*, 6.
18. New Visions for Public Schools, "The Portal by New Visions."
19. Woulfin and Rigby, "Coaching for Coherence."
20. Richard Paquin Morel and Cynthia Coburn, "Access, Activation, and Influence: How Brokers Mediate Social Capital Among Professional Development Providers," *American Educational Research Journal* 56, no. 2 (April 2019): 247–88, https://doi.org/10.3102/0002831218788528.
21. Marcia H. Davis, Martha Abele Mac Iver, et al., "Implementation of an Early Warning Indicator and Intervention System," *Preventing School Failure: Alternative Education for Children and Youth* 63, no. 1 (January 2, 2019): 77–88, https://doi.org/10.1080/1045988X.2018.1506977.
22. However, Meisha Ross Porter had a short tenure chancellor of the New York City Department of Education, only from March to December 2021.
23. #DegreesNYC, "About #DegreesNYC," #DegreesNYC, 2022, https://www.degreesnyc.org/about.
24. Research Alliance for New York City Schools, "Projects | Supporting the #DegreesNYC Data Co-Op and Learning Network| NYU Steinhardt," NYU Steinhardt, 2021, https://steinhardt.nyu.edu/research-alliance/research/projects/supporting-degreesnyc-data-co-op-and-learning-network.
25. New Visions for Public Schools, "The Portal by New Visions."
26. In contrast to New Visions in New York, the NCS did not have its own charter school network.
27. Anthony S. Bryk, "2014 AERA Distinguished Lecture: Accelerating How We Learn to Improve," *Educational Researcher* 44, no. 9 (December 1, 2015): 469, https://doi.org/10.3102/0013189X15621543.
28. William Penuel et al., "Principles of Collaborative Education Research with Stakeholders: Toward Requirements for a New Research and Development Infrastructure," *Review of Educational Research* 90 (July 3, 2020): 1–48, https://doi.org/10.3102/0034654320938126.
29. Scott, "The Politics of Venture Philanthropy in Charter School Policy and Advocacy."
30. Kenneth J. Saltman, *The Gift of Education: Public Education and Venture Philanthropy* (New York, NY: Palgrave MacMillan, 2010); Reich, *Just Giving*.

31. Hess and Henig, *The New Education Philanthropy*, 2.
32. The philanthropic manager requested anonymity and was the only research participant who requested anonymity after being asked if they were willing to be identified. Interviews with school participants were anonymous by default.
33. Alan J. Daly, ed., *Social Network Theory and Educational Change* (Cambridge, MA: Harvard Education Press, 2010).
34. Frank, Zhao, and Borman, "Social Capital and the Diffusion of Innovations Within Organizations"; Song and Miskel, "Who Are the Influentials?"; E. N. Bridwell-Mitchell, "Them That's Got: How Tie Formation in Partnership Networks Gives High Schools Differential Access to Social Capital," *American Educational Research Journal* 54, no. 6 (December 1, 2017): 1221–55, https://doi.org/10.3102/0002831217717815; Huriya Jabbar et al., "It's Who You Know: The Role of Social Networks in a Changing Labor Market," *American Educational Research Journal* 57, no. 4 (August 1, 2020): 1485–1524, https://doi.org/10.3102/0002831219879092.

## Chapter 5

1. Payne, *So Much Reform, So Little Change.*
2. Trinidad, "Teacher Response Process to Bureaucratic Control"; Verena Wolf and Daniel Beverungen, "Conceptualizing the Impact of Workarounds—An Organizational Routines' Perspective," in *Proceedings of the 27th European Conference on Information Systems (ECIS)* (Stockholm-Uppsala, Sweden, 2019), https://ris.uni-paderborn.de/record/9676.
3. Anthony S. Bryk, "Organizing Schools for Improvement," *Phi Delta Kappan* 91, no. 7 (April 1, 2010): 23–30, https://doi.org/10.1177/003172171009100705; Bryk and Schneider, *Trust in Schools*; Olli-Pekka Malinen and Hannu Savolainen, "The Effect of Perceived School Climate and Teacher Efficacy in Behavior Management on Job Satisfaction and Burnout: A Longitudinal Study," *Teaching and Teacher Education* 60 (November 1, 2016): 144–52, https://doi.org/10.1016/j.tate.2016.08.012; Jose Eos Trinidad, "Material Resources, School Climate, and Achievement Variations in the Philippines: Insights from PISA 2018," *International Journal of Educational Development* 75 (May 1, 2020): 1–9, https://doi.org/10.1016/j.ijedudev.2020.102174; Jessica L. Grayson and Heather K. Alvarez, "School Climate Factors Relating to Teacher Burnout: A Mediator Model," *Teaching and Teacher Education* 24, no. 5 (July 1, 2008): 1349–63, https://doi.org/10.1016/j.tate.2007.06.005.
4. Becker, "Organizational Routines"; Tim Hallett and Amelia Hawbaker, "The Case for an Inhabited Institutionalism in Organizational Research: Interaction, Coupling, and Change Reconsidered," *Theory and Society* 50, no. 1 (January 2021): 1–32, https://doi.org/10.1007/s11186-020-09412-2; Lance D. Fusarelli, "Tightly Coupled Policy in Loosely Coupled Systems: Institutional Capacity and Organizational Change," *Journal of Educational Administration* 40, no. 6 (January 1, 2002): 561–75, https://doi.org/10.1108/09578230210446045.
5. Tim Hallett and Marc J. Ventresca, "Inhabited Institutions: Social Interactions and Organizational Forms in Gouldner's Patterns of Industrial Bureaucracy," *Theory and Society* 35, no. 2 (April 2006): 213–36, https://doi.org/10.1007/s11186-006-9003-z.
6. Claus Rerup and Martha S. Feldman, "Routines as a Source of Change in Organizational Schemata: The Role of Trial-and-Error Learning," *Academy of Management Journal* 54, no. 3 (June 2011): 577–610, https://doi.org/10.5465/amj.2011.61968107.
7. Ewald Terhart, "Teacher Resistance against School Reform: Reflecting an Inconvenient Truth," *School Leadership & Management* 33, no. 5 (November 1, 2013): 486–500, https://doi.org/10.1080/13632434.2013.793494; Monty Neill, "The Testing Resistance and Reform Movement," *Monthly Review* 67, no. 10 (March 2, 2016): 8–28, https://doi.org/10.14452/MR-067-10-2016-03_2.
8. Kathryn Bell McKenzie and James Joseph Scheurich, "Teacher Resistance to Improvement of Schools with Diverse Students," *International Journal of Leadership in Education* 11, no. 2 (April 1, 2008): 117, https://doi.org/10.1080/13603120801950122; Diamond and Spillane, "High-Stakes Accountability in Urban Elementary Schools"; Kristen Erichsen and John Reynolds, "Public School Accountability, Workplace Culture, and Teacher Morale," *Social Science Research* 85 (January 1, 2020), https://doi.org/10.1016/j.ssresearch.2019.102347.

9. Sarah Brayne, *Predict and Surveil: Data, Discretion, and the Future of Policing* (Oxford, UK: Oxford University Press, 2020); Meg Caven, "Quantification, Inequality, and the Contestation of School Closures in Philadelphia," *Sociology of Education* 92, no. 1 (January 1, 2019): 21–40, https://doi.org/10.1177/0038040718815167; Mennicken and Espeland, "What's New with Numbers?"
10. Mac Iver and Messel, "The ABCs of Keeping On Track to Graduation."
11. Lessard et al., "Shades of Disengagement."
12. Battin-Pearson et al., "Predictors of Early High School Dropout"; Valerie E. Lee and David T. Burkam, "Dropping Out of High School: The Role of School Organization and Structure," *American Educational Research Journal* 40, no. 2 (January 1, 2003): 353–93, https://doi.org/10.3102/00028312040002353.
13. Dee and Jacob, "The Impact of No Child Left Behind on Student Achievement"; Hursh, "Assessing No Child Left Behind and the Rise of Neoliberal Education Policies."
14. Neal and Schanzenbach, "Left Behind by Design."
15. Jennings, "Below the Bubble."
16. Hibel and Penn, "Bad Apples or Bad Orchards?"; Jacob and Levitt, "Rotten Apples."
17. Jenny Nagaoka, Alex Seeskin, and Vanessa M Coca, *The Educational Attainment of Chicago Public Schools Students: 2016* (Chicago, IL: University of Chicago Consortium on School Research, 2016).
18. Peurach and Glazer, "Reconsidering Replication."
19. Frank, Zhao, and Borman, "Social Capital and the Diffusion of Innovations Within Organizations."
20. Coburn and Russell, "District Policy and Teachers' Social Networks"; Cynthia E. Coburn, Willow S. Mata, and Linda Choi, "The Embeddedness of Teachers' Social Networks: Evidence from a Study of Mathematics Reform," *Sociology of Education* 86, no. 4 (October 1, 2013): 311–42, https://doi.org/10.1177/0038040713501147.
21. Sherer and Spillane, "Constancy and Change in Work Practice in Schools," 611–12.
22. Becker, "Organizational Routines."
23. Richard R. Nelson and Sidney G. Winter, *An Evolutionary Theory of Economic Change* (Cambridge, MA: Harvard University Press, 1982); Michael T. Hannan and John Freeman, "Structural Inertia and Organizational Change," *American Sociological Review* 49, no. 2 (1984): 149–64, https://doi.org/10.2307/2095567.
24. Sangyoon Yi, Thorbjørn Knudsen, and Markus C. Becker, "Inertia in Routines: A Hidden Source of Organizational Variation," *Organization Science* 27, no. 3 (June 2016): 782–800, https://doi.org/10.1287/orsc.2016.1059; Feldman and Pentland, "Reconceptualizing Organizational Routines as a Source of Flexibility and Change."
25. James P. Spillane, Leigh Mesler Parise, and Jennifer Zoltners Sherer, "Organizational Routines as Coupling Mechanisms: Policy, School Administration, and the Technical Core," *American Educational Research Journal* 48, no. 3 (June 1, 2011): 586–619, https://doi.org/10.3102/0002831210385102.
26. Bailey et al., "Persistence and Fadeout in the Impacts of Child and Adolescent Interventions," 9.
27. Baharav and Sipes, "Early Warning Indicator Systems in Action: Considerations from Identification to Supports."
28. Allensworth, *Graduation and Dropout Trends in Chicago: A Look at Cohorts of Students from 1991 through 2004.*
29. Markku Jahnukainen and Tiina Itkonen, "Tiered Intervention: History and Trends in Finland and the United States," *European Journal of Special Needs Education* 31, no. 1 (January 2, 2016): 140–50, https://doi.org/10.1080/08856257.2015.1108042.
30. Hank Fien, David J. Chard, and Scott K. Baker, "Can the Evidence Revolution and Multi-Tiered Systems of Support Improve Education Equity and Reading Achievement?," *Reading Research Quarterly* 56, no. S1 (2021): S105–18, https://doi.org/10.1002/rrq.391.
31. Orlando Patterson, "Making Sense of Culture," *Annual Review of Sociology* 40, no. 1 (July 30, 2014): 1–30, https://doi.org/10.1146/annurev-soc-071913-043123.
32. John W. Meyer and Brian Rowan, "Institutionalized Organizations: Formal Structure as Myth and Ceremony," *American Journal of Sociology* 83, no. 2 (September 1, 1977): 340–63, https://doi.org/10.1086/226550; John W. Meyer, "The Effects of Education as an Institution," *American Journal of Sociology* 83, no. 1 (July 1977): 55–77, https://doi.org/10.1086/226506; Karl

E. Weick, "Educational Organizations as Loosely Coupled Systems," *Administrative Science Quarterly* 21, no. 1 (1976): 1–19, https://doi.org/10.2307/2391875; Jianping Shen, Xingyuan Gao, and Jiangang Xia, "School as a Loosely Coupled Organization? An Empirical Examination Using National SASS 2003–04 Data," *Educational Management Administration & Leadership* 45, no. 4 (July 1, 2017): 657–81, https://doi.org/10.1177/1741143216628533; Viki M. Young, "Teachers' Use of Data: Loose Coupling, Agenda Setting, and Team Norms," *American Journal of Education* 112, no. 4 (August 2006): 521–48, https://doi.org/10.1086/505058.

33. The principal and school are not named in accordance with my research protocol that only organizations are named. No schools in Chicago, Philadelphia, or New York are identified for this research.
34. Sarah Brayne, "Big Data Surveillance: The Case of Policing," *American Sociological Review* 82, no. 5 (2017): 977–1008; Sarah Brayne and Angèle Christin, "Technologies of Crime Prediction: The Reception of Algorithms in Policing and Criminal Courts," *Social Problems* online first (March 5, 2020): 1–17, https://doi.org/10.1093/socpro/spaa004; Ruha Benjamin, *Race After Technology: Abolitionist Tools for the New Jim Code* (Cambridge, UK: Polity Press, 2019); Sara Safransky, "Geographies of Algorithmic Violence: Redlining the Smart City," *International Journal of Urban and Regional Research* 44, no. 2 (March 2020): 200–218, https://doi.org/10.1111/1468-2427.12833; Cathy O'Neil, *Weapons of Math Destruction: How Big Data Increases Inequality and Threatens Democracy* (New York, NY: Crown, 2016); Aaron Shapiro, "Predictive Policing for Reform? Indeterminacy and Intervention in Big Data Policing," *Surveillance & Society* 17, no. 3/4 (September 7, 2019): 456–72, https://doi.org/10.24908/ss.v17i3/4.10410.
35. Diamond and Spillane, "High-Stakes Accountability in Urban Elementary Schools"; David Gillborn, Paul Warmington, and Sean Demack, "QuantCrit: Education, Policy, 'Big Data' and Principles for a Critical Race Theory of Statistics," *Race Ethnicity and Education* 21, no. 2 (March 4, 2018): 158–79, https://doi.org/10.1080/13613324.2017.1377417.
36. Barbara Turnbull, "Teacher Participation and Buy-in: Implications for School Reform Initiatives," *Learning Environments Research* 5, no. 3 (October 1, 2002): 235–52, https://doi.org/10.1023/A:1021981622041; Angela Booker, "Designing for a Productive Politics of Participation in Research Practice Partnerships," *Educational Policy* 37, no. 1 (January 1, 2023): 225–49, https://doi.org/10.1177/08959048221134586; Jasmin-Olga Sarafidou and Georgios Chatzioannidis, "Teacher Participation in Decision Making and Its Impact on School and Teachers," *International Journal of Educational Management* 27, no. 2 (January 1, 2013): 170–83, https://doi.org/10.1108/09513541311297586.
37. Hallett and Hawbaker, "The Case for an Inhabited Institutionalism in Organizational Research"; Hallett and Ventresca, "Inhabited Institutions."

## Chapter 6

1. Ash Amin and Nigel Thrift, "Neo-Marshallian Nodes in Global Networks," *International Journal of Urban and Regional Research* 16, no. 4 (December 1992): 571–87, https://doi.org/10.1111/j.1468-2427.1992.tb00197.x.
2. Kevin Loughran, "The Philadelphia Negro and the Canon of Classical Urban Theory," *Du Bois Review: Social Science Research on Race* 12, no. 2 (2015): 249–67, https://doi.org/10.1017/S1742058X15000132; Micere Keels, Julia Burdick-Will, and Sara Keene, "The Effects of Gentrification on Neighborhood Public Schools," *City & Community* 12, no. 3 (September 1, 2013): 238–59, https://doi.org/10.1111/cico.12027; Neil Smith, "New Globalism, New Urbanism: Gentrification as Global Urban Strategy," *Antipode* 34, no. 3 (June 2002): 427–50, https://doi.org/10.1111/1467-8330.00249; Julia Burdick-Will et al., "Socially-Structured Mobility Networks and School Segregation Dynamics: The Role of Emergent Consideration Sets," *American Sociological Review* 85, no. 4 (August 1, 2020): 675–708, https://doi.org/10.1177/0003122420934739.
3. Christof Brandtner, "Green American City: Civic Capacity and the Distributed Adoption of Urban Innovations," *American Journal of Sociology* 128, no. 3 (November 2022): 627–79, https://doi.org/10.1086/722965.

4. Corinne M. Herlihy and James J. Kemple, *The Talent Development Middle School Model: Context, Components, and Initial Impacts on Students' Performance and Attendance* (New York, NY: MDRC, 2004); Kemple, Herlihy, and Smith, *Making Progress Toward Graduation.*
5. Kemple, Herlihy, and Smith, *Making Progress Toward Graduation*, xi.
6. Kemple, Segeritz, and Stephenson, "Building On-Track Indicators for High School Graduation and College Readiness."
7. Melissa Roderick, Jenny Nagaoka, and Vanessa Coca, "College Readiness for All: The Challenge for Urban High Schools," *The Future of Children* 19, no. 1 (2009): 185–210; Melissa Roderick, Vanessa Coca, and Jenny Nagaoka, "Potholes on the Road to College: High School Effects in Shaping Urban Students' Participation in College Application, Four-Year College Enrollment, and College Match," *Sociology of Education* 84, no. 3 (July 1, 2011): 178–211, https://doi.org/10.1177/0038040711411280.
8. See the NCS website: https://ncs.uchicago.edu/page/national-freshman-success-institute-improving-high-school-graduation-rates.
9. In 2023, the five-day workshop was divided into a three-day workshop in June and a two-day workshop in October.
10. See the Diplomas Now website: https://new.every1graduates.org/tools-and-models/diplomas-now/.
11. See the Connecticut RISE Network website: https://www.ctrise.org/what-we-do/improvement-networks/. The name RISE stood for resources, innovations, systems, and empowerment.
12. See https://www.ctrise.org/get-involved/coaching-and-professional-learning/freshman-focus-network/.
13. Joel Knudson and Mark Garibaldi, *None of Us Are as Good as All of Us: Early Lessons From the CORE Districts* (Washington, DC: American Institutes for Research, 2015).
14. See the CORE Districts LinkedIn page: https://www.linkedin.com/company/core-districts/.
15. See the CORE Districts website: https://coredistricts.org/opportunities-to-participate/school-improvement/#:~:text=On%20%E2%80%93%20Track,can%20be%20shared%20across%20schools.
16. Allensworth and Easton, *The On-Track Indicator as a Predictor of High School Graduation*; Balfanz, Herzog, and Mac Iver, "Preventing Student Disengagement and Keeping Students on the Graduation Path in Urban Middle-Grades Schools."
17. Phillips et al., "Using Research to Improve College Readiness."
18. Frazelle and Nagel, *A Practitioner's Guide to Implementing Early Warning Systems*, 2.
19. Carl et al., "Theory and Application of Early Warning Systems for High School and Beyond."
20. Hansen, "Information as Intervention."
21. Todd Feathers, "This Dropout Warning System Flags 'High-Risk' Students. The False Alarms Might Hurt Them Instead," *Chalkbeat*, April 27, 2023, https://www.chalkbeat.org/2023/4/27/23699361/dropout-early-warning-system-dews-student-dropouts-race-income-data; Feathers, "How Wisconsin Uses Race and Income to Label Students 'High Risk'"; Perdomo et al., "Difficult Lessons on Social Prediction from Wisconsin Public Schools."
22. Andrea Jean Thiner, "Minnesota Early Indicator and Response System Impact on Graduation Rates: An Analysis of an Early Warning Intervention and Monitoring Systems in an Alternative Learning Center" (Thesis, Fargo, ND, North Dakota State University, 2021), https://library.ndsu.edu/ir/handle/10365/31987.
23. Todd Feathers, "This Dropout Warning System Flags 'High-Risk' Students"; Feathers, "How Wisconsin Uses Race and Income to Label Students 'High Risk'"; Perdomo et al., "Difficult Lessons on Social Prediction from Wisconsin Public Schools."
24. See the REL and IES website: https://ies.ed.gov/ncee/rel/About/.
25. Arthur Burke, *Early Identification of High School Graduation Outcomes in Oregon Leadership Network Schools. REL 2015-079* (Portland, OR: Regional Educational Laboratory at Education Northwest, 2015), https://eric.ed.gov/?id=ED556119.
26. Theresa Deussen, Havala Hanson, and Biraj Bisht, *Are Two Commonly Used Early Warning Indicators Accurate Predictors of Dropout for English Learner Students? Evidence from Six Districts in Washington State. REL 2017-261* (Washington, DC: Regional Educational Laboratory Northwest, 2017), https://eric.ed.gov/?id=ED573197.
27. David Stuit et al., *Identifying Early Warning Indicators in Three Ohio School Districts. REL 2016-118* (Washington, DC: Regional Educational Laboratory Midwest, 2016), https://eric.ed.gov/?id=ED566958.

28. Faria et al., *Getting Students On Track for Graduation*.
29. See the GRAD Partnership website: https://www.gradpartnership.org/.
30. Brandtner, "Green American City"; Bridwell-Mitchell, "Them That's Got"; Bridwell-Mitchell, Jack, and Childs, "The Social Structure of School Resource Disparities."

# Conclusion

1. Frederick M. Hess, *Spinning Wheels: The Politics of Urban School Reform* (Washington, DC: Brookings Institution Press, 2011); Brent R. Keltner, *Funding Comprehensive School Reform* (Santa Barbara, CA: RAND Corporation, 1998), https://www.rand.org/pubs/issue_papers/IP175.html.
2. Charles M. Payne, *So Much Reform, So Little Change: The Persistence of Failure in Urban Schools* (Cambridge, MA: Harvard Education Press, 2008).
3. Haridimos Tsoukas and Robert Chia, "On Organizational Becoming: Rethinking Organizational Change," *Organization Science* 13, no. 5 (October 2002): 567–82, https://doi.org/10.1287/orsc.13.5.567.7810.
4. James P. Spillane et al., "Striving for Coherence, Struggling with Incoherence: A Comparative Study of Six Educational Systems Organizing for Instruction," *Educational Evaluation and Policy Analysis* 44, no. 4 (December 1, 2022): 567–92, https://doi.org/10.3102/01623737221093382.
5. John W. Meyer and Brian Rowan, "Institutionalized Organizations: Formal Structure as Myth and Ceremony," *American Journal of Sociology* 83, no. 2 (1977): 340–63; Karl E. Weick, "Educational Organizations as Loosely Coupled Systems," *Administrative Science Quarterly* 21, no. 1 (1976): 1–19, https://doi.org/10.2307/2391875; J. Douglas Orton and Karl E. Weick, "Loosely Coupled Systems: A Reconceptualization," *The Academy of Management Review* 15, no. 2 (1990): 203–23, https://doi.org/10.2307/258154.
6. John B. Diamond, "Accountability Policy, School Organization, and Classroom Practice: Partial Recoupling and Educational Opportunity," *Education and Urban Society* 44, no. 2 (March 1, 2012): 151–82, https://doi.org/10.1177/0013124511431569.
7. Cory Koedel, Kata Mihaly, and Jonah E. Rockoff, "Value-Added Modeling: A Review," *Economics of Education Review* 47 (August 1, 2015): 180–95, https://doi.org/10.1016/j.econedurev.2015.01.006.
8. Kimberlee C. Everson, "Value-Added Modeling and Educational Accountability: Are We Answering the Real Questions?," *Review of Educational Research* 87, no. 1 (February 1, 2017): 35–70, https://doi.org/10.3102/0034654316637199.
9. Theodore M. Porter, *Trust in Numbers: The Pursuit of Objectivity in Science and Public Life* (Princeton, NJ: Princeton University Press, 1996); Elizabeth Popp Berman, *Thinking Like an Economist: How Efficiency Replaced Equality in U.S. Public Policy* (Princeton, NJ: Princeton University Press, 2022).
10. Zachary Griffen and Aaron Panofsky, "Ambivalent Economizations: The Case of Value Added Modeling in Teacher Evaluation," *Theory and Society* 50, no. 3 (April 1, 2021): 527–28, https://doi.org/10.1007/s11186-020-09417-x.
11. Ibid., 529.
12. See the TFA website at https://www.teachforamerica.org/where-we-work.
13. See the TNTP website at https://tntp.org/what-we-do.
14. See the NYC Teaching Fellows website at https://nycteachingfellows.org/.
15. See the South Carolina Department of Education website at https://ed.sc.gov/educators/alternative-certification/teachcharleston/.
16. Priya G. La Londe, T. Jameson Brewer, and Christopher A. Lubienski, "Teach for America and Teach for All: Creating an Intermediary Organization Network for Global Education Reform," *Education Policy Analysis Archives* 23, no. 47 (April 20, 2015): 3, https://eric.ed.gov/?id=EJ1070361.
17. Kerry Kretchmar, Beth Sondel, and Joseph J. Ferrare, "The Power of the Network: Teach For America's Impact on the Deregulation of Teacher Education," *Educational Policy* 32, no. 3 (May 1, 2018): 423–53, https://doi.org/10.1177/0895904816637687; Kerry Kretchmar, Beth Sondel, and Joseph J. Ferrare, "Mapping the Terrain: Teach For America, Charter School Reform, and Corporate Sponsorship," *Journal of Education Policy* 29, no. 6 (November 2, 2014): 742–59, https://doi.org/10.1080/02680939.2014.880812; Tina Trujillo, Janelle Scott, and Marialena

Rivera, "Follow the Yellow Brick Road: Teach For America and the Making of Educational Leaders," *American Journal of Education* 123, no. 3 (May 2017): 353–91, https://doi.org/10.1086/691232.

18. Steven Glazerman, Daniel Mayer, and Paul Decker, "Alternative Routes to Teaching: The Impacts of Teach for America on Student Achievement and Other Outcomes," *Journal of Policy Analysis and Management* 25, no. 1 (2006): 75–96, https://doi.org/10.1002/pam.20157; Trujillo, Scott, and Rivera, "Follow the Yellow Brick Road"; David Labaree, "Teach for America and Teacher Ed: Heads They Win, Tails We Lose," *Journal of Teacher Education* 61, no. 1–2 (January 1, 2010): 48–55, https://doi.org/10.1177/0022487109347317.
19. Mark Berends, "Sociology and School Choice: What We Know After Two Decades of Charter Schools," *Annual Review of Sociology* 41, no. 1 (2015): 159–80, https://doi.org/10.1146/annurev-soc-073014-112340.
20. Tong Tong et al., "Charter Schools: An Alternative Option in American Schooling," *Encyclopedia* 3, no. 1 (March 2023): 362–70, https://doi.org/10.3390/encyclopedia3010022.
21. Diane Ravitch, *The Death and Life of the Great American School System: How Testing and Choice Are Undermining Education* (New York, NY: Basic Books, 2016); Janelle Scott, "The Politics of Venture Philanthropy in Charter School Policy and Advocacy," *Educational Policy* 23, no. 1 (January 1, 2009): 106–36, https://doi.org/10.1177/0895904808328531; Zachary W. Oberfield, *Are Charters Different?: Public Education, Teachers, and the Charter School Debate* (Cambridge, MA: Harvard Education Press, 2017).
22. National Center for Education Statistics, "Public Charter School Enrollment," in *Condition of Education* (Washington, DC: U.S. Department of Education, Institute of Education Sciences, 2023), https://nces.ed.gov/programs/coe/indicator/cgb.
23. Brayden G King, Elisabeth S. Clemens, and Melissa Fry, "Identity Realization and Organizational Forms: Differentiation and Consolidation of Identities Among Arizona's Charter Schools," *Organization Science* 22, no. 3 (June 1, 2011): 554–72, https://doi.org/10.1287/orsc.1100.0548.
24. Jaren R. Haber, "Sorting Schools: A Computational Analysis of Charter School Identities and Stratification," *Sociology of Education* 94, no. 1 (January 1, 2021): 43–64, https://doi.org/10.1177/0038040720953218.
25. Joseph J. Ferrare and R. Renee Setari, "Converging on Choice: The Interstate Flow of Foundation Dollars to Charter School Organizations," *Educational Researcher* 47, no. 1 (January 1, 2018): 34–45, https://doi.org/10.3102/0013189X17736524.
26. Joanne W. Golann, *Scripting the Moves: Culture and Control in a "No-Excuses" Charter School* (Princeton, NJ: Princeton University Press, 2021).
27. Linda A. Renzulli, "Organizational Environments and the Emergence of Charter Schools in the United States," *Sociology of Education* 78, no. 1 (January 1, 2005): 1–26, https://doi.org/10.1177/003804070507800101.
28. Tim Craig, "Moms for Liberty Has Turned 'Parental Rights' into a Rallying Cry for Conservative Parents," *Washington Post*, October 15, 2021, https://www.washingtonpost.com/national/moms-for-liberty-parents-rights/2021/10/14/bf3d9ccc-286a-11ec-8831-a31e7b3de188_story.html.
29. See the Moms for Liberty website at https://www.momsforliberty.org/about/.
30. Lonnie Lusardo, "Moms for Liberty Spreads Its Anti-LGBTQ+ Hatred to the Northwest," *The Seattle Times*, June 13, 2023, https://www.seattletimes.com/opinion/moms-for-liberty-spreads-its-anti-lgbtq-hatred-to-the-northwest/.
31. Paige Williams, "The Right-Wing Mothers Fuelling the School- Board Wars," *Annals of Education*, 2022, 1–17.
32. Ibid.
33. InfluenceWatch, "Moms Demand Action for Gun Sense," *InfluenceWatch*, 2023, https://www.influencewatch.org/organization/moms-demand-action-for-gun-sense/.
34. Barbara DeSanto, "Moms Demand Action: Using Public Relations to Combat Gun Violence," in *Public Relations Cases* (New York City: Routledge, 2022).
35. InfluenceWatch, "Moms Demand Action for Gun Sense."
36. See the Moms Demand Action website at https://momsdemandaction.org/about/chapters/.
37. See https://momsdemandaction.org/moms-demand-action-successfully-pressures-starbucks-to-stop-allowing-guns-in-stores/.

38. Kimberly J. Morgan and Andrea Louise Campbell, *The Delegated Welfare State: Medicare, Markets, and the Governance of Social Policy*, Oxford Studies in Postwar American Political Development (New York: Oxford University Press, 2011), 6.
39. Tracy L. Steffes, *School, Society, and State: A New Education to Govern Modern America, 1890–1940* (Chicago and London: University of Chicago Press, 2011).
40. Monica Prasad, "Problem-Solving Sociology," *Contemporary Sociology: A Journal of Reviews* 47, no. 4 (July 2018): 393–98, https://doi.org/10.1177/0094306118779810.

## Appendix

1. Susan Bush-Mecenas, "'The Business of Teaching and Learning': Institutionalizing Equity in Educational Organizations Through Continuous Improvement," *American Educational Research Journal* 59, no. 3 (June 1, 2022): 461–99, https://doi.org/10.3102/00028312221074404.
2. Included in the 73 actors were three educators in New York City, inclusive of one principal and two teachers.

# Index

*For the benefit of digital users, indexed terms that span two pages (e.g., 52–53) may, on occasion, appear on only one of those pages.*